BACK DOOR INTO HERMETICS

About the Authors

Mark Rasmus began his journey into Hermetics during the late 1970s when he met his first mentor, William Cook Edwards. Since then Mark has combined his expertise with martial arts and Hermetics to create the Elastic Force System. Considered a living master of applied Hermeticism, Mark has taught thousands of students tai chi, qi gong, wing chun and other internal martial arts, and Hermetics, over the course of more than three decades. Mark has travelled extensively, especially throughout Asia.

Jake Senn has studied Hermetics and the works of Franz Bardon since his early teens. As a child, Jake would spend much of his free time with a wide variety of nature spirits around his home in the Pacific Northwest wilderness. Jake travelled to Thailand in 2018 for an extended stay, in order to study Hermetics with Mark Rasmus. Jake teaches a variety of subjects online, ranging from basic meditation to a 20+ hour course on emotional intelligence based upon the four elements. Jake graduated from the University of Washington with a Degree in Comparative Religion, having focused his studies on Eastern religions and ancient Christian Gnosticism. Jake currently lives in La Jolla, California.

Back Door Into
Hermetics

A Guide to Becoming Initiated
into the Mysteries

Mark Rasmus · Jake Senn

Thailand

Copyright © Mark Rasmus, Jake Senn 2020

This book is copyright. Apart from any fair dealing for the purpose of private study, research, criticism, or review, as permitted under the Copyright Act, no part may be reproduced by any process without written permission. Enquiries should be made to the publisher.

First edition
published 2020
by Mark Rasmus, Jake Senn

For further information please visit our websites:

Mark Rasmus
www.markrasmus.org

Jake Senn
www.jakesenn.com/hermetics

Edited by Paul Hardacre
Book design and typeset by Marissa Newell
in Arno Pro and Univers LT Std
Images sourced from www.freepik.com

*This book is in dedication and service to the next generation
of people who decide to walk the Hermetic path.
May the path of Light guide and protect.*

Contents

Introduction: The Practice of Hermetics

On Creating a Mental Stream of Practice as the First Cornerstone of Success	15
Working with Others to Accelerate Success	15
How to Measure the Results of Energy Games with the Elements	16
Developing a Holographic Stream	18
On Constructing and Executing a Mental Plan	19
Mechanics of Delivery	19
Time Continuums in Relation to Mechanics of Delivery	20
On Deconstructing the Limitations of Books	20
On Your Training Environment	22

Part 1: Theory

Chapter 1: Your Journal	**27**
Your Journal is the Initiation Text	28
Examples of Uses of Your Journal	28
Examples of Questions One May Ask Themselves in a Journal	29
Observing the Macrocosm and Microcosm Through Your Journal	29
On the Metaphysical Layers of the Journal	31
Chapter 2: Sucess and Failure	**35**
Principle of Transmission	36
Mechanics of Opening Space	36
On Giving Others Your Best	39
On Self-Initiating	40

On Maintaining a Like-Minded Community	42
The Crown Technique	42
Principles of Hosting a Spiritual Circle	43
On Precepts and Vows	45
Five Buddhist Moral Precepts Metaphysical Breakdown	45
The Three Transformations and Pillar of Light Exercise	52
"May the Path of Light Guide and Protect"	57
Practicing Mona	58

Chapter 3: Pore Breathing Guided Meditation Practice	**61**
Floating the Bones	61
Electric Phase	62
Magnetic Phase	66
Questions from this Guided Practice Session	68

Chapter 4: Akasha	**73**
Akashic Breathing	73

Chapter 5: Non-Dual Light	**79**
Astral Light	79
Mental Light	80
Non-Dual Light Mastery	83

Part 2: The Mental, Astral and Physical Streams of Practice

Preliminaries to Mind Stream Training	**97**
Introduction	97
On Awakening the Spirit for Training	98

Mental Stream	**101**
Step One	101
Step Two	104
Stopwatch Technique	105
Step Three	106

Bridging the Sense Gates into Mental Wandering	*107*
From Creativity to Sensitivity	*108*
Step Four	109
Step Five	110
Step Six	111
Step Seven	117
Fire	*119*
Water	*120*
Air	*121*
Earth	*122*
Step Eight	123
Mental wandering	*123*
Step Nine	126
Step Ten	137
Astral Stream: Steps One through Ten	**143**
Steps One to Three	143
The Astral Black and White Soul Mirror	*144*
Step Four: Astral Training	147
Working with the Elements and Fundamentals	*150*
Step Five	156
Step Six	160
Step Seven: Sense Gates	164
Sight	*164*
Sound	*165*
Feeling	*167*
Taste	*167*
Smell	*167*
Step Eight: The Electric and Magnetic Fluid	168
The Great Moment of Now	*168*
The Electric and the Magnetic	*169*
Inward Electric Fluid	*169*
Step Nine: Astral Travel and Leaving the Physical Body Matrix	170
Step Ten: Astral Training Paths of Self Realization	173

Physical Stream: Steps One through Ten	**177**
Step One	177
Garden of Eden Diet	*178*
Step Two: Asanas	181
Step Three: Accumulating Vital Power	182
Step Four	187
Step Five	189
Step Six: Creating Elementals from	
Universal Light, from Akasha or the Four Elements	193
Kabbalistic Creation of Elementals	*198*
On Larvae and Phantoms	*208*
Step Seven	209
Step Eight	214
Fluid condensers	*219*
Step Nine	221
Akashic Volting	*223*
Step Ten	227

PART 3: CAUSATION CHAINS

On Reverse Engineering Any Skill for Causation Chains	230
Causation Chain of Clairvoyance: Complex Breakdown of Causation Chain for Understanding the Underlying Mechanics of All Causation Chains	231
Causation Chain of Prayer	240
Causation Chain of Samadhi	244
Causation Chain of Inner Knowing	245
Causation Chain of Working with a Group	246
Causation Chain of Invocation and Evocation	247
Causation Chain of Equalizing with the Planetary Spheres	251
Causation Chain of Hermetic Evolution	252
Working with Akashic Beings, Beings of the Sun Sphere, and Bringing Them to Non-Dual Light	256

Part 4: Conclusion, Resources and Index

Conclusion 263
Resources 267
Index 269

Introduction

The Practice of Hermetics

In the beginning of the initiation process, it is important to understand the psychology of what we are doing. When the mind concentrates on any one meditation object, every aspect of concentration is strengthened. By simply concentrating on an object, your proficiency in every exercise in Franz Bardon's *Initiation into Hermetics* – the groundwork of this book – is improved.

Throughout both this book and Bardon's texts, every exercise is connected to every other exercise. The practice is like a net: when we lift one part of the net up, every other part of the net is raised too. We want to remain closely aware of this inter-association. If we allow difficulty in one exercise to halt our progress and momentum, our proficiency in every other exercise degrades. You have to keep the stream of progress flowing at all times.

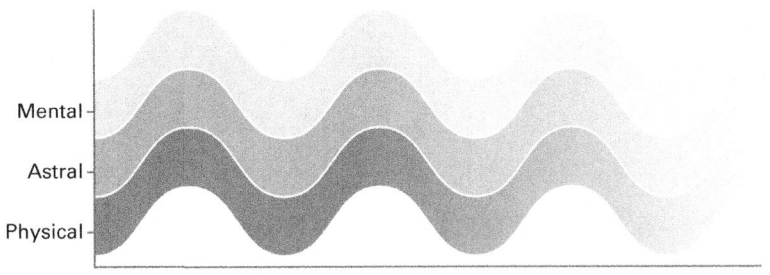

The Mind Streams

By practicing exercises that are enjoyable and those in which you have excelled, you will develop a flow that generates momentum for succeeding in all of the other exercises. When people approach exercises by following the common adage, "Do only one exercise at a time," there will be more failure than success. Those who follow this adage are taking a backward step, and may eventually give up. If one is doing the exercises that they are successful at, then all of their weaknesses will continuously dissolve as they practice. By doing the exercises that are fun and enjoyable, we gain free energy and that free energy keeps our training focused and promotes the achievements of our highest goals.

On Creating a Mental Stream of Practice as the First Cornerstone of Success

When approaching all of the mental exercises as a stream, align all of the exercises from steps one to ten and set a timer. Go through each exercise one at a time, a couple of minutes each, and establish a flow. The exercises that you are successful at, simply do more of them. At first, it may seem counterintuitive not to work on your weaknesses, but those weaknesses will naturally dissolve by concentrating on your strengths. We never ignore our weaknesses, but neither do we have to focus all of our attention on them. There is a curve of success in these exercises, and we measure our success by looking at that curve and putting more time into the exercises that are giving us gains, concentration and results.

This principle of one path affecting all paths is a foundation of success and needs to be reinforced from the beginning. For example, when working with the astral energies, categorize anything pertaining to the Water element by putting them into one session and build the Water element on the top – whether it is transforming personality traits, self-hypnosis, increasing energy flow, or your ability to be intuitive. Separate out all of the exercises that relate to that one frequency and the variations of that frequency, and practice them in a stream. Then move to the Fire element and repeat the process – categorizing all of the astral training that relates to the Fire element and putting them into one session. Break down the exercises, set a timer, and work through the exercises sequentially. Start with a couple of minutes on each exercise and then work with longer time periods. Create sequences and practice each of the other elements as well.

We are always building a central core frequency inside ourselves and allowing different expressions of that frequency to express astrally and spread through the exercises. We can organize these frequencies into topics, categories, elemental groups, and so forth. You'll find that you will raise the frequency of anything that accompanies that particular energy, topic, category, or elemental you're working with. Everything rises together when working with this method.

Working with Others to Accelerate Success

When working with others in the physical, we turn all of the exercises into practical games so that we are having fun. With a training partner, we can touch a person's fascia, and through their fascia, touch their base (either the bottom of their feet or the root of their spine), relax ourselves underneath them through feeling, and extend our vital energy to affect their balance or to have other effects on their body. Exercises that give measurable results, give measurable success and accumulate energy quickly. Measurable exercises rapidly accumulate faith and an understanding of how the process works. Once you begin to see the causation chains you are set on a path to success.

When the vital energy is stronger and you can move people around with it, you will realize how easy it is to move the consciousness of diseases, to pull negative energy out of a person, to control an environment, and influence the energy field of a person. Play a lot of energy games where the result is measurable and improve on that result.

> Note: If you want to learn more about partner-based energetic exercises and practice, train with Mark in person or take his online Elastic Force course at **www.markrasmus.org** or on YouTube **www.youtube.com/user/SifuMarkRasmus**

How to Measure the Results of Energy Games with the Elements

Air element	Improve the understanding of what you are doing
Water element	Get more cohesion into your plan of what you are doing
Fire element	Use more willpower to produce greater effect
Earth element	Balance all other elements out as manifestation, discerning that your attachment and will is unified to get the best results

Start from the beginning by doing simple partner exercises like vital breathing into people, floating them off their point of balance, extending energy to push people over, and working with their energy fields. The possibilities are as numerous as you allow creativity in your day-to-day life.

When you can influence another person's energy field, your ability to influence yourself increases. As the ability to influence yourself increases, it reflects and will be able to affect others more efficiently. That can be used for teaching, for healing, for counseling – whatever application you feel that is going to benefit yourself and the Consciousness.

INTRODUCTION 17

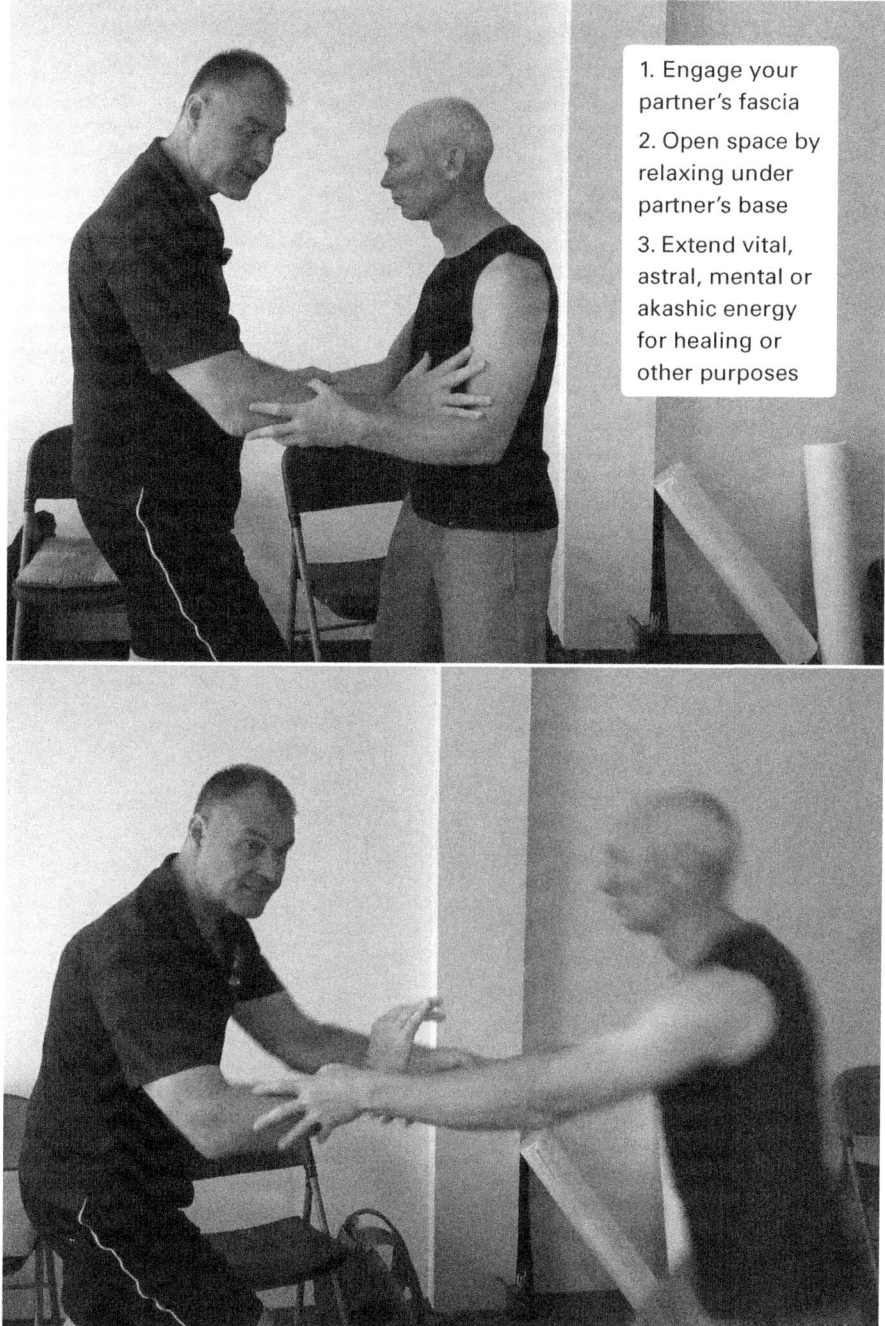

1. Engage your partner's fascia
2. Open space by relaxing under partner's base
3. Extend vital, astral, mental or akashic energy for healing or other purposes

Partner-based energetic exercises

This way of looking at the initiation process is not very traditional. It is not the way presented by Franz Bardon in *Initiation into Hermetics*, but it gives results quickly.

Developing a Holographic Stream

When you are developing a new training plan, understand the outline of Bardon's book and note the systematic approach in the way that he presented it. The first correction you need to make is to see everything within the book as a holographic stream and that the past, present and future are connected. Energy is continuously moving. Things that you are going to achieve in the future can be touched now, and things from the past are morphing into the future. We want to look at our training in a way that any effort we are investing now is changing the vibration of every other skill we have. We do not have to look at our practice as a linear progression. It is not solely by doing x input, one gets y output. When we practice, all of our different skills are being changed.

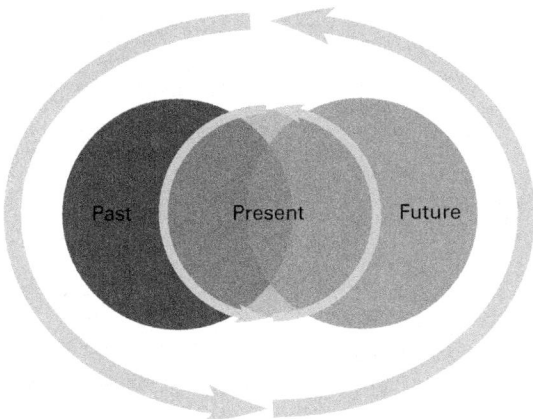

Holographic Stream

Taking a holographic approach by releasing time, you are allowed to work on your strengths, thereby fixing your weaknesses. We are setting aside our habit of conceptualizing progress purely in terms of linear time. You do not have to go to the weakness to fix it – instead, work at the weakness from the periphery through your strengths. Once you have worked through the exercises and started to develop your own mindstreams – mentally, astrally and physically – and found your way of practicing, then you can start steering towards your goals. Initially you will start doing this without thinking too much – you might visualize that you want to be better at a particular sport, so you visualize yourself playing that sport. You get two benefits by doing this: firstly the visualization practice, and secondly you improve your ability in that sport. We do this unconsciously all of the time – it is a natural process.

On Constructing and Executing a Mental Plan

When we are looking at our goals, we look at our mental plan. What is the frequency of that goal? What is the timing? What is the space required for this particular thing to take place? Then we ask ourselves to look at the personality of the energy. We work with an elemental balance of it and understand how to produce an astral environment in which we can work with that energy. Then we look into the physical environment, mechanics – the delivery. The following is an example of executing the mechanics of delivery:

> *"When my daughter was young, and I wanted her to sleep when she was awake late at night, I would do a bedtime story for her. So I tune my vocal cords into the theta-range, into a monotone, into a very, very deep astral space, then as I read the story, her mind would pull into the astral space, her brainwave patterns would start moving into theta, and then she started drifting off. It was being delivered through the vocal cords and through the feeling. So tuning the vocal cords in the feeling of that particular energy allowed her to have a deep, deep rest. It basically dissolved the static of what was preventing her from falling asleep."*

Mechanics of Delivery
The mechanics of delivery depend on the type of energy that we want to generate. The type of energy that we want to generate is what the delivery will be based on. Is the delivery through feeling? Is it through sound? Is it through sight? And so forth. We need to look at the mechanics of what we are delivering. If you were generating a field of energy, you would open your

joints electrically and magnetically, to stimulate the vital force to support that field. Then you need to relax into the astral plane to accumulate that in the astral field so that the physical space would start building that particular intent within it. So, you will look at the mechanics of your body as well as the mechanics of the environment. Do you need a particular environment to generate that energy? Is it a place of nature that is better for that particular function, exercise and outcome? Do you need a sacred space? Perhaps it is better to practice in the temple, stand upon a vortex, be under a waterfall, etc. Consider the physical environment, which will amplify the effects of what you want to do.

Time Continuums in Relation to Mechanics of Delivery
Physically, astrally and mentally we have three different time continuums. The physical world is in the present moment and is restricted to space and time. The astral realm is still restricted to space but has a slowed time continuum because the astral realm is released of time. The mental realm is released of space. The mind can place itself on the moon and back in its body instantaneously. The mind does not travel through linear space as it does not have those restrictions. Those laws within each one of these realms are different. So, as we develop our training system to achieve our goals, we have to take into consideration what each one of these laws and these bodies are doing.

Restrictions	Physical	Astral	Mental	Akasha
Time	Time	Released of Time	Time	Timeless
Space	Space	Space	Released of Space	Spaceless

On Deconstructing the Limitations of Books

Now we are looking at the deconstruction of books as a limited form. We can take the information in Bardon's book and reformulate it so that it flows, streams and individualizes it for ourselves in a way that is unique for our life path. As soon as we engage something in the form of a book and deconstruct it, the book automatically forms limitations. As a natural consequence of books as a medium, there are boundaries – it is going to work for some people and not work for others. Therefore, this book is to be approached in such a way that the reader individualizes each exercise as they encounter it, in order to suit their life's purpose. The *Initiation into Hermetics* text has tools to fulfill our life's purpose with a high level of efficiency. One needs to recognize before starting the exercises our life's most important questions: "What is my life's purpose? What direction do I want to go?" By knowing our life's purpose and direction, we can use every exercise within the book to create a magnetic pull to the fulfillment of our life purpose. The moment you start reading, you are individualizing. This individualizing generates great success and brings you into resonance with your purpose and direction. It brings you into resonance with what you are meant to be doing and how to do it efficiently. You are magnetizing your astral body to propel you towards those experiences. Everything is manifesting at an accelerated rate because of the stream that you are building.

You may try removing the word 'magician' and being a magician from your identity and replacing that word with an identity that suits your life's purpose. For example, you might be a healer, so you will write instead of being a 'magician', being a 'healer'. Then once you have identified your life's purpose – to be a healer – you start taking the exercises from the text and overlapping them onto the blueprint of the healer. So you have two blueprints: one encompassing your tools and the other your purpose. You take all of the tools, adjust them to the purpose and do each exercise in accordance with how to be a great healer. This will change every exercise and give it a different flavor. No exercise will be a 'universal' exercise anymore. These will be 'specific' exercises which make healers develop quickly. For example, to individualize an exercise of visualizing, visualize the purpose of what you want to be using your energies for – i.e. what are your goals? Visualization exercises will then be more about astrally programming and goal-setting than they are about visualization, which makes it easy. The visual aspects will naturally pop-up.

You may need to look at how to make each exercise mentally stream from one to the next towards your life's purpose, your fulfillment, and achieving the highest level of that purpose. Each of the astral exercises are the same. Again, each exercise is manifesting an astral ego consciousness that is a master of a particular skill, that is working in service for humanity and is developing to raise in the group consciousness through that particular direction. What kind of physical body do you need to develop for that purpose? What is the lifestyle in the physical that you need? What is the physical way that you need to live your life that is required? Make those adjustments using those tools to match that life's purpose. Consider this type of thinking before engaging in the book.

On Your Training Environment

For the spiritual journey, you require two things – the correct information and the correct environment in which to apply that information. If you are getting information from a book, then you need a nurturing environment where you can practice those techniques that is quiet and where you can move into that frequency of truth to develop it. If you are using a spiritual school like a Buddhist or a magical school, it is important not to get trapped by the organization, religion or system.

A spiritual teacher is just a tour guide. When you go on a tour, the teacher points out the important things for your development – that is all that teachers are there for. Teachers are there for your self-realization, to help you realize that you need nothing outside of your own spiritual essence for your spiritual development. They are there to stimulate your intuition so that you come into your own power – this is important on the spiritual path. You do not need a spiritual doctrine, you do not need any framework, you do not need any organization, you do not need to submit yourself to anyone, because you are a master within your own right and need to recognize that.

Once you have finished the learning 'tour' with a spiritual teacher, and if that spiritual teacher has done their job well, you will realize that everything you need is within you, and that the teacher is not needed any more. The teacher may become a friend, but it is certainly not a lifetime commitment. It is a short-term commitment to the teacher and it produces the conditions in which your growth can be accelerated.

In order for you to achieve mastery, you need to be treated like a master. The teacher should project to the student that the student is a master as well. In the beginning, the teacher is talking to the part of the student that is a master. The teacher stimulates that divine spark within the spirit of the student. The stimulating of that divine spark to become self-aware is within the normal consciousness of the student. This relationship is very important. If there is a hierarchical structure, if a student feels inferior or any of these problems come up, then that particular teacher is simply not for you. You need to feel empowered by the space and the people that you are practicing with.

Part 1
Theory

Chapter 1

Your Journal

Journaling is the decider between success and failure within your practice. If the journal is ignored, then the insight into your development – into what is working and what is not working – simply is not there. **Your journal is your teaching manual.** Any true initiate is practicing for the benefit of the next generation. In its essence, being an initiate is founded upon the principle of evolution. Evolution is the group consciousness-raising frequency from one generation to the next. Evolution is not about you as an individual. It is about the group consciousness of the planet. It is about the group consciousness on both a microcosmic and macrocosmic level. In order to generate this evolution rapidly, you have to feed the stream of that evolution into the next generation and practice and work for their benefit. So if you are a teacher, you train all of your practices for the benefit of your future students. If you are a healer, you practice all of your healing skills for the benefit of your future patients, and for the people you are going to teach to heal in the future. The practices that you are doing are for the next generation. Your skill is not for you, it is part of the group consciousness and part of the evolutionary curve of the planet. When you recognize this and make a vow that you will practice for the benefit of the next generation, automatically your stream moves forward in time and pulls you forward. Your skills will develop at a far more accelerated rate astrally. If you are clinging to your own ego and your own individual power, then you will not be able to fully reap the benefits of this accelerated process.

One other aspect that happens is that the skills that you are going to achieve in the future manifest now. They get pulled into the present moment.

That energy being brought to the present moment is a huge accelerator. Whatever abilities you are going to have later in life, you can have now. This process is a huge benefactor. It allows you to move forward at a much more accelerated rate.

Your Journal is the Initiation Text

Journaling allows you to see this process of development for the group consciousness. It allows you to document this process. It allows you to take every exercise that you are working with and graph it, refine it and produce a teaching method which is better than what you started with. When you start practicing this, you are a beginner. And as you develop your skills, you become intermediate, then advanced, and then at a teacher's level. Your journal will have all these processes written down. Your journal will detail how you produce results, how you can produce better results in your students, and how the next generation can evolve. **Your journal is the initiation text.** It is the teaching manual.

When Franz Bardon wrote his first book, *Initiation into Hermetics*, it was a long time ago. It was written within a certain group consciousness, within a certain era and for a certain audience. Bardon knew very well that there were many powers that were going to misuse this knowledge once they got their hands on it, so he protected it. Bardon stated things like, "Don't move on to the next exercise until you've mastered this one," knowing very well that the stream would stop and when the stream stops, you stagnate. In reality, you are journaling to accelerate the speed of your stream. Journaling allows you to do things such as graphing results, detailing what works, showing what does not work and how to utilize the moon phases and regulate what you are practicing. Through journaling one is able to measure what is needed for success.

Examples of Uses of Your Journal
All of these realizations for one's highest development are written in your journal. When reading your journal, you will have moments of clarity. For example: "When I eat 'x' items, my practice is better. When I practice with 'x' person, our energy joins together as an amplifier, we both grow faster together than as individuals." And then groups of energy, again, are amplified

when you are working with groups using sacred geometry to position each person in the room. Geometric structures will also amplify the speed of vibration of the group. These are simply examples of things that you may discover through working with your journal.

When you journal, for example, you may note how you position each person in the room during a group practice and say, "Look at the group." The way the tuning forks for all the resonance with each other, they were all bouncing off each other with the sacred geometry. If the sacred geometry is clear, precise and exact, the energy vibrates faster and more efficiently. You may draw the geometric patterns on the floor; a triangle for three people, a square for four people, and so forth. You may find that by positioning the numbers of people in the exact position for the sacred geometry – when the group practices, the energy will vibrate faster, transform quickly, and will both raise and ascend in resonance with the universal laws. Again, this is written in your journal. If you are taking great care with your journal, you will find insight that cannot be found from any other book or teacher.

Examples of Questions One May Ask Themselves in a Journal
- How do you regulate the times of day you practice different exercises in order to have the highest growth rates?
- How do you regulate food to speed up your progress?
- How do you regulate the people around you to speed up this process?
- How do you control the environment to speed up the process of growth?
- What are the layers of this exercise? What layers of each aspect reveal themselves? Physical? Astral? Mental? Akashic? Light?

Observing the Macrocosm and Microcosm Through Your Journal

Another aspect of journaling that is important is the ability to scale things down from the macro into the micro. You might have the macro outlined in an exercise where you observe your thoughts arise and fall away. That is the first section in Bardon's book. Your journal will give you the other 99% of insight on that particular exercise. In the first mental exercise of *Initiation into Hermetics* you observe the rising and falling of thoughts. There are thoughts that you see with your eyes and they fall away from the description of the book. In your journal, you may have noted that there is a mental space and that you have given your own description. There are certain thoughts which may arise that are astrally charged emotionally that interrupt your ability to observe. Write them down and you will notice every now and then that you get absorbed in a story. You get into a creative cycle of making a story and realize that you are not meant to touch your thoughts. You then break that creative cycle and go into dissolving – the releasing or destructive cycle – and let that energy go. By observing the rising and falling of thoughts, you learn the creative processes found in the three bodies that engaged to make a story. And you discover the release process, how the three bodies disengaged to release and dissolve energy. Right there, you have the mechanism of healing, the mechanism for growth, and so forth.

The bigger picture of what the initiation text is pointing at is written in the contents of your journal. Every time you practice an exercise you are getting the complete picture of what the byproducts of that exercise are. What are you learning about from your journal? You will end up having it written into an entire book on esoteric psychology just from documenting your experiences with the first few exercises. That is not written in the *Initiation into Hermetics* text. So your journal is the true initiation text. That is where all of the information about the initiation is. There are myriad books of knowledge written within your journal. You should be writing at least one page, perhaps several pages, when you journal each day. That knowledge, as it unfolds, gives a large reservoir of detail and processes. It gives you an intuitive intellect into how the initiation process works and is critical for one's development.

If you are someone who is not interested in teaching or are a person who is practicing for pure enjoyment – which is to practice and not journal your progress – you will find that your training will become one-sided. You will develop a feeling for how to do things but you will not be able to verbalize them, to fully intellectualize what you are doing. So you will be incapable of sharing the process with someone else even though you can touch them and say, "Oh, this is the Fire element," and you give them that feeling. But your process of how you explain will be no more than to imagine the color red, imagine the heat, and breathe it into them so that they may equalize with the feeling because you have not been journaling. As you journal, you will see intellectually the different aspects of the Fire element from different angles. This allows you to generate a type of intuitive intellect that can define many different processes for developing the same thing. So you can help different people learn in different ways. Journaling is important for teaching, but less important if you are simply an individual enjoying the path. You can get away with not journaling to a small degree, but your progress will definitely not be as fast.

If you are working on releasing mechanisms, such as vipassana, journaling becomes less important. If you are working on creative mechanisms, then journaling becomes extremely important. If you want to work with high magic, you must journal. If you are aiming towards Nirvana and releasing everything you touch to allow the mind to refine to the higher levels of consciousness, you do not really need to journal too much, because you are letting go of everything you touch anyway. Journaling an individualized process in teaching mechanisms.

On the Metaphysical Layers of the Journal

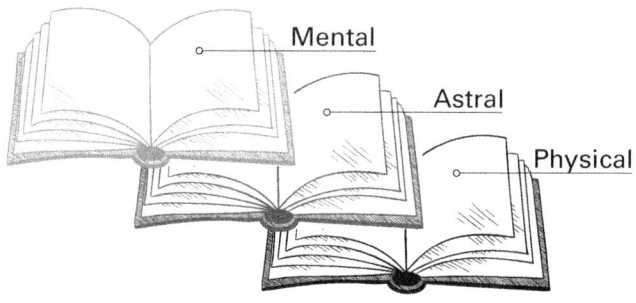

Three Layers of your Journal

We have several different journals. The first journal is obviously a **physical journal**, which you write after you practice, maybe during a practice or training classes. This journal is a link to the astral energy set that you experienced. The **astral journal** is the energy underlying your physical journal; it encompasses the experiences that you are trying to relay. The physical words are just a key to those experiences. When you have a practice session, you have an astral experience and then you write it down. That writing is a key to the re-awakening of that astral energy. When you have read it, you open up that key to remember it. If you mentally transfer into that memory, then you can re-experience this astral energy. That is stored in your journal. When you are journaling, you should have a pen that is only used for that one purpose and charge that pen with Akashic light, so that it can store that experience all the way deep in the Akasha and that knowledge becomes accessible from the Akasha.

Your **mental journal** is the aspect of your journaling that carries over with your spirit after you leave the body. The astral form obviously dies someday and it stays in the book. In general, if it is a part of your body, it moves back into the elements, into the physical and astral worlds. The physical journal itself carries the astral fluid. The mental journal is the only journal you carry after you move on to your next life. The mental journal is a part of your spiritual property. That mental journal is engraved in your mental body. It is a part of your spiritual heritage and skillset; a part of what you have developed, and the work and effort that you have put into spiritual development. This spiritual journal is important because there is only one of these three journals which continues after you leave the body. In order to refine that, we need to look at every exercise we do as a reflection of life, as a reflection of universal life. For example, if we are working with nature spirit energies, shamanistic animal spirits and so forth, there is a certain center of gravity within that energy. So, the astral field of that energy has a strong connection to the physical world and the spiritual essence of that is also a similar frequency.

If you are working on a shamanistic level, your spiritual journal will have a magnetic attachment to the physical world. That astral space is very close to the physical. If the exercises you practice are invoked through prayer from universal light, from the Brotherhood of Light for example, then that light travels through the three bodies as you both write and practice; the energy and information being written down in the journal are of light. It creates a center of gravity of energy inside that journal, which pulls you up to that level of the Brotherhood of Light at the end of your incarnation.

The things that you write in your journal stay forever. They stay with your spirit for a long time and they are not extinguished until you achieve Nirvana, until you are dissolved into that highest level. Your journal writing forms a type of center of gravity. If you have spent several incarnations in a lower center of gravity, you have to do several incarnations on a highest center to offset it, because that information written into your journal is permanent. You cannot just delete it. You cannot go into the Akasha and wipe it out. It stays within the spiritual, it is engraved inside the spirit and it is engraved in a spiritual frequency. When you are filling out your physical journal, there needs to be a deep sense of connection to light and a deep reverence and seriousness in how you address your journal, because this has lasting effects. It is going to have a profound effect on your next incarnation and many incarnations after that. You want that energy stream to have a deep sacredness to it.

Chapter 2

Sucess and Failure

There are several key factors which we will cover in this chapter regarding the subject of success and failure on the Hermetic path. The following are a few, but not all, noteworthy components of universal practice, in no particular order:

1. Maintaining a journal
2. Principle of transmission
3. Supportive group environment
4. Maintenance of precepts, dedications or vows
5. Directly working with and equalizing with Akasha and non-dual light

As discussed in the previous chapter, the maintaining of a practice journal is essential as it serves countless purposes in attaining our highest aspirations throughout many lifetimes.

The maintenance of precepts and vows provides a safety net and acts as a tuning fork to the highest universal truths.

The principle of transmission is useful to not only benefit ourselves in this lifetime via those who have walked the path before us, but also to ensure that the next generation is even more evolved. In the same way that we stand on the shoulders of giants in the sciences, such as Sir Isaac Newton for physics or Charles Darwin for evolutionary biology, we too are supported by the work of those who walked the spiritual path for the benefit of all sentient beings. It is by the transmission of love and physical matter in the form of food and water provided by our parents that we get nurturing into physical reality when we enter the world. It is by the transmission of knowledge from teachers that we grow fully into our intellectual capacity until we can stand our own ground. Therefore, as we have observed in the rest of our lives, the next transmission into the subtle realities of life are assisted by those who have walked the spiritual path in this lifetime.

A supportive group environment acts as a massive catalyst. Having even one person that confirms the development of spiritual faculties as a normal part of human development can enable our subconscious to both normalize and help develop our faculties.

One can develop Akasha and non-dual light by equalizing with it through samadhi, as described in later sections, or through taking ownership of the feeling through the transmission of someone who already has attained non-dual light and Akasha. There is much more to be said in this chapter and yet it is up to the reader to invoke their own genius so that they may arrive at the answers they need for their development.

Principle of Transmission

The mental-astral-physical bodies link together to form protective energy; the mental and astral matrices need to increase magnetic fluid and that develops top protective chi or Wei Chi, as it is called in Chinese medicine. This protective energy is measured by the amount of magnetic fluid within the mental-astral matrix. The astral matrix is the most important for health and the mental matrix is the most important for intellectual thinking, analysis and so forth.

When teaching information, demagnetize the student's mental matrix so that it is neutral and soften their astral matrix. We do not want to neutralize the astral matrix because the person's health is at risk – we want to soften it, not neutralize it. We do this by simply creating more space when we feel the relationship between the person's willpower and balance in relation to their body.

Mechanics of Opening Space

In tai chi, when touching a person's fascia, we feel the interconnectedness of their body. We feel a relationship between their balance and strength. As we separate their balance and strength, we begin to feel a gap. That gap

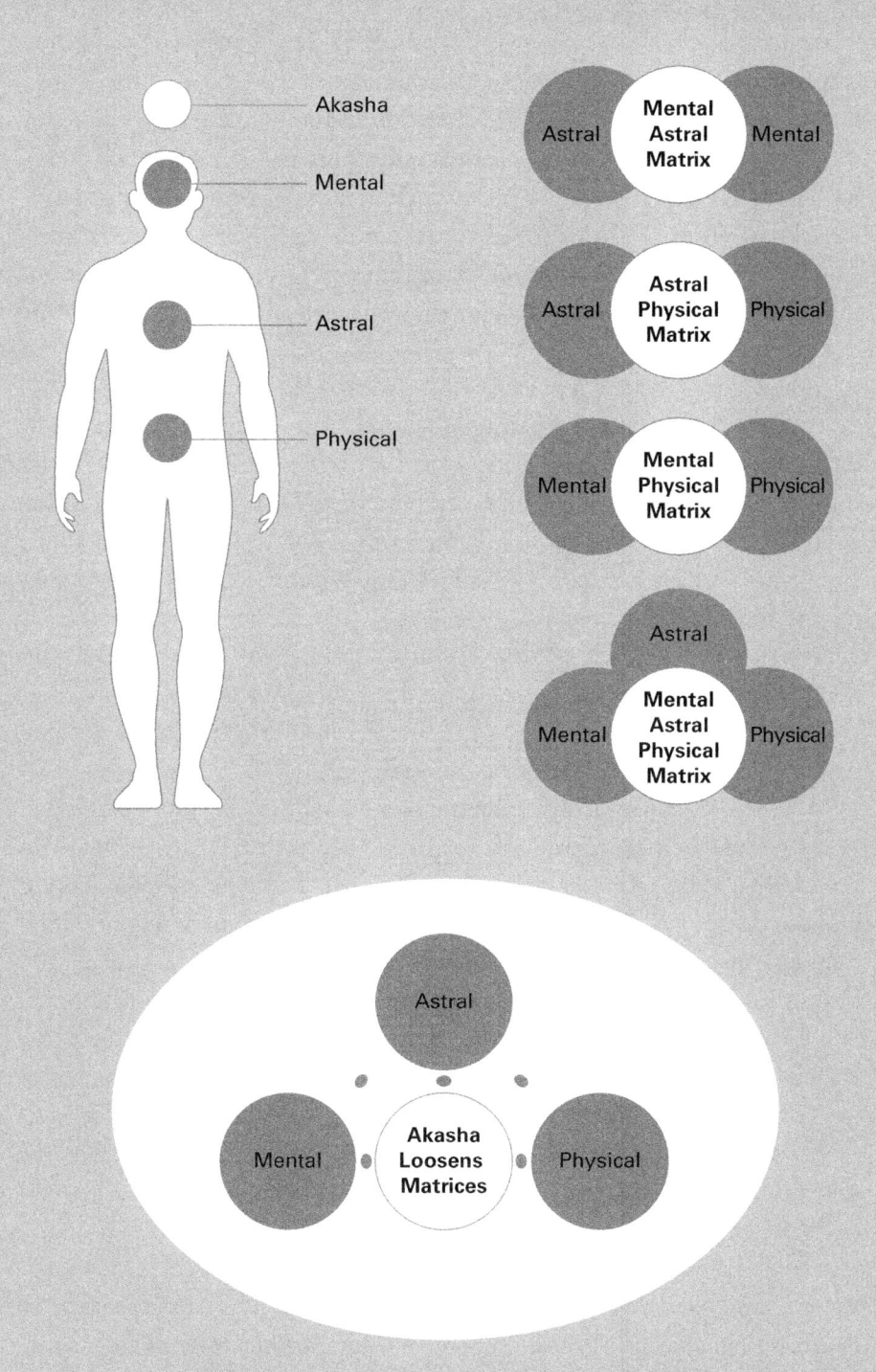

Matrices in the body

is the mental matrix. We thin their mental matrix out by expanding it into the space around them. We then have a large window where we can enter directly into their astral subconscious mind. This astral subconscious door has a lot to do with space and pressure. When it has a small space, the matrix has a lot of pressure. When we expand it into a big space, it has lower pressure and it is much easier to transmit, to heal, to communicate information, to hypnotize behavioral condition, whatever is needed for the benefit of that person.

When you are teaching a piece of information, you need to do two things: firstly, you need to take the feeling – the outcome – of what the process of information is about, and secondly, you must transmit that feeling through the mental matrix into their astral subconscious. Thus you are creating an energetic charge in their astral subconscious. Then you have to give them a process that they can follow – such as a meditation exercise – in order to release the result. So they act upon it, they practice the exercise, and the energy that you implant into their subconscious then releases itself. This relationship between the conscious and unconscious minds, where they synchronize and give almost magical effects, is important. You can get students to a high level quickly using this method.

When you are physically touching someone, it is easy to engage their fascia, engage their base, generate a slight compression of life force into their bones, then pull back and release. All of that elastic pressure pops and their balance comes out. Then, you slip straight through the mental matrix into their energy fields and expand, opening everything up. When you are not able to physically touch the person, you need to use energy in the room. You create more energy in the room than what their mental matrix is, and it sucks in the mental matrix into the space of the room. This automatically opens them up and makes them float.

Most people have a similar type of energy in the mental matrix – it is not vastly different, just slightly different. There is a small spectrum of energy of the mental matrix that you can breathe into the room, in order to make everyone float inside of it. Once you have opened this up, and if you understand what this is, you will immediately understand how cults function. If someone can breathe a type of light into the mental matrix to every person in the room, this is what generates a cult. It creates cultish behavior; people will act in unusual ways when people are floating within whatever patterns the cult leader is facilitating through the group. Everyone will be jumping around with those patterns and acting in a particular way, thinking and feeling in that particular way. This can be very easily misused as a cult means. Be clear about both your ethics and precepts.

On Giving Others Your Best
As a teacher, it is important for your ethics to transmit purely what the teachings are, especially since people are in a highly vulnerable, programmable state. Only give them your best. This is for many reasons, the first being that if you give them a lesson at your best, that energy transmission to the person pulls the center of gravity of your consciousness to a higher state. You are giving that person a transmission of a certain frequency, so the stream of that energy reflects back at you, it mirrors back to you. Give people your best and ensure that the constant stream is a platform of your best for you to stand on, to continually rise to higher levels. The merit field reflecting through that particular transmission will propel you upwards in the same way that they are being pulled to that level. The act of helping others rise up in frequency creates an upward pressure for you to rise up as well. It is a vacuum which rises you to the next level as you rise someone else up to the next level. This multiplication effect of, say, teaching a thousand people and elevating their frequency creates an upward vacuum that pulls on your crown, pulls you to a higher frequency, is far greater than what you gave them – because of the great consciousness effect. For example, teaching a hundred people in energetic work every day will automatically elevate your frequency whether you know what you are doing or not. It can appear ironic that a qigong teacher could stand in front of a hundred people with zero skill and a few years later they have achieved empty force. This is because the group's energy is projecting and willing the teacher's subconscious to act, feel and perform in a certain way. And that person's unconscious starts acting, performing in that way, to meet the expectations of the group that is projecting onto the teacher.

Now, this very often how cults are formed. People like to be sheep. It is unfortunate that there are people who do not seek self-mastery. When you have enough of them following a teacher, they will project and put themselves into that position whether you want them to or not. You will find that if you are teaching in an environment for more than 12 months, and those same people are there for more than 12 months, you will have very strong cultish behavior forming whether you want it or not. Normally you can neutralize this effect by dissolving those behaviors and every time you see any cultish behaviors coming out, just raise those behaviors energetically up through the person's chakra, connect them to the light, reinforce this seed of mastery – that they are the master, not the sheep. This way, you can bypass most of these side effects.

When teaching in suburbia, most of the people in suburbia are sheep, not masters. If you are teaching and creating a teacher's course, then you are going to have masters coming, and it is then much easier to neutralize those types of behavior. But this is something that you have to manage as it arises when you teach. Because anyone who is following through Bardon's work is a teacher. Normal people, living day to day life, do not do this sort of work. It is too difficult and requires far too much commitment. It is a calling, something your spirit tells you to do and then you practice it. When you have that calling, you are a teacher. You have a special place in the world and you are here to do something unique. Thus, you practice and allow that quality of mastery to flow through you.

On Self-Initiating

Some people work on the *Initiation into Hermetics* text on their own. This is the most difficult way to succeed with the work. For example, the text is pointing out and describing what an orange tastes like, but it does not give you an orange to taste, as it is a book. You have to create an orange and taste it. So this is all reliance on the impossible. It is something that is difficult. This is mainly because the ego gets lost. The quality of the release is not pure, one's conviction isn't pure – it is a difficult way to get success in initiation.

When you are in a group of people practicing initiation and someone in that group has been initiated, this initiate has been given an orange and knows what it tastes like. This initiate can give you an orange so that you may taste it. It is a clear transmission of one frequency from one generation to the next. It saves you decades of messing around and decades of having to develop samadhi to take charge of Akasha, and so forth. It is much quicker to get into a practice group. There are few practice groups out there for

Hermetics. If you are fortunate enough to get connected to one, and work with one, take advantage of it straight away.

You may also consider going to Vajrayana Buddhist groups, such as Tibetan Buddhist groups or Shingon Buddhist groups, because the deities that they are working with have a Bodhisattva vow. The Bodhisattva vow is non-dual, meaning the entities you will be practicing with within groups are doing it for the benefit of all sentient beings; therefore, there is no accounting. You do not owe them anything when working with them. This is a way of working with these high frequencies. While it is not exactly the same as Hermetics, it takes you to non-dual light quickly and once you have entered non-dual light you can bring energies down through non-dual light and they can manifest themselves through those three points. You can make quick progression in the initiation texts on your own by getting into that state. Working with non-dual light is extraordinarily important. Find someone who can transmit that to you. Having said that, there are many people who work with non-dual light that do not know that they are working with it. This is very often found in high level meditators, yogis and Tibetan lamas, and some teachers in Vajrayana Buddhism in Japan have a radiance of this non-dual light.

The difference between dual light and non-dual light is that when non-dual light is sensed and felt, it has an underlying feeling of infinity when connecting to it. Non-dual light does not have any boundaries, it just keeps going. With dual light – such as astral light – you feel its radiance, its heat, its strength, its form, and it has limitations. With non-dual light, when you touch it and you release yourself into it, it is forever, because there is no sense of ending to it. This is what you are after. If you can equalize your center of gravity to experience non-dual light, then you can pass samsara in this incarnation. Then you have the freedom of choice. That freedom of choice is whether one wants to incarnate again or not. Because your will is equalized with very subtle light and the flux within non-dual light is so small, there is no gravitational samsaric force to pull you into another incarnation. Non-dual light is really the platform that you want to stand on as quickly as possible.

In order to train this, release time to get into the astral, release space to get in the mental, release consciousness in the state of infinity, enter into the Akasha, and investigate the nature of your own essence of mind, essence of spirit, which is non-dual light, through Akasha, and then you touch that quality of light and the universal mind which is composed of it. That is where we want to stand as a platform for practice.

On Maintaining a Like-Minded Community

Now we are going to look at the training environment in relation to the people that you live with, practice with, work with, and share your life with. There are these rings of openness. How much does your heart open to the people in your house? How much does your heart open to your neighbors? How much does your heart open to your practice group? How much does your heart open to your colleagues at work? You have this degree of openness and this is a two-way exchange of energy. In this energy exchange, you influence them and they influence you. The astral bodies are mixed. This mixing of the astral body is happening unconsciously based upon love. If you really care for someone, and you are totally open to them, they have a profound effect on you and vice versa.

The Crown Technique

This openness to your environment is a double-edged sword. You want to be expanding and having a feeling of being omnipresent and connected, being in connection with your environment, into nature, into the planet. But you do not want to be receiving negative flow back from your openness. Because, of course, all of these energy streams are both positive and negative. All we need to do is connect these circles of energy to the positive side and not allow the negative feedback to be received. We do this through the law of resonance. There is a technique called 'the crown'. Visualise each person you meet with a crown around their head and each point of the crown is the positive aspect of them. You look at them and feel that the person has virtues, has a work ethic, is very athletic, good at this skill, or at that skill, and each point has a positive aspect. Then you identify this person every time you see them. You look at their crown and say, "Oh yeah, Jack has these qualities ... Jessica has those qualities," and that becomes your identity, your tuning forks, how you perceive that person.

By reinforcing these positive attributes and labeling people with positive qualities, you activate those qualities within your crown. You become open to that person through the points of their crown. It becomes an energetic exchange, that you tune in to the best which that person has to offer, and the best they have to offer affects you. The rest of it, you do not really see it, care about it, engage it or nurture it. You will only nurture the highest, most benevolent qualities of a person.

On an unconscious level, that person will feel nurtured on a high level every time they meet you. Every time they see you, they will feel that they really like you and they will not know why. It is because you are bringing out their best, seeing the best in them, radiating light into their crown, and nurturing their highest qualities. In this way, through each of your circles, you can create a positive return stream without their negativity.

If you make a judgment that someone is this and they are that, then those same judgments become a negative mirror of what you get back from them. When you see them, you get a reflection of those judgments. There is a subtle negative vibration, the law of resonance reflects back on you. Those judgments become your property. They manifest within you, they become your feelings, and they bring you down. Clearly, we don't want to possess these judgments. Neither do we want to be brought down. By putting a crown around every person you meet, placing high frequency qualities on that crown, and looking at the crown every time you see the person, those frequencies will be mirrored back at you. These qualities will come into your perception, astral body and your physiology.

This principle of the crown is important – the qualities within the crown become more refined as you work with people that you spiritually practice with. There is a saying, "Wish for others what you wish for yourself." You cannot wish for something that a person does not have. You have to come into resonance with something that they do have and amplify it. If you are developing wealth, you have to look at a person – they do not have to be monetarily wealthy, but they have to be wealthy in some way or another – then look at that tuning fork and amplify it within them and it will reflect to be amplified within you. Whether it is monetary wealth, a wealth of knowledge or insight, you need to look at how that tuning fork vibrates, how to amplify it, and how it reflects. Bring these principles into daily use.

Principles of Hosting a Spiritual Circle
In your spiritual circle, the principle of amplification becomes vitally

important. When two people who are clairvoyant come together, there is amplification. When three people come together, you have three times three, you get the power of nine and so forth. If you have four, a power of sixteen. If you have ten people, that is a power of a hundred. This is because each person's tuning fork is hitting each other person's tuning fork and vibrating back and forth between every person in the room. If you have ten people generating a field, its power is equal to a hundred people working individually. That means that clairvoyance development hits a critical mass and everyone in that group starts to experience high levels of clairvoyance.

Try working within a group, whether you are a teacher or a group leader, and ensure that the crown that each person is wearing has high frequency spiritual qualities. Educate each person in this group to really perceive these qualities, identify them, and then allow each person in the group to express their skills. If someone is very good at a particular skill, allow them to lead the group in the development of that particular skill. If someone is naturally clairvoyant and you are doing a clairvoyant exercise say, "Okay, Charlie, you've got a really good clairvoyance skill. Would you like to lead this exercise?" Everyone will look at Charlie and will tune into Charlie's clairvoyance as he leads the exercise. Everyone's crown will start to awaken with clairvoyance because Charlie has that skill. If there are ten people in the room and each person has a different skill, they can awaken that skill

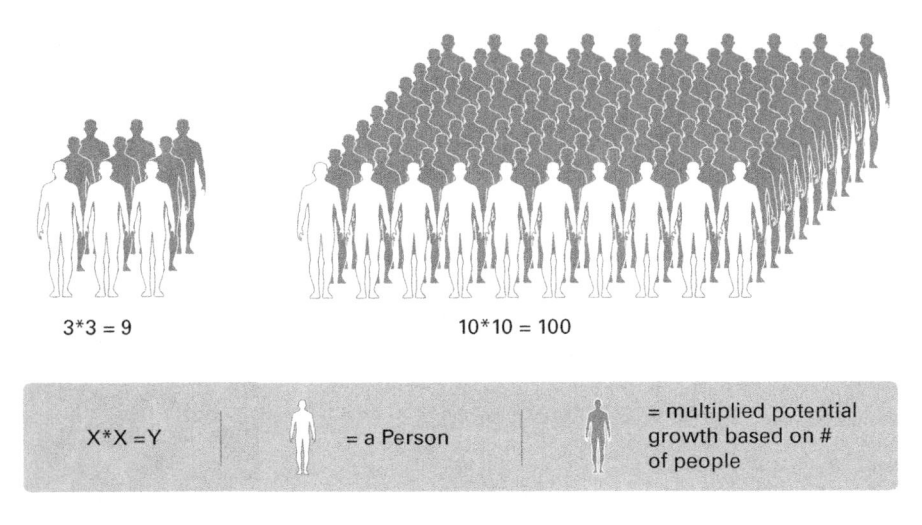

$3*3 = 9$ $10*10 = 100$

$X*X = Y$ = a Person   = multiplied potential growth based on # of people

Amplification process

within every other person in the room until each person has all ten skills.

This amplification process is valuable. It would take many years to get to the same place as you can get to in a few months in a very good group environment. So, it is important to understand what every person's skills are, what their background is, and to find their crown. What are those points on the crown, what are their peaks? Be sure to reduce people talking about their skills and bragging, getting feedback and acknowledgment from their peers. That is a weakness. When people try to get validation from others, they need help to cut that craving of validation straight away when it arises. Be sure to warn everybody in the group about it. As soon as you have a group sharing individual experiences, there is an unconscious need for approval that will result in people embellishing their experiences when they should not share what they just went through. We need to counter this from the beginning and keep all of the experiences as being absolutely normal. There is nothing special about clairvoyance, it is normal. If it is special, it is hard to achieve. If it is normal, it is easy to achieve. So you keep everything within the realms of normality, even though these are metaphysical skill sets, and then it will be normal for everyone to achieve them. There is no embellishment, there is no making anything sound more glorious than it actually is. It is something simple. It is just clairvoyance.

On Precepts and Vows

Vows and precepts are the rules that you make to govern yourself. Abrahamic faiths have the Ten Commandments and Buddhists have five moral precepts. When you design your own precepts, you have to base it on the type of physics. Each precept is a tuning fork. The precepts you create are not dogma, they are a positive life enhancement. Precepts are energy emanators, receivers and transmitters that generate in your internal environment, which is the point of your practice. Precepts are also a safety net. So we want to look at these tuning forks, how we and why we build them, and how they generate an internal environment in which we can grow and accelerate.

Five Buddhist Moral Precepts Metaphysical Breakdown
Let us look at something as simple as **"to abstain from false speech"** or "thou shalt not lie." This is a negative precept that we cannot do something;

we cannot have a tuning fork based on the negative. What we can do is instead generate the tuning fork of truth. How do we do this?

You may have already started to do it by creating the black/white soul mirror, looking at personality and how you think, feel, act and define your personality. By being true to yourself while creating your soul mirrors, you can then also look at the truth of how you think and feel about others, how you act towards others, and how you speak; you will only speak in the resonance of truth. One builds this receiver and transmitter antenna of truth. Of course, universal knowledge is based on truth. Part of this tuning fork is getting to know the fabric of the universal rules and to understand these rules, so the truth is possibly the most important precept or tuning fork. We want to see the truth within ourselves, within universal teachings, and universal knowledge within the Dharma if you are a Buddhist, or within the *Bible* if you are a Christian. Whatever your doctrine is, you want to go to the essence of the truth of the doctrine. Living in the pure essence of the truth allows your perceptions to see the truth. Information will align itself with truth into your consciousness, so you will understand things in different ways than other people who are not living in resonance with the truth.

Let us look at **"to abstain from taking what is not given"** otherwise known as "thou shalt not steal." Again, we cannot exclude something that is not a tuning fork. We have to build a tuning fork that has ethics and a perfect accounting, that when anything is out of balance in ourselves, we have to have a tuning fork that is charitable. Many have realized that charitability has nothing to do with money. It is teaching a person how to fish, not giving that person a fish – so it is sharing knowledge. Sharing knowledge is being charitable, because knowledge is what allows people to create a good life for themselves and develop themselves physically, astrally and spiritually. Sharing knowledge is charitability.

With this tuning fork of integrity, you are building a positive accounting system where during every interaction you have with other people, you will ensure that they get more out of the interaction than you. With this tuning fork, continually giving is universal. Thus, you continually create an environment of receiving. If during every business interaction you do more for the person that you are working with than what you receive, then there is automatically a type of gratitude from that person, a type of well-being where they are nourishing your spirit, your astral relationship and your connection to the community. Of course, your business is going to be better because of this interaction. Whether it is a social or a business interaction – whatever it might be – there is always a sense of giving that exponentially grows with that interaction. You will always have good luck following you everywhere and people will love you for it. So, this tuning fork of integrity is in the environment. When you choose to practice, the energy coming through and the energy around you nurtures that practice. The physical environment you sit upon is charged with nurturing your spiritual practice. If you went in the opposite direction, where you are out of your integrity and there is a sense of lying, stealing and fraud within your thinking, feeling and actions, then automatically the three bodies are going to contract into survival mode. You will be disconnected from your environment. Your ego-making will draw you into yourself. Spiritual growth is completely the opposite of contraction. The spiritual grows as the mind expands, the astral field expands, the body opens and you are unified, omnipresent and connected to your environment.

The "to abstain from taking what is not given" or "thou shalt not steal" rule is more about integrity, staying on the side of integrity and looking at the way you interact with other people, making them grow. We are all connected and if you are generating growth for others, then we all grow at an accelerated rate. We are helping that connected web. If you are constantly within your integrity, then energy radiates out and will constantly be radiating back to its source.

When you go further into precepts, we have **"to abstain from intoxicants as tending to cloud the mind"** or "thou shalt not take intoxicants." Intoxicants are things that turn a master into a slave. Anything that is addictive and prevents you from being in charge and instead puts a substance in charge, whether it is alcohol, drugs or anything that puts you on a merry-go-round. If you cannot get off until the drug is out of your system, it puts you into a state of slavery. That is something that you have to be careful about and it is not just because you waste all of your time, mess with your brain chemistry and reduce your ability to practice properly in the future. It can also open up holes in the mental-astral matrix, in your aura. Those holes create a gateway for negative forces, negative information, delusion and types of nonsense to flow through your consciousness. You will not be able to tell that they are not true, that they are illusory. These holes in your aura can generate conspiracy beliefs and all types of delusions because these holes in the aura are connected to lower astral realms, as all drugs of that nature are nature-spirit oriented and connected to the lower realms. Beings of lower realms do not know any more about reality than you, they just know about lower realms. They do not know about higher spiritual laws or about the fabric of creation; they have no concept of the highest universal laws. So they can perfectly give you lies, they can perfectly translate those lies for the holes in the aura and form religious beliefs around it. And then everyone involved with substances can dance around the fire and bang on drums and that is all fun. As we are well aware as Hermeticists, this does not mean that it has anything at all to do with universal truth. It is no higher frequency than the physical world around you because it is a material practice of the physical world. The drugs have physical properties layered upon it and the spiritual entities connected to that drug exist just above the physical. These spirits do not know any more about the highest spiritual laws than you – in all probability, they know less. If you have any confliction about this, try observing those who have regularly consumed drugs and the results of their progress. Consider the various spiritual masters and how many advocated against drug usage or had not allotted any importance to such substances.

Have a concise look at intoxicants, with a simple example being coffee. How addicted are you to coffee? When you have a cup of coffee, does it make you a slave to all the caffeine in your body? Or does caffeine just stimulate more concentration and growth? What does it do for you? Really look at everything you take into your body and get to know it inside out and back to front. You will find some things that are addictive are maybe beneficial, and some things that are addictive may be detrimental. It is for you to decide and closely look at each one of these different qualities.

Another tuning fork is "**right sexual conduct**." Like integrity, every sexual interaction you have needs to be a positive growth experience for both parties. This means that every sexual interaction you have with a person that you are involved with needs to have a positive effect on them, where they feel better from that encounter. It is important that they feel they have grown from the experience, that the interaction nurtures their spirit, that they feel good about it on the inside – in the spirit – and in their body; that all three bodies are harmonized and they see benefit from that interaction. If you are just engaging their body and not the astral-mental, then it is very limited.

In all probability, it will work against your development. Every sexual interaction has an etheric body connection. Your etheric body becomes linked to the person you have intercourse with and if you do not know how to use the Akasha and dissolve that connection, that energy will continue to leak. Behavior patterns, types of thinking, feeling and actions will leak between the two people unknowingly. A lot of the qualities that you have inside you do not actually belong to you, they belong to someone else. Someone else is nurturing them and you are experiencing them. If you identify with those qualities – you start thinking, feeling and acting them out – you are taking on other people's karma. This is the trickiest part of sexual interaction with people. You need to dissolve those connections afterward. Before, during and after, there has to be a stream of positive mental growth, positive astral growth and positive physical change, and then any disconnection you need to do afterward must also be considered.

The last of the most fundamental precepts is "thou shalt not kill." In Buddhism it is called "**non-harming.**" When you look at the precept as a tuning fork, it has to be a tuning fork which generates something. In this case, we are generating love, a type of connection to our environment. In the same way that you take care of your own body – you wash your body, your clothes, yourself, you keep yourself warm and protect your body – you want that particular type of feeling to extend from you and into your environment: to plants, animals, the house you sleep in, the people around you, and the earth. Everything needs to have a feeling of connection to you. Your consciousness is a part of that consciousness and there is a unified intermingling of all of these consciousnesses into a unified mind. This type of thinking totally eliminated killing other animals. When we do kill another animal, there is a huge contraction – like a rhythmic whiplash – in your etheric body. This generates a type of survival instinct in your mental-astral-physical bodies which makes your three bodies cling together – a type of deep fear in the psyche that disconnects us from the environment, and as this disconnects there is an extreme contraction of the self. We want our practice to be an expansion of the mental, astral and physical bodies; this feeling of release and letting go, of relaxation. We want to be connected, we want to have a connection to all of these different levels. As soon as you generate harmfulness you compete against yourself in a fighting type of way. When you kill an animal or harm someone there is an extreme contraction in the three bodies.

When something dies there is a whiplash through the Akasha and you and your etheric body feel that. Your body contracts back into itself and we want to minimize that type of effect. When you eat meat, you are the cause of the death of the animal. One might say, "No, someone killed the animal a long time ago, and eventually made its way to the supermarket shelf. I then purchased it." Remembering supply and demand, if everybody stops eating meat, there would be no more animals killed. So, there is an astral stream. When you create a demand, supply fills that demand. The astral stream cannot be relinquished by saying that the animal's death happened in the past – it does not work that way. By eating meat now, you are connecting to the energy of the death of the animal in the past when it was killed, and your path is responsible for that karma. That karma will flow towards you, through you. Recognizing this type of energy is important. If you are eating meat, you are killing animals. If you choose to eat meat, you should raise the spirit of the animal you have eaten into either non-dual light or the Brotherhood of Light. Since you are connected to the animal, your spirit vibrates the animal's spirit up to a higher level. You are paying the animal for its life by raising its frequency into the light. This is okay if that is your way. Bless the animal, give thanks to the animal and give it a prayer to raise the frequency of the animal. This type of prayer can move the animal from animal reincarnation into a human incarnation, which is a big challenge for an animal's spirit by itself. When it is done to the correct spirit, with the right approach, it can be very beneficial for the animal, even though it is giving its life for you.

Another precept that is unusual, in Buddhism for example, is not to sleep on a high, luxurious bed. It has more to do with the word 'high' than 'luxurious'. When you have any thermal environment like the ground, the floor in a concrete building, you have an earth current running through, which is about a foot (30 cm) radiation of the earth current. If you sleep within that one foot radiation, you will find that the earth's currents will balance out your astral body. You will get very deep sleep, a very profound sense of healing, and when you get up in the morning to meditate, you will have a deep calm and deep stillness. This is amplified if your body is actually grounded and connected to the earth while you sleep. So, whether you have a grounding thermal mat underneath your sheet or something similar, it amplifies the thermal effect, it discharges all of the static in your body and creates a neutral pH environment which allows your mind to have peacefulness.

When we look at the principle of grounding when you are at home, you should be barefoot and walking on the ground so that static is discharging out of your body. That grounding process is amplified when you have a shower, but a five minute shower is not long enough – it takes a good 45 minutes to ground yourself. If you walk on the beach, it is a very powerful grounding process. When you go for a swim, it is a very powerful grounding process. Swimming is not just good for you because you are swimming, it is good for you because you are in the water and grounding yourself for the amount of time that you are there. When you are fully grounded in the water while you are exercising it generates a double benefit. The chemistry, the oxidation, the chemicals that are running through your body are all being continually grounded while exercising. That does not happen with normal exercise. Exercising underwater is fantastic, wherever it may be and whether it is swimming or any other type of exercise.

Precepts like not wearing jewelry are about a projection of hierarchy. When someone wears jewelry, they have a status associated with themselves. For anyone who looks at the jewelry, they become status-related to it. So, this status is just a projection from people. This becomes a problem when you are a teacher. In Buddhism, the monks are not allowed to wear jewelry because they do not want to change the hierarchy and projection from other people.

Whatever precepts you choose to follow, you need to look at them based on vibrational energetic laws. What is the law of this particular precept? How does it work? How does it create an environment for practice? Does it benefit me or not? Wearing an amulet that is highly charged with energy is very beneficial, but the amulet can be under your shirt so no one sees it. It is jewelry, but energetically it is going to regulate your field. It may have protection around it. It may have mindfulness charged into it. Perhaps it has an energy reservoir connected to your etheric body. The jewelry may be balancing the elements all the time. It may be giving you connected inspiration to light, bringing you into resonance with your universal truth so that your environment is aligned to it as well. It makes up a whole range of functions. That type of jewelry is excellent. It brings a huge amount of value for wearing it or an amulet around your neck.

Give some thought to your precepts. Design them energetically based on laws of energy and vibration. Once you have designed them, commit yourself to your precepts. Say to yourself, "Okay, I'm going to test this precept for one month or one year, and thoroughly test it." Journal the results, document them well. Remember, you are not only documenting the results for yourself, but for whether you can recommend it for the next generation. If you develop a type of precept – a type of life code, a type of causation chain that gives you value in your practice – of course, you want to be sure that this is the most effective way to do it. Then you can share it with other people so they can benefit as well. It is pointless keeping a precept to yourself. Remember, precepts affect your past, present and future. All of the changes that you create within yourself now are going to be energetically connected to you after you leave this body. Your spirit is still going to be nourished by those hundreds – if not thousands – of people that are being touched by the information you give them. And when you reincarnate to your next body, you will have this light coming into you, nourishing your spirit, and you will not even know why. It is because of all of those people who are still alive and who benefited from the information you shared during your last incarnation. Your spirit is being nurtured in this incarnation and you get somewhat of a 'free ride'. For some, life is easy. It is because of what they did in their past incarnation, it is still floating through their spirit in this incarnation. These effects are important to document and become sensitive to. If you wonder why something is happening to you in this life and you observe the Akashic stream of that event, very often it will connect to past lives. You will observe the streams of thinking, feeling and causation from that past life streaming through your spirit into this life. Parts of this stream may be positive, or perhaps negative, it depends upon your situation.

The Three Transformations and Pillar of Light Exercise

The Three Transformations exercise is not in Bardon's book, but it is an excellent exercise and a natural byproduct of studying his text and working with his system.

The first transformation is moving energy from your vital field into your astral field. It is a simple process of charging yourself through vital breathing, becoming filled with life force. Then you slow down the time continuum of that life force. There are several ways you can do that. You can vital breathe in, pause, stop the breath, stop the mind, enter into a state of stillness, then breathe that stillness in, and then breathe that stillness out. Follow this cycle. At the end and beginning of each breath, stop, engage the stillness, and slow everything down through the in- and the out-breath.

You will find after one or two minutes of doing this, the life force would have slowed right down and dropped you into the astral body. This first transformation from vital to astral can be transformed within the same space or can be transformed from your physical center of gravity up to your astral center of gravity.

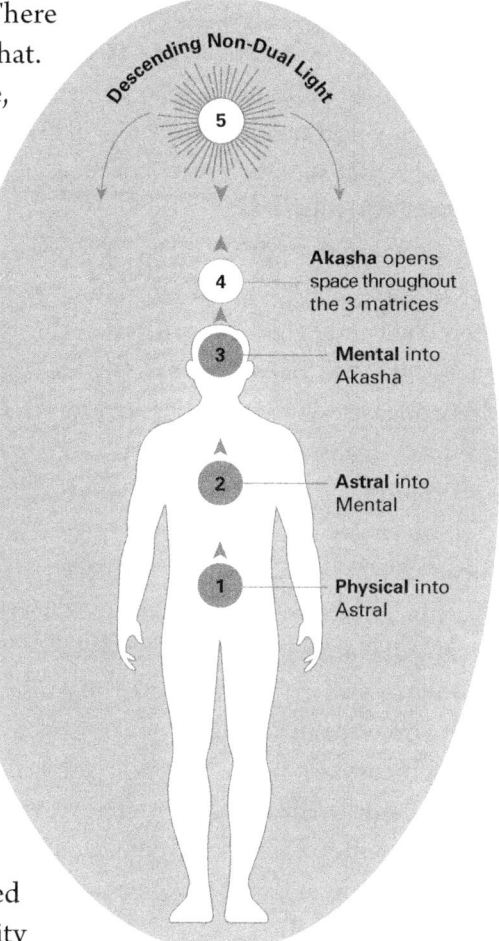

The Three Transformations

If you look at a Taoist alchemical model for energy transformation, you vital breathe, then you slow the energy down and it bubbles into astral energy. That energy will steam up from the physical center of gravity to the astral center of gravity. The astral center of gravity then condenses into form and this is a heart center. You want to transform it up to the mental center of gravity that has released all form. We feel the edges of the form of the energy we are working with, we feather them off and release space. As you release space the energy starts to spread, and as the energy spreads we relax and release it up to the center of gravity of the mental body.

There is this transformation of the vital energy to the astral and the astral up to the mental. To get this transformation, we need to recognize that this astral energy is mind substance. It has mind and it has form. We want to take the power out of the form, relax it into the mind substance and then increase the mental power. This awareness of relaxing the energy from a form state into a mental state is a particular feeling and it is something that cannot really be verbalized. If you are working with a group which is doing it, you feel it and you know that is how it is done. If you do not have the luck to be in a group – meaning that you cannot experience what others are doing – then you need to go to the idea that the astral field is subject to form. This energy that has been built astrally has edges. Then you have to recognize those edges and recognize the mental energy, or relax the edges and feather them off to absorb the energy into the mind. This is a feeling skill. Feel it, and you transform it through the type of relaxation.

The center of gravity of the mental body is in the pineal gland within the center of the head. The energy will rise up to that point. Again, using the three centers of gravity is an option, it is a choice. You choose to do that because it is actually easier to move it along the central axis than to transform within the same space of where the energy is.

If you want to have energy connect to the physical when you do all of the transformations within your physical center of gravity, you can transform energy to the astral-mental planes that are strongly connected to your physical center. This can also be used to affect the physical center of other people. Through the physical center, you can transform and work with the astral-mental bodies.

By sinking the chi, as they call astral energy in the Taoist alchemical models, we are transforming energy in the space of our physical body all the way into Akasha (known as wuji in Taoist traditions). That energy is anchored in the physical world for physical effects to take place. So this works very well for people who are practicing systems of qigong and standing practice, and tai chi. Fundamentally it is the same, they are just using that model to generate a particular outcome in their energy work.

We are working up the vibrational scale. We release time, moving it up through the astral body, releasing space, moving it up through the mental body. Now we need to Akashically breathe. To breathe Akasha, we have to release time and space together and go into that infinity quality that is worked on in Step Five and Step One mental training. That stillness, that vacuum, we need to bring that into the whole body and pore breathe. When you stop pore breathing there is a stillness. This stillness creates a low pressure environment. Wherever there is a lower pressure environment through strong concentration, you are going to accumulate Akasha. You are also going to generate a lot of energy movement if you open space in a low pressure environment with high pressure around it.

You can use Akasha for summoning and moving large amounts of energy, or you can use it for transforming energy up through the crown to open and clean the crown chakra. Akasha, when it is viewed clairvoyantly, is dark violet in color. This dark violet color that is accumulating around a person's field, we want to add that straight into a visualization. When you move into this feeling of stillness – into this mental vacuum – associated with the dark violet color, and then breathe that vacuity in and out through the pores of the body, this vacuum will naturally build Akasha throughout the three bodies. In the etheric body itself, it will increase its intensity of vacuity.

Once we have caught a feeling of that Akashic substance, we want to raise that Akashic substance up through the crown and funnel up about a hand-span above the crown to open up the crown chakra. Only this timeless, spaceless, infinity quality can open the crown chakra completely. The crown can be opened vitally a small amount, can be opened astrally a small amount, can be opened mentally a small amount. But in order for the crown to open in a large amount you need Akasha, you need wuji training.

The fastest way to develop Akasha is to work with people who have already got it. For example, as soon as a teacher starts breathing into the room, you are breathing it in, your mind gets anchored. That Akasha is found in a slow, low pressure environment. Since you have a taste of Akasha, then you can repeat it. If you have been in that group a few times and you remember it well, your subconscious remembers, your spirit remembers, and it just starts aligning to that Akashic field and functioning through it. If you have not had a group in which you can get a feel for Akasha, you need to develop it yourself. To do this, you need to master samadhi. That means your one-pointedness of concentration has to be so strong that a vacuum builds around your mind. If you are solely focused on an object, then time is going to slow down naturally. Your mind becomes still, space is going to expand naturally. Your mind will become more stable within that release of space. Then the Akasha is going to accumulate around you and the meditation object. Once you are aware of that deeply profound Akashic substance accumulating around your samadhi, you simply move your mind like a feather to that Akasha substance and begin breathing it in and out, and then you have wuji or Akasha. This can take anywhere from one or two to ten years, depending upon the person's merit field, their karma. If one has done this type of work in past lives, it arises relatively quickly due to resonance. If one has not, they may have a solid decade of hard work to put into it. Clearly, the easiest way to take ownership of this particular type of energy is to train with people who already have it and it will similarly transfer quickly through people who are simply breathing it into the room. When you are inside of Akasha, you do not have a body – you are an Akashic substance and you breathe that substance into the room so that everybody in the room can amplify the depth of the vacuity of the Akasha. This amplifies everyone else's gains as well.

Try energetically drawing a circle and have everyone in a group stand in a circle, and for each one to take a turn to sit in the circle and build Akasha as a group. Then have each person add to the vacuity of that circle, the vacuum of that circle. This way, everyone's skills are amplified, magnified many times over with each session they practice. There is a huge benefit to working with Akasha in groups due to the amplification effect.

Once you have streamed Akasha up through the crown and suspended the head from above, you accumulate it a handspan above the crown. Once it is accumulated a handspan above the crown, you have a low pressure environment above the crown and a high pressure environment inside your body. Your physical body is subject to time-space, your astral body subject to space. But it is running on a much slower time continuum. Your mental body is subject to the present moment in time because it is stuck in this body and a subject to the space of this body, but the essence of spirit is not subject to time and space. Of course, moving through the crown, moving through infinity, we move it to the Akasha. We have the strongest emptiness of vacuum above the crown and the strongest form in a physical center of gravity. This creates a feeling of being pulled upwards. In this vacuum, high pressure moves towards low pressure. So, the physical body is high pressure, the astral is a bit less, the mental energy is a bit less, and above the crown is a zero state of pressure. Energy is going to want to rise up your central axis. Energy will start naturally transforming up through the three bodies to that point a handspan above your crown. So, we transform all of these lower energies to the height, relaxing and releasing them upwards to that point.

"May the Path of Light Guide and Protect"
Once we are at this point, we are within that zero state in an Akashic vacuum. To get to this next stage of non-dual primordial light, you cannot intend it because the nature of primordial light is non-dual – it is something that exists outside of that zero state; a light waiting to come into form. But what we can do is to create a type of prayer. We invite that light in with a strong vacuity, the vacuum in the prayer. By making a prayer, "May the path of light and guide and protect," you can invite light down from this primordial non-dual light into your crown chakra and lubricate it with Akasha so that it flows through the three bodies. Akasha increases the flow rate, but it decreases the density of the form. Anytime it is too slow, create a little bit of Akasha and it will speed up the process. Then it is just a matter of increasing its substance, so that it increases inside the form. Remember that form is dependent on emptiness and the emptiness is dependent on a form. When you increase Akasha underneath the power, it makes the power amplify and becomes stronger. When you decrease Akasha underneath the power, the power loses its strength and decreases to match the Akasha. It is like a mirror. So, by increasing the Akasha underneath something powerful, it increases in its power output. You can decrease physical power and the Akasha underneath it will also decrease, so you can affect both sides – you can affect each other from either side. Affect the form, you affect Akasha. Affect the Akasha, you affect the form.

Let us say that you tune in to life force and you breathe Akasha underneath life force with the intent to amplify the life force, so then the power of the life force amplifies. You can draw life force directly out of Akasha – it is an amplification process. It is much easier to amplify Akasha than it is to amplify life force. Life force has natural physical boundaries as it is subject to the laws of physics. The metaphysics say that you can only pull this much up. But when you pull more Akasha through, those laws are being regulated by the Akasha and are not being regulated by physical form. Those laws that you are using are outside of normal time and space, which breaks the physical laws and work deeper into the astral-spiritual in Akashic laws. This generates different physical outcomes. This is the fundamentals of magic:

that we are manipulating Akasha underneath the form to amplify or decrease the energies that we are working with to create various types of effects.

Practicing Mona
Once you are working with Akasha for a few months, when you are inside of Akasha and you recognize your own consciousness, you can allow Akasha to collapse into your own consciousness. You will find that there is only light and space, infinite empty space, and this light of your consciousness, when you are incarnated in the body, has a center of gravity and hovers around the pineal gland. William Cook Edwards referred to this as the mona and he called it a pure spirit. Now, this pure spirit is only accessible by equalizing with the Akashic substance underlying a spirit, and then you come into the essence, into that light. It is like a sun shining in the center gravity of your mental body.

Of course, if you are working with non-dual light and even releasing into it, there will not be a shape or a body, there will just be the beingness of light consciousness. This forms a type of vibrational scale where, when you first enter into the universal light of the astral, you have a definite form. When you go into the light of the mental body, you have a form but it is much more like a silhouette, like a center of gravity of radiation. It is more like you see the silhouette because it is a life force connected to your mental body that keeps you alive and connects to the physical. When you stop working up through Akasha into non-dual light, you enter into the non-dual light with a shape of a body, but as you go up the vibrational scale, there is no body – it is just mind substance. You can sense that the presence of intelligence is everywhere around you, that you are in a space of mind, but there are no bodies to be found. You cannot see the shape of an individual unless that entity wishes to express themselves as a shape. The higher the frequency, the less form or residue of past incarnations there is.

These higher non-dual light realms are just light, but you can sense consciousness – it exists within them. As we come to the lower non-dual light realms, we have shapes of individual spiritual identities that exist among those levels. As you come into the mental body, you have the shape of your current incarnation. As you come into the astral, you have a dense form of light and then in the physical, we have life force and radiation of physical objects.

Ultimately, everything is light – yet there is a vibrational scale that you must first navigate through by the releasing of time for the astral, and the releasing of space for the mental. Then you explore the residues of consciousness left for the Akasha, followed by the non-dual light realms, up to the pure mind state. There is a definite scale that you can perceive and get a sense of. Your intuitive intellect will recognize that is how it works. This is a vibrational scale. Once you sense the scale, you sense the conditions upon which you can elevate yourself and ascend up that scale.

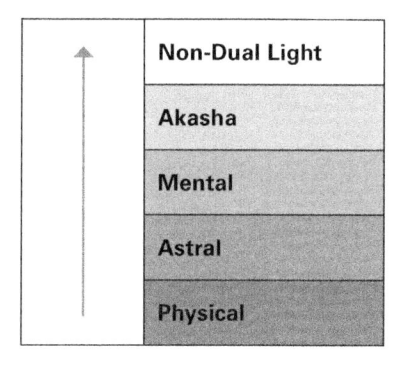

↑	
	Non-Dual Light
	Akasha
	Mental
	Astral
	Physical

Chapter 3

Pore Breathing Guided Meditation Practice

Pore breathing is a fundamental idea, it is simply breathing life force through the pores. Inflate your body like a balloon on the in-breath, relax and release on the out-breath. Whether you are holding the energy in or letting the energy out, that is the basics of pore breathing. What brings pore breathing up to the next level is breathing into the bones. The way the bones are connected to the muscles and the tissues need to be loosened. You want your bones floating in a fluid. The bones have a floating quality to them; the life force is bridging between the bone marrow in the bone and the muscle fascia. If the muscles are holding on too tightly to the bone, then the energy does not transform between the internal storage mechanisms of the physical body. Then you will get an overheating type of effect that is going to happen because the energy cannot radiate properly.

Floating the Bones

We call this breathing method 'floating the bones'. We are going to go through a series of exercises for how to pore breathe and all different types and functions of pore breathing. We are going to break these down into categories. This is the most fundamental basic training in qigong or any kind of energy or chemical work. We have to develop this relationship as a bridge between the breath, the skeletal structure, the muscles, and the fascia, and how the system of the body absorbs and radiates energy.

When the body is very relaxed, and the bones are floating inside the fascia-muscle connection, then there is a straightforward path of radiation of energy out of it. When the muscles are grabbing the bone and holding on, there is a high amount of resistance, and there is no radiation. The energy cannot comfortably radiate outwards. We soften this connection between the bone and the muscle. That hollow space, which we are charging with energy, allows radiation to take place.

Electric Phase

Straighten your spine. Raise your hands up as if you are holding a ball. We do this to become sensitive to energy. You have to have a focal point outside of the body. If your focal point is inside the body, your nervous system is going to control your mind and you are not going to feel much. But when the focal point is between the hands and the ball is between the hands, it is outside of the body, so your senses start becoming active. Your spirit senses start becoming active, your astral senses start becoming active, and you bypass your nervous system, which controls your ordinary day-to-day experiences. So, we want to direct the center of attention to the ball between the hands, breathe in through the pores, inflate your whole body like a balloon, and then breathe out into the ball.

A few things are happening here – we are expanding the mental space as we breathe in and inflating the ball, and as we breathe out we are creating and condensing the mental space in the ball. This expansion and contraction creates contrast. Contrast amplifies the feeling.

Inflate like a balloon on the in-breath, then condense energy through the ball now. The further away you are inflating, feel the diaphragm movement. As the diaphragm breathes in, allow yourself to stretch your body. Allow that stretch to permeate the whole body on the in-breath as you inflate like a balloon. The diaphragm releases. That feeling of release through stretch permeates through the fingers and into the ball. There is synchronicity between the fingers and the ribs – as the ribcage expands on the in-breath, fingers expand; when you release, fingers release. This amplifies feelings further and helps synchronize your breath. The diaphragm-rib movement with the fingers expanding and contracting the ball in resonance to the breath. Move into breathing directly into the ball to bypass the body altogether.

Your breath is still in resonance with expanding and contracting the ball. You are almost ignoring the body. Just expanding the ball on the in-breath, and establishing that electromagnetic feeling between the hands. It is a fluidic and magnetic quality between the hands. Tune the fascia muscles of the whole body to this quality. Starting from the hands, breathe into the hands, give them a stretch, and breathe out, and we tune the stretch in the fingers. Because we are working with the space between the hands, you can naturally feel the ball as you tune into the fingers.

As soon as you have that magnetic quality in the fingers, tune the wrists. Stretching the wrists open. After you tune your wrists, your forearms are going to come in. Relaxing your muscles and tuning the forearms, work up to the elbows and up to your shoulders. And the shoulders connect to the scapulae, the spine – holding the ball through the arms, and through the back of your neck.

You use the chi ball as the tuning fork for your awareness. Maintain that magnetic quality between the hands and bring your whole body into resonance with that feeling. Bring it down the spine, stretch the spine, and bring the spine into resonance with that magnetic feeling, releasing the muscles. Feel the ribcage, release the ribcage. Release the hips, feel the way the muscles are connected to the pelvis, and tune your fascia down to your legs. Stretch that magnetic feeling. As soon as you have reached the feet, scan through the whole body – your jaw, your facial muscles – looking for points of tension to release. Now feel all of the muscles and the fascia, tune them into the fundamental level of the feeling of life force, breathing directly into the bones. You breathe through the pores, into the bones, and from the bones out through the pores.

In that space between the bones and the pores, release that space. Release the muscles, the fascia, the tension, the gripping between the bones and the pores. Breathe into the bones. As you breathe out, relax everything between the bones. And you work through the rest of your body, releasing all of these layers.

This time, breathe into the bones and as you breathe out, open your joints a little bit more than usual to create a stretch. Use that stretch to condense that vital energy in the bone. Breathe into the bone and into the bone marrow with a firm intent. On your in-breath, relax, and inflate the body like a balloon, suck the energy into the bone. As you breathe out, condense, and open the joints, stretching your fascia, so that it puts pressure on the bone and squeezes your bones gently. There is no muscle contraction – engage your joints to create a squeezing effect on the bones. Condense energy into the bones. Give your bones a load of energy so you can feel pressure on the bones, feeling radiation coming out of the bones, and imagine your bones are full of light and glowing.

Then we move on to floating the bones. Because there is a space between the bones and the muscles, you want to fill that space with life force. You are going to wave the hand in micro-movement – very, very small – and you are going to let that wave around through the whole body. Whatever bone-muscle relations you are working on, relax around the bone and create waves of fluid between your muscle and your bone. Just float the bone in that fluid. Very gently waving. Still holding the ball. Very softly waving your hand across.

Now, identify the feeling of drawing the life force into the pores and disconnect your breaths from that process. As you are breathing in and breathing that life force into the pores, draw the life force into the pores, but forget about your breaths. Start sucking it in and bring it into the bones for about one minute. Allow yourself to be like a vacuum, pulling that life force in. With pure mind intent, draw it in, fill the bones, make the marrow bubble, have the bones start radiating light, and then your bones will start to heat, your spine will warm up for a little bit. And then you will start to get hot with radiant energy. Draw the life force in, and your body starts to overheat. Your marrow will begin to glow, keep sucking it in.

Then float the bones again. Move the bones inside that radiant light, relax more the layers of muscles and fascia around the bones. In tai chi, it is called the 'sung' – it means to relax. But in this particular case, it is a by-product of our practice. Simply float the bones inside that energy, wave the energy side to side, release, and the fascia loosens … sway your knees in and out, just a few millimeters, so that the bone can move, and float the bones. Increase the will within the quality of relaxation – the quality of letting go – and you want that vital light to radiate further, until it starts radiating out through the pores and all the layers. Allow yourself to be totally relaxed.

Change the wave in your spine, feel the muscles connecting into your spine relaxing and releasing. Use that radiation of light from the bones to release the muscle and fascia tension gripping the bone and allow everything to float. Relax in that magnetic fluid. As the bones are floating, breathe into the bones to generate an inflation from the bone through all of the layers. As we breathe out, we are going to have a deep relaxation of letting go. It is as if you are dropping the tension out of your body. So, breathe into the bones, radiate that light, and breathe out, let go. Let all of the muscles hang and release tension in the rhythmic contraction. Make that light bright, suck energy in, and then release. Let all muscles hang, let all tensions drop. With any type of loosening exercise, you breathe in to generate the upward movement, radiate the light, and breathe out to drop, release the muscles, release the tension. So, when you breathe in, you inflate and open and when you close the breath, you release. You can apply that to any loosening exercise. As the feet drop, we drop the tension to the floor, to the ground, and let the muscles hang. With your next breath of vital force, it will increase the density of that light, as it is less resistant. When you breathe in, you feel the body open that light, and as you drop while exhaling, the tension falls away. The next breath of vital force is less resistant, with more light and more radiation.

After you have completed a session, you want to empty that energy out of the body. You can put that energy into a water bottle, an amulet, a picture or an image – wherever you want it. But, since we are still doing an exercise, we are going to keep that energy in. Normally you would discharge the excess energy out, so that your body does not overheat.

For one minute breathe and feel your hands. There should be a silky powdery quality to your fingers. That is some type of chemical that your body produces that is highly charged with vital essence, so it is very valuable. With this energy, you may want to massage the eyelids or if you have any aching joints or body pains, rub that local area. If you hold onto this energy, you may get a side effect of raptures, headaches, insomnia, irritability, no sleep, or emotional instability. You have to remove that energy from your body, especially if you are using the method that continually sucks the energy in. That energy is not going out, it is pressing out through your marrow until it becomes bright. Typically, when you breathe light force in and breathe it out, there is a self-stabilizing thing inside the energy. It takes what it needs and releases what it does not and self-stabilizes, creating pressure. And you keep sucking the energy in through your will and creating pressure. By floating the bones, you can absorb far more of that energy than usual, just by relaxing and releasing. Some Taoist qigong systems have metaphors like standing like a tree and the wind passes through you. There is a small micro-movement in your body as your bones float with life force. It is like wind making the leaves move, and that is the key to any type of standing practice: you are making the bones radiate with life force, and you are floating the bones and letting all the fascia ripple, radiate and move. There are small micro-movements everywhere inside your body and you release the tension. You are not building power in your shoulders to hold your arms up. You are continually rippling energy through you, and the bones need to literally be doing this inside the body, swimming like a fish. This is so that they totally release the tension between the bones.

Magnetic Phase

The previous exercises were primarily electric, and now we are going to move on to the magnetic exercises. With the magnetic phase, we pull the joints open gently. As we pull the joints open, we suck energy in a similar way to the electric, but our mind is in a magnetic state. We do not have the joints stretched open and pulling energy to radiate. We are pulling the joints open, holding the magnetic feeling, and continually sucking magnetic fluid into the bones. The same principle of floating the bones still applies.

Go back into the vital breathing. Suck that energy in through the pores and the bones and start to feel a subtle tension from keeping the joints pulled open. Begin floating the bones, creating a wave through that subtle tension and loosening it up before you draw the energy in. Through these small micro-movements that we are doing, we want to develop a relationship between the mind intent, the energy and the movement. You do this so that your mind is completely fused into the world of energy. As you move the energy in these waves, your body floats inside those waves. So, if I want to do a tai chi form, my mind will fuse into the feeling of chi, I will have radiated that out, and the bones would float inside that feeling of chi so my body would move to produce that form. Our mind moves the chi and the chi moves the body. You have got to get the mind wholly fused into the feeling of energy. We are floating that energy around the bones, and the bones are floating inside of that energy. That generates these ripple waves in movement. Then the qigong becomes an engine of power. This bridge is important if you are going to put movement into a framework.

The mind radiates the energy, the energy radiates through the bones, the bones float and move, and the rest of the body responds accordingly.

The mind, energy, bones, and the rest of the body work through the fluid. That fluid will activate fascia and switch off muscles, and there is a minimum amount of muscles applied and a maximum amount of fascia connection.

There comes the point when you start feeling the fluid radiating around you. You want to radiate this sphere around the body of fluid. So now we do not need to pull it all the way through the bones, you just pull it into the sphere. Just fill that sphere up, so that everything equalizes and floats inside the sphere. As your body is floating in the spherical fluid, there is the specific point at which you use the same amount of will to suck energy in, and the energy floating slows down. To pull more energy in the fluid, you will float. It is like your body just gets full.

Now you are going to use mental pressure to take it beyond fullness and pressurize that form. It is a type of will that overloads the energy system with more magnetism than it can cope with. When you overload the energy system with more than what it can cope with, you will become immune to that level of energy. So, I want you to take all the deep will of your willpower, pull that energy in and hold that state of will and keep factoring it in, keep sucking it into the body, increase your will, increase your focus, increase your whole body into the energy moving. So what we are going to do is start from the fingers and the toes and grip the ground with your toes and create a fist with your fingers. Pulling the stretch of the body open – you pull your wrists open, you pull your elbows open, you pull your spine open, you pull all of the joints open, and with that pulling open, you squeeze the bones. You seal that energy into the bones and relax that feeling. If you are overheating, going into the ocean will demagnetize it and take you back to a neutral state. If you are in the shower, you will also demagnetize. When you have contact with water, it demagnetizes the body and takes your body into a neutral state. So, it is a good idea that before you do this type of exercise, you charge the bones with that energy, you burn it up during the exercise, and then find a balance point at the end to revitalize your body and bring yourself back to balance.

You will find that if you are doing a type of running exercise, you are going to be leaning much more towards the electric with the short bursts. It will be more towards the Air element with prolonged, extended exercise, and the magnetic type of activities will require a high amount of coordination, flow, internal timing through your body movement, and so forth. So, with energy work type exercises, you have a strong magnetic quality to it, and tai chi will form a magnetic quality to it. Running and weight training are Air and Fire type of exercises. If you want to work on bone density, you use the Earth element. If you are doing a deadlift at the gym where you lift a weight up and you relax the pressure into the bones, you do the marrow breathing, electromagnetic energy – which is Earth – will condense the bones and your bones get super strong. Try to do your gym training as early in the day as possible, because I have found that there is an eight hour bubbling that happens after a workout. If I work out at 12:00 p.m., I could sleep after 8:00 p.m. If I work out at 3:00 p.m., it is going to be around 11:00 p.m. or midnight. So do not train after 4:00 pm, because you will not be able to go to sleep before midnight. You just have that cycle in your body. Check the periods in your body and how you wish to train yourself.

Bring your awareness into your marrow, feel that density of energy that is in your marrow. You breathe into it. Now we are going to express it through the elements. For the Air element, we breathe electromagnetic in as an underlying feeling. Then we simply stretch all the fascia of the body upwards very gently, float the bones upwards, and we rock the bones backward and forwards and let everything sink. Feel the wave of the spine falling backward and allow everything to rise. Shoulders have a slight forward and backward micro-movement, all the joints of the body are falling backward, and that will loosen everything up with an upward stretch. Arms stay up, and as you stretch floating upwards, feel the stream of the life force into the bones, have the stretch regulate the frequency in there, and steam all of the energy in your body out. Just float everything upwards. When you come back to your body, all of that energy, you want to put it into an amulet. Pick up an amulet, raise it with your left hand. Feel the energy you built, electromagnetic, electric-magnetic, Air element, and so forth, and put it into the amulet with your chosen function.

Questions from this Guided Practice Session

Student: So, there is no benefit to store this energy at the end of the session?
Mark: Yes, you can draw the energy into your etheric body, and center in

that physical feeling, affect the physical, and work it through the physical layer. You are all storing automatically in the above it, to a degree, so your mind is doing all the work. So you are getting mental spirit automatically. Your astral is there if you are doing vital and relax into it, you get a bubbling of the astral. So, the level above – you are getting the effect on the level above.

Student: This combining of two or more energies, is it just really the same thing as multiple letter use in Kabbalah?
Mark: It is similar. This exercise is more about generating a platform through Kabbalah so that you will get the strength and the vital force in relation to the elements. When you start doing Kabbalistic work, it is all far easier to be done, since the foundation inside you is already built through this exercise.

Student: Does a swimming pool work for demagnetizing or just the ocean?
Mark: Using a shower works, as does a bathtub. A shower does not work as well, but it does work. Let us say you had time to build up the Fire element and did the 462 repetitions and your body, your marrow is bubbling, overheating, pumped up, and then you did a little bit of movement work. And then all of a sudden the phone rings – something has happened, and you are distracted, and you are doing something else. The energy moves into your astral body from your vital field. Once it is in the astral body, it is already metabolized, and it is overheating the system. Then you cannot just breathe it out any more because it is already converted and has changed state. So the way you have brought it in, you cannot take it out in the same way. You have got to follow through. It is a bit like that cold or flu. If you feel it coming, you vital breathe, gone – you do not get the cold or the flu, you catch it in that first quarter. But once it hits that critical mass point, all you can do is speed it up. You cannot stop it. So you have got to boost your immune system before it catches you and you feel that it is just coming. With these energies, once the energy flows into your astral and it is being metabolized by your body, then it is difficult to remove. The ocean is the only thing that would remove it, where I could really get that cramps in my stomach from overheating, and I go sit in the sea at 6:00 pm or 7:00 pm and just lay there and float and 20 minutes later, cramps would settle, and the heat would be gone, and I could say, "Finally." It took that long. It is only a matter of a few

minutes and breathe out. Your astral body has to be demagnetized and all your vital field. Your vital field is easy to flush any energy out, but the astral field, it has got this pattern – this critical mass thing – that is holding on. The same will apply for any oppressive emotional state that you are going through. Sit in the ocean and just make a prayer to the spirit of the water to dissolve it, lay in there for 20 minutes and just demagnetize your astral body.

Waterfalls are different. They are more powerful than the ocean in one way, because of the direction of the negative ions are produced from crashing and cleaning of the waterfall. The spirit of the water kind of ignores that your physical body is in the way, and it just passes through you. So, as it is washing your astral body at an incredibly fast rate, wherein the ocean, the rhythm, the energy waves of the sea pass through your physical body and they do so just to be there. Just have that rhythmic swing and have the flow of the tide. When you are in the waterfall, it is just hammering through you. You cannot get the same effect in the shower, because you do not have that same volume of water, the consciousness of that water hitting the same spot for hundreds or thousands of years, the astral plane is not built. When you put the shower on, and the astral field is switched on, there is an unconscious flow.

> *"Waterfalls are special. For example, If you go to any waterfall in Japan and you switch your clairvoyance on, you will notice that there are Shinto spirits dressed in white around the waterfalls, practicing. That is quite normal. I was practicing on one waterfall and there was a spirit standing there who said, 'You shouldn't be there,' and I said, 'Why shouldn't I be? I enjoy practicing under this waterfall.' And then later, while I was practicing, there was a snake who came up and bit me on foot. The funniest thing is that the video recorder is on as I was recording with my friend, and I scream, 'Ouch! There are two big fang marks on my foot.' It was some type of water snake."* – Mark's personal story

Student: We condense both electric fluid and magnetic fluid … if you do that in equal amounts, does it kind of balance out?

Mark: It does equal out. We start with electromagnetic, but because of this will of the mind, it turns out electric, and then you condense the vital force. It starts off as electromagnetic, and then it just starts swinging towards electric by itself. It radiates electric light and then it switches to the magnetic to balance it out. But again, you do not leave this in your body too long. When you want to go for a run, you want to go to the gym, you want to train, you want to practice it and it will move as a vital force and it will get metabolized into your muscles, into your fascia, and make you powerful. You have got to convert the energy into a functional form. When it is in a raw form, as condensed energy, it is not useful, it is just fuel and there is too much of it, and it is seeking to express itself. And it is a fuel that you cannot store. It is not storable, so it has to be used straight away. That is why Bardon says you have to release it at the end of the session so that you do not overheat. The best way to release this is to use it. Because by using it, you convert between the states, it stores in your energy memory, it stores in your feeling, your power, all your cells get charged up. You need some sort of activity. That is why you do qigong first, and you do your tai chi form, because the act of doing the form permeates all the layers of the muscle and it gets absorbed. Then you do your push hands, it condenses in your fascia, you tap your body, it condenses in the bones, so it gets used and transformed into a function. And that function has an energy memory of radiating light and you get powerful. So this is a pre-exercise to any type of human movement exercise, where you are going to do some sort of activity. When you are going to climb a mountain and you do this with the Air element first, float yourself in the Air element, so the bones are floating in air, and you will then feel light when you are climbing up the mountain. And you can continue the exercise as you are walking. You can adapt it to suit your needs.

Student: Can electric and magnetic phases stay, expand and contract all at the same time?

Mark: Yeah, when you are doing the expansion radiation for the electric, you open the joints and stretch out, when you start sucking electric fluid in, the feeling is all magnetic when you are drawing in. Still, your body is in electrical state, your mind is pulling on electric and you are focusing on the radiation of light. The magnetic radiates light, but it is more like a blue aura, like a starshine, and then there is a soft blue through the color when you are drawing that magnetic fluid in. The electric has more of a silver, gold reflective radiance coming out, so it sparkles.

Student: The radiation is just an aspect of one releasing energy?

Mark: Correct. You can switch a lightbulb on and it is going to radiate. Energy is going to keep going out. But it maintains the center of gravity of the light with itself. You can build energy, not lose energy, because light radiates, and chi is light. The most important part of energy storage and use is applying it to something, building it into a skill, so that you build it into a function and do something with it. Clairvoyance has light. It is the light of clairvoyance, an energy which produces clairvoyance. So everything, whether it is a qualitative or quantitative skill, has a type of energy that makes that skill radiate and become functional. Without energy, it cannot work. So, when we are doing three transformations, connecting through universal light, and then making a prayer and inviting clairvoyant light down, that light hits the third eye, changes shape, and then starts to radiate as your energy field transforms it. And that is a type of energy, a substance – a clairvoyant substance.

Chapter 4

Akasha

Akashic Breathing

The prerequisite for Akashic breathing is that you have done the astral breathing to release time; you have done Step One mental training, where you have mental vacuity and you have become comfortable with that. You put the elements to the four regions of the body to generate a stillness in your solar plexus, and you have relaxed your mind into that void in your solar plexus. The reason why we use the solar plexus: above the solar plexus is electric and below the solar plexus is magnetic. There is electromagnetic balance at that point and that is the most still part of your body when you balance the elements out. It is easy to contract the mind into that stillness and that still-point in the exercise.

From there, you take the mental vacuity which you developed in Step One mental training, you take the astral vacuity which you have developed in balancing the elements and the four regions and sinking into that stillness, and you take those two in the quality of releasing time. Now we put them all together and release time and space together through the pores. You breathe timelessness in and then spacelessness out through the pores. As you move into this rhythm of timelessness in and spacelessness out, those two qualities start overlapping.

As they overlap they blend and we get this infinity quality coming in and out of the pores. You quickly realize that you are building a vacuum in your mind, you are making a vacuum in your astral body, and you are building a vacuum under your physical body. The side effect of this vacuum is a slight feeling of drunkenness like you are losing your balance. If you were to rock your body weight forward and backward, you would feel a lag between your mental, astral and physical forms – that there would be a gap forming between them. You can use this as a test when you are doing the Akashic breathing to see how much Akasha has arisen and how it has affected your three bodies.

Once you have rocked forward and backward and you have identified that you have the Akasha feeling there, then we spin it in a circle. You just keep breathing that Akasha in and out and spinning it around your body. As you spin it around the body, the mental body occupies the outermost layer of that spin, the astral stretches out towards it. Then the physical feeling of balance is moving around the physical body. These three bodies are stretching out and you can spin them around your physical form while you are Akashic breathing.

The reason why we rock back and forth is that it creates a physical state of balance being on the edge and your mind is extending and breathing the Akasha substance, which allows for that Akasha to penetrate into the gap, into the middle astral matrix between your middle astral physical bodies. As it penetrates into the matrix and as the matrix is dissolved, it is much easier to enter into Akashic trance. Once you have achieved that Akashic feeling in Akashic trance, then you stop the spinning. You center the Akasha and just pore breathe the Akasha in and out, create more mental and physical space around you, and you can be in a cosmic trance without moving your body. But it is much easier to enter Akasha with the forward-backward sway and a rotational sway, sensing the gaps between the bodies and breathing into those gaps to enlarge them, to go deeper into Akashic trance.

Once we have established these three stages of the practice, then we can increase the Akasha within whatever we want. For example, we can place a meditation object in front of us, put our hands over the meditation object and begin breathing Akasha into the object. We continue to do this until the object starts to flicker. It appears and disappears, where you can see through the object and then it reappears again. These flickers last a fraction of a second, but there is a clearer view straight through the object. This is as the mind goes into the Akashic substance of the object, and then the law of rhythm pulls you back to form, it appears and disappears. These are the first signs that you are able to produce Akasha within that object within the physical world and for it to begin to affect your perceptions.

This stage is very important because this flickering in and out of form is what opens the door to spiritual light, to non-dual light. You have to enter through the Akasha into the essence of the fabric of your own spirit, to touch the non-dual substance of your own spirit. To do this, we take this Akasha quality, raise it up through the crown, and as we stream the Akasha up through the crown, having released time and space and inside that infinity quality, the crown chakra opens. As the crown chakra opens, we get a polarity differential because we are streaming all this up, a handspan above the crown. We have a vacuum above the crown and we have pressure below, your lower energies of the physical and the astral body will start pulling upwards. Those energies will begin to rise up through the crown.

Once we have stabilized this rising feeling and have a head suspended from above, then we enter into prayer. When you pray, you are praying to something greater than the ego that is making the prayer. You are humbling yourself, but you are not humbling yourself to anything outside. You are humbling yourself to the essence of your own being. The essence of your spirit is a vibrational match to God. It is a vibrational match to the Tao; it is a vibrational match to the universal mind. The essence of you is a tuning fork that vibrationally matches the highest frequencies that exists. It is that part of your being which you are praying to. The prayer does not move outside of oneself, it stays within the essence of spirit.

As we make this prayer we state, "May the path of light guide and protect." Your intuition comes into a form of guidance and protection; if there is a problem on the right, you step to the left. You come to a state where you are protected through your actions intuitively and naturally. You may step to the left and not know there was danger on the right, or maybe you do know there is danger but you intuitively just take that path. Our own intuition is a form of protection. The guidance is in relation to a spiritual path. The path of light is what raises the vibration of your spirit.

Everything you need to know is contained within the essence of your own spirit. It is built into our spiritual nature to evolve. As the essence of spirit is a vibrational match to the universal mind, everything that touches universal mind is emanating out of the essence of our own spirit, so we do not need a doctrine, group or religion, or when you do a sitting within stillness, enter that intuitive state of releasing and all of the information we need will release from within the essence of our own spirit.

We invite this white light that we've entered through prayer from that place just outside of the body a span above our head. we invite that white light down through the crown. As it moves through the crown, we create the space and release it to move through the third eye, through the astral body, and through the physical body down the central axis, down to the feet. We pour it through the three bodies into the earth. From heaven, we let the light enter into man, and from man, we let it enter into earth. We create a stream of lines like we are standing under a waterfall or a pillar of light. This light, as it passes through, moves from a non-dual state to a dual state.

When we remain in the state of prayer as it comes into form, it has a purification effect. It polarizes every particle, every cell, every chemical in your body to the highest, to its best. As it tunes each part of your body to its best, your life's purpose becomes obvious, your intuition gets stimulated, and all the higher skills that make who you are in the direction you are going in pertinent, they all come up. They always become obvious when you are working with this light. You want to watch this light through the three bodies, so the best of who and what you are becomes polarized and you start seeing, feeling and experiencing life through that best part of you.

This white light exercise is very simple: cultivate the Akasha, raise it through the crown, suspend the head, make a prayer, "May the path of light guide and protect," invite that white light back down, and let it wash through the three bodies. After about 10 or 15 minutes of washing through the three bodies, you will find a part of your mental body is equalized with that light; that you have got a mental body charge of light, an astral body charge of light, and a part of your physical cells are charged with light. Once you feel that equalization, relax your mind up to the crown into that light and release your awareness up through the crown into this Universal light.

Once you have developed this universal light properly through the Akasha, it becomes a non-dual light. It is light that is seeking to come into creation. When the mind enters into that primordial light there is a strong sense of dissolving of the self – the normal part that you identify as you is not present, it is not there. It is your spirit that is there, and as you enter into that light, you will start to find that the way you identify with spirit as having a body starts to dissolve; that the shape of your spirit dissolves, that all there is mind and light.

As this dissolving happens, you should go with it. If you try to hold on to the shape or identity of the spirit, it will pull you into an astral state of having a supernatural ego. If you let go of the form of the spirit and let your spirit move into the formless infinite light, then you let go of those lower attachments and the center of gravity of your mental body takes on non-dual light.

The value appears in this when you move into your next incarnation cycle, when this body ages and lets go of life, the astral body falls away, the physical body falls away, and the spirit separates. The center of gravity of spirit – if it is in a non-dual light state – will equalize to that non-dual light state immediately. You will float into it. When you float into non-dual light and if you have equalized with it, you will have achieved complete agency and freedom of choice. For example, you can choose to work within this light and develop yourself further, perhaps reincarnate in the path of service, whichever is more important. You have choices because the force of samsara does not exceed the will of your spirit inside of that non-dual light.

But if your mind had been focusing on form in its meditative practices, the samsara force, due to those laws of samsara and form, would pull you into another reincarnation. We want to get to this non-dual light state as quickly as possible within our spiritual practice, so that we do not have any hindrances for our advanced development. When you get into the non-dual light state – you hit critical mass, you can sit within it – then your future incarnation is assured to have a very high level of agency and freedom of choice. This is the primary reason that we work with Akasha, and this is how we use Akasha to access non-dual light.

Chapter 5

Non-Dual Light

Astral Light

We have many different types of light, because everything in the universe is energy and energy is light. To break these different types of lights into categories, we need a vibrational scale of some type. We can look at the physical forms of light that are functioning inside of time and space in the physical world. Astral light is a form of light that can slow down in frequency and maintain form. This astral light, as it becomes slower and slower, increases in its spiritual intensity. Slower forms of astral light are essentially of a higher frequency and are, in fact, the faster forms of astral light. When these slower forms of astral light come closer to the physical world and become denser, this light is actually sped up. There is a mirror effect inside this. On one side the vibrations are slow, yet they are actually much faster than they appear. This happens because of the light's reference point. We are looking from the physical and from a physical state of perception and you are looking at a frequency of vibration. It appears to go slower and slower and slower when you are looking at it from the physical world. But once you are equalized with that astral light there is a normalization of it. When you go deeper into the astral light, the lights are actually vibrating faster and faster and faster. The speed of that light and the intensity is continuously growing faster as you go deeper into its form. It is not a process that you can intellectualize through the normal intellect. Sometimes through working with this light you will recognize that there is a reversal process taking place within light as you work through the astral

– that is, higher levels of light appear slower, but they are vibrating faster. This insight you can only really get when you are inside of that astral light and experiencing it directly.

Mental Light

When we go into the mental light, it takes on a mind substance that moves from form to mind. From the astral perspective, it cannot be vibrating. If it is not subject to space, how can something vibrate? Mind substance has a type of vibration within it that is not subject to form. We do not need to intellectualize or make sense of it. When you place your awareness in the mental plane, and you feel a density of light and vibration within the mental plane, you can relax and release up that vibrational scale. As you do this, there is a sense of a greater vastness of space to higher frequencies of vibrations within mind substance. So, as the light becomes thinner, it becomes more intense. It can only be experienced if you have equalized it. If the energy rises in frequency and you are not raising in frequency, it will disappear. You simply will not be able to see it. Your mind needs to rise up in that frequency with the light in order to see the intensity and vastness of that light increase. So, we have this mind substance principle, where we have these different types of light that function within the mind substance.

Most people, if they really summon their will, can concentrate for a short period of time at a high level – and they are not able to do that for very long. So by summoning all your inner light, you can focus on a meditation object for a minute or two, make everything sit still, and achieve a very satisfactory result. But a normal person is unable to maintain that for an extended period of time, because that mental light becomes exhausted – it runs out of energy, it starts to dim. And as soon as it starts to dim, the 'monkey mind' switch is on, and the consciousness drops into the astral, and it starts bouncing around with all these emotional ideas and memories and so forth. This happens to normal people in their thinking processes. The concentration of the mental body and the concentration of the astral body – they are very different. The mental body is a much cleaner, clearer type of stillness with vast space. The concentration of the astral body can be lateral thinking, multi-tasking, mathematical calculations, and so forth. It still has an active static analytical component to it. A mental body concentration bridges into true samadhi, where the mind is accumulating stillness, underlying as one-pointedness. And this light – the light of samadhi – has an extremely high value. All the mental training exercises of Bardon's book are forms of samadhi and vipassana. So one may ask themselves how to develop these types of lights within the mental body, and refine them.

As discussed in the introduction of this book, when you take an ice bath or use ice water to splash your face with, you will find that these actions awaken your spirit. These actions can pull your spirit from your mental body into your physical body so that you can practice. This is an easy way to get in touch with your spirit. This way you know exactly what part of your being you are cultivating when you do your meditation practice, as the will pulls you up to that higher state of the mental plane very quickly through ice water. From the light of the mental plane, we need to develop Akasha to work with high levels of light, because we need to release time and space together to create a quality of infinity. This is in order to get to the essence of the underlying fabric of mind, or to the mona as some call it. And to reach the mona, we need to release time, space and enter into infinity. This is for the divine light of the spirit to awaken and become present. That divine light of the spirit is simply a consciousness that is able to move through Akasha unhindered. When normal forms of consciousness touch Akasha, the matrices which normally give oneself stability dissolve and the consciousness floats. For an analogy, it is as if one gets pulled into the water and their light is like a cork on the ocean, floating at the surface. Whereas the mana is able to move through Akasha unhindered. It is the mind substance that is beyond time, beyond space and that can only be engaged in through these qualities of infinity to touch the pure spirit.

Once we have worked into the mana, then we are engaging from levels of non-dual light into the singular light. This is the light that moves from zero to the one, but it is not vibrating yet – its rate of flux, its rate of movement, is so small that one's spiritual consciousness can sit within it without any static and can unify with it comfortably. Once you have touched on this non-dual light, it normally will reflect three astral bodies in the form of heat. So, if you sit in the mana, your astral body will get hot and you will feel a lot of power surging through the three bodies and your body will start to overheat physically and astrally. This is a good sign because that light has a purifying effect. That heat is burning resistance and resistance expresses itself in the form of heat. So this light passing through has a very beneficial purifying effect.

As we work with passing light through the three bodies, you will find that your craving – everything from the types of things you think about, your emotions, your physical cravings – start to polarise. They start to rise in frequency and change to a higher state. This will be so if you have made some type of vow for your spiritual development. So, if you are a Buddhist and you have taken refuge in the Buddha, and you have this aspiration for an enlightenment, that light recognizes that it is blueprinted for that vow, that higher aspiration. It will just pull your cravings towards them. If you have not taken any aspiration at all, the light can do whatever it wants. If you have a craving for a physical thing, it will activate the physical thing and simply give it to you and you will find yourself with that craving standing in front of you and it is like, "Ah, the light produces whatever I want it to produce." So, when you bring light through, you have to recognize this as a light of creation that creates everything. It will manifest itself according to the will of the creator, which is you. So, having vows in place when you are working with these types of non-dual light will ensure that these types of light will manifest according to the needs of your spiritual development, not the needs of your ego. And you need to decide what they are and put them in place because you are the creator, you are making this happen. You are bringing this light through into the physical world. We need a very clear, concise intent on what it is going to do and what is going to manifest and what it is going to create.

The laws are different for people who work with non-dual light, compared with people who work with normal vibrational light, because they are in a state of creation – they are bringing energy into the world that did not exist before; it was not physically already there. If a person breathes astral light in and out, they are basically coming to resonance, which is something that already is and they are just accumulating it, directing it, streaming it, according to their particular function. They might build a reservoir for magical use and so forth. When you are bringing light from the non-dual state through the mental-astral body, and it is becoming dual, the fabric or the mental programming – the value placed within that light – will generate your karmic field. This is the energy that makes your mental-astral body emanate, like a tuning fork, like an antenna sending information out and pulling information, pulling astral feelings out, pulling astral experiences in, emanating physical experiences, and gathering new physical experiences. So the vow that you placed within this light – we are wording it using the word 'vow' because it requires a very firm will. Light is very unstable. As soon as it starts to vibrate, it takes the path of least resistance, and it scatters outward into creation. It is seeking to express itself. So, when you take a vow, you put it on railway tracks, and you go. This is what this energy is going to do, and it follows your vow. It is bound to those railway tracks. It cannot scatter, dissipate, fuel fantasies, and so forth. It will only vibrate through the will of your mind, the will of your vow. This is important because light is very unstable. One would think that the light of creation is the emanation of God, but remember, when you touch mana, you are God. How stable are you? How stable is your astral body? How stable is your physical body? That light is just going to follow the stability of you because you are made in the image of the creator.

This vibration elimination, it will just radiate you outwards. So having these vows in place and only letting light pass through you when you engaged in a vow of some type, that will create a return path for ascension, for energy to pull your mental body up that path, back to the source of that light. So we are essentially making a two-way energy movement. You bring something down, which is a benefit to humanity, and the same energetic return pulls your mental body up. It is a two-way pump.

Non-Dual Light Mastery

Let us have a look at the process of getting into white light practice. There are several stages that first need to be undertaken.

The first is separating the mind intent from the observer, so we have got to release intention within the mind. This practice is very simple: you sit quietly, watch your thoughts arise and fall away, and get a distinct separation between the observer and the observed. This is an essential foundation practice. As all intuitive information is flowing, you are not allowed to touch it – you just have to observe it arise, observe it fall away, without the mind intending. As you do this first exercise, there is a type of mental vacuity which forms where the observer becomes further and further away from the observed, and you end up in a still space. This is the accumulation of Akasha, that is a byproduct of the observing type of concentration. It is a very soft form of Akasha. As there are many different types of Akasha, which are byproducts of different practices, this type of observing generates a very soft form of Akasha and is essential for our practice.

The second exercise is one-pointedness, where you select a thought form that passes by, you stop it and hold that thought form in your awareness, and let everything else disappear. There is just that thought form, your awareness engaging it, and you put a tunnel vision onto that one thought form. You go through four stages of this process: the first is you discern that there is a thought form there; the second is you attach to it and you identify, "I am this thought form," and the third is you strengthen your will to increase the unification with that thought form, before finally you find a balance point between that part of you which is observing, that part of you which is identifying and your willpower. And this balance point in the Earth element is essential for mastering samadhi.

From those two exercises, we move on to mental vacuity. So, when you are doing the first two, there is a stillness which arises as a byproduct of the exercise. In the first one, it is your mind, the observer moves further and further away from the observed. In the second exercise, the stillness accumulates in the object that you are observing and the object starts to disappear. It is a much sharper type of emptiness. The emptiness almost has a sheen to it, a gloss to it. So it is like a sword – a very sharp type of emptiness. These two exercises generate a yin and yang relationship to emptiness, to stillness. One is soft and dissolving and the other is sharp and cutting. We want to investigate the yin-yang relationship to Akasha and just sit within that still feeling, sit within the Akasha.

Now, this initial type of Akasha is an Akasha of mental space. It is the emptiness underlying the mental world, underlying the spirit, underlying thought forms, underlying all mental structures. This first type of Akasha generates a doorway to the higher and the lower levels of Akasha. This is the easiest one to attain.

Once you have spent time sitting in the stillness and exploring this yin-yang relationship of Akasha – one being soft and dissolving and the other being sharp and attentive – we move from those exercises to whole body vital breathing.

Whole body vital breathing is a preliminary exercise for mastering the elements. So, with Fire, Air, Water and Earth, we take the vital breathing exercise and we swing the vital energy towards one of the elements. If you work with the Fire element, for example, you invite the whole body to pore breathe, you stretch the joints open, slightly expanding them from the center with a strong will, and then the vital energy will begin to heat. It will take on the form of the Fire element and the fire will build within you. If you pull the joints open, very similar to if you are grabbing a door handle and pulling a door open – that is, pulling muscles you use to pull the joints open while you are doing whole body pore breathing – your body becomes more magnetic and the life force will swing towards the magnetic Water pole. And that feeling of energy will totally reverse the polarity. Then you practice switching onto the electric, the Fire and then back to the magnetic, the Water and feel the rhythmic flow between those two polarities. When you can control that rhythmic flow, you can then control the fuels of your emotions. That allows you to choose to have equanimity or not within your astral body.

The mental training exercise that we started with generates a mental equanimity on the surface, but it does not settle the energies underneath the surface – it does not get deep into your astral body and generates stillness there. So, we need a method in which to bring the astral body into equanimity that makes you have to master the elements.

From there, we do the whole body pore breathing, then we stretch in our gravity up to the chest and we just gently stretch all the joints upwards, creating a feeling of lightness throughout the body. As we create that feeling of lightness, the center of gravity rises, the whole body feels like it wants to float in the air like a balloon, and we just encourage that feeling. As you strengthen that floating quality within the Air element, your whole body will become very buoyant and stretched. You are stretching the spine upwards, the head upwards, and the whole body is moving in an upward Air element and state.

From there, we continue that exercise until you have engaged the Air element and the Akasha starts accumulating around the Air element that you are so concentrated on that feeling, you become aware of its Akasha and the feeling. This same measurement applies to all the elements. When you become so concentrated in the Fire element, the Akasha accumulates around the Fire element; when you become so concentrated on Water, Water and Akasha start melding together. And the same for Air and then Earth. So, when you are doing the Earth element, you feel gravity acting on your body. You generate a stretch very similar to the Air element, but you let gravity pass through the body and you hang all the muscles, you let the joints open up, and you let everything sink downwards. So your center of gravity is on the bottom of the joints and centring more on the legs.

This feeling of heaviness of gravity, you just allow your life force to move with that feeling and you increase gravity acting on your body. This generates a groundedness, increases the connection between the mental-astral-physical bodies, increases magnetic fluid and protective Chi, your protective energy. Your energy system's protection is based upon the mental-astral matrix magnetic fluid. If it is very strong you can access very high reserves of energy for your immune system; when those mental-astral matrices are weak or have holes in them, your immune system has less energy to access and you will be leaking energy.

So, the Earth element and the Water element both increase the magnetic fluid within the mental-astral matrix, which is essential for health.

Once you have developed those four elements, we begin breathing them into the four regions. So, you increase the Fire element into the head region, the Air element to the chest region, and the Water element in the abdominal area, and then in the legs, buttocks and hips you will do the Earth element. As you build each one of those elements, you meditate on each of those areas coming into equanimity and each of those elements acts like a magnet. You build a Fire element in the head region and the Fire of the rest of the body just naturally equalizes as a side effect. Same with the chest in the Air and the abdominal area for the Water and the Earth region.

Once you practice this exercise a few times and you can hold those elements in the four regions, and you have meditated on each of those four elements coming into equanimity and balance, let your awareness soften into your solar plexus. Once you have softened into the solar plexus and found that center point, allow the mind to become smaller and smaller. Take the feeling of the mental body's softness within the stillness and sharpness – within the stillness of the first two exercises – and move into that stillness within your solar plexus with a feeling of contraction, like you are sinking inwards, allowing the mind to continually shrink. This feeling of shrinking inwards connects to a feeling of infinity, where you are sinking infinitely inwards, becoming smaller and smaller. It would not matter whether you are practicing infinitely going outwards or inwards, infinity is infinity. But the breaking point is much easier to reach on an inward contraction than it is on an outward expansion. When you are moving outwards, there always feels like there is more. When you are moving inwards, the structure reaches a point where it just breaks and you drop into that infinity quality much more quickly. So, we connect this concept to our mental training.

We connect this feeling of the astral body and the breathing of the elements into the feeling in your solar plexus, then let your awareness contract inwards, until you find a still space. The still space can be applied to any object. So, you can pick up a ball, catch the ball, feel the ball, feel the center of gravity of the ball, then relax your awareness and sink inwards into the center of gravity of the ball. You move into its Akashic center, not just its physical center, but you use the awareness of a physical center to find the Akashic link to control that particular object. With this type of training you want to use a wide variety of objects for finding centers, and mentally transferring into those centers.

As you are doing this exercise and jumping between practicing within your own body and then practicing that on external objects, you will quickly find that the mental body becomes flexible and is able to move into the still point of any object. We are using the solar plexus not because it is the center of the body, but because it is a junction point of the active and passive elements of the body. The Fire and Air above the solar plexus which are active, and the Water and Earth below the solar plexus which are passive. So, right at the junction point there is an equalization of the elements, which is the stillest part of your body to access Akasha. If I use my physical center of gravity, that is not the stillest part of my body. There is electromagnetic static there. If we instead balance the elements in the four regions and then let the mind sink into the solar plexus, we can achieve access to that still point quickly.

Once we have achieved that stillness through the solar plexus, through different objects, then you can move to your physical center of gravity and then find your physical center and move into the stillness of your physical body. You can go to the stillness of your astral body and in the heart center, or you can go to the center of gravity in the mental body – to the pineal gland, to the center of the head – or you can go on to the center of gravity in your etheric Akashic body above the crown. Depending on what you want to influence and what function you want to have through the exercise is where you access Akasha.

If you want to use Akasha to affect the physical world, you go to your physical center of gravity, enter into the Akashic trance, and then you radiate energy from the Akasha through the physical center of gravity, through the mechanical framework, and then radiate it out through the energy layers as per the result you want.

Once you have been working with that infinity quality in various objects within the different centers of gravity in your mental, astral and physical bodies, from there we want to put that inward sinking quality into your pore breathing. As you breathe in, you release time, as you breathe out, you release space. As you breathe in again you draw that stillness in and as you breathe out you enter into that infinity quality. You can practice this two-breath cycle. You should be able to drop into Akasha within a week or two of this practice.

As you pore breathe this infinity quality in and out of the pores, you cannot sense Akasha, because it is an empty space. The mind simply cannot comprehend – it is beyond the mind. What you can sense is the effect that the Akasha does have upon the mind, the environment and the different layers of your energy bodies. So, to your perception, as you breathe Akasha in and out, it will appear to be a substance and what appears to be the substance is the effect of the Akasha or the Akasha itself. So the effect of the Akasha for most people, when they start Akasha work, is that there will be a slight feeling of drunkenness, being slightly displaced between the mental-astral-physical bodies. There will be a state of relaxation, with the mind moving in and out of the physical form. Some people will get light-headed and 'spacey', whereas others will have out-of-body experiences. For the most part, there is a general sense of drunkenness which starts to appear.

If you sway your center of balance forward and backwards in your chair or, say, on the mat that you are sitting on, you are going to notice a lag between the mental body, the astral body and the physical body. As your intent moves and you move your physical body, the three bodies are going to be separate. This is a type of measurement of how much Akasha you have accumulated. You can see how separate the three bodies are. If you want to accumulate more Akasha, breathe into that gap, breathe into the separateness of the bodies. So, you just increased the Akasha within those bodies and moved through that door, through your field; bypass its resistance and you can then enter deeper into Akashic trance.

As you become more familiar with this Akashic trance, you can start to draw energy from it. Enter Akashic trance, equalize your mind with the Akasha, and then draw vital energy in and out of your body. As you do this, you will pull vital force directly out of the Akasha through your pores into your body. This way, you will be acting as a creative being.

As you train this process of breathing Akasha in and out, you are going to find that there is a ramping up in the quantitative volume of the Akasha and the quality of the Akasha. The first exercise started with observing the rising and the falling away of thoughts and you accumulated a soft form of Akasha this way. It is at this point where that accumulation becomes important, because as you breathe the Akasha in and you observe it, you have to pay attention to it very softly – like moving a feather, as it comes in and out. And as you pay attention to it, it increases qualitatively. If you apply the sharp will of drawing the Akasha in and out, as in the second exercise, you end up with a quantitative form of Akasha as a byproduct. So it is important to develop this Akashic trance and Akasha qualities qualitatively, where you just simply observe: you do not release, you do not intend, the mind is not in any form of clarity, as you are simply sitting quietly and watching. As the mind watches the Akasha, it moves deeper into it and equalizes with it. With this type of training the mind intent needs a deep softness within. We are continually letting go of time, space and intent, and we are not looking for the volume of that drunken feeling. We are not trying to manifest the Akasha. We are trying to move the mind into it and let the mental body become more flexible so that it equalizes with Akasha; so it understands Akasha and knows what it is.

Then, in order to get the volume, we apply intent. We have qualitatively had an experience and we gently, from that qualitative experience, increase our willpower within that feeling. As we increase the will, the Akasha naturally accumulates. In order to sense Akasha, you need to move it. If Akasha just accumulates within a fixed space, there will be a tendency for the perception and the will to reach a point where it cannot move or generate anymore. If you move the Akasha, it gives you an amplified sensation of the Akasha and allows you to accumulate a much larger amount of it. With the pore breathing, for instance, you move the Akasha in and out through the pores. Because you are moving it, you get a quantitative awareness which gives you a sense of volume, which you can then increase. When you are observing it, you get a qualitative awareness which has little to no volume, but there is a huge expanse of consciousness. These two qualities need to be brought together and harmonised.

Once we have reached this point in the training where we have been working with the whole body pore breathing of Akasha, we fill the whole body with Akasha and then we qualitatively observe it and quantitatively build it. Again, we qualitatively observe it, and quantitatively build it. We rhythmically move backwards and forwards until we reach a still point within that energy, where those two qualities are balanced. Then we softly let the Akasha float up, just by observing the Akasha and moving it up through the crown. We suspend the head from above and we sit about a hand span above the crown and let all that Akasha accumulate at that point.

Once we are at that point, we want to enter into prayer. Prayer is basically creating a sense of reverence towards something greater than yourself. So, we are going to make the assumption that there is a universal consciousness, a God – something far greater in quality and quantity than our own spirit. And we are going to generate a reverence and deep humility towards that. As we make that feeling of deep humility, we make a small prayer and we say: "May the path of light guide and protect." As we make that prayer with a deep sense of stillness and reverence, this reflects what is in the essence of the spirit and generates a connection to a type of light. What we are looking for is a non-dual light, not a dual light. So we have got to work through these levels of stillness, of releasing time and space; work through these levels of Akasha to access the essences of our own spirits. We want to access that essence from above your crown. As we invite that light to appear, it connects us to what is called in Hermetics the 'Brotherhood of Light', which is basically a vast ocean of light, of energy in its primordial state that is unmanifested. Practitioners who have reached a state of concentration where they are able to access primordial light are able to equalize with the Brotherhood of Light. It can only be accessed once you have undergone Akasha training and it has to be done so in a gentle and soft way, through deep and profound prayer.

Once you have worked through that stage of the Akasha – that deep profound prayer and inviting that light to arise – then you can let that light down from above the crown into the mental body, into the astral body, in the physical body. To increase the flow of light, you increase the vacuity. So you just lubricate that light with Akasha. You breathe Akasha in through the pores and it will stream through your body rapidly. If it hits resistance in any part of your body, then you just simply wash the Akasha through that resistance. As that light permeates, you just relax it through the mental body and it will permeate through the mental. Again, lubricating any resistance in the mental body with Akasha and with that prayer. Then you bring it into time and space of the astral body. So this time continuum gets closer and closer to the physical as it comes to the physical body, but each layer of the astral body has a different time to it. So we go from a slow time to a time closer to the physical rhythm, as we move down through the astral layers – again, using Akasha to lubricate, dissolve resistance to the light, and allowing that light to shine down through the astral layers of the astral body. Once it reaches a critical mass, you will have a brightness within the mental, a brightness within the astral, then it will overflow into your physical cells, into your physical form, and your physical body will take on a gentle glow. Very similar to when you look at a woman who is pregnant, their vital force has a glow to it – it is emanating physically and that light will take on that glow. Some people are very conscious of it, if they are in practicing light, while other people will just have a feeling for it.

Once you have brought it to the physical body, you want to connect it to your feet or your ground to the physical earth. If you are sitting in a chair, you want to feel your bones and your feet at the same time, pass it through the chair and pass it through your feet. As it passes to the earth, just let it permeate and charge the space around where you are sitting to about an arm's reach around you. So, once that space where you are sitting is saturated with light, from there where you want to continue that energy all the way down, deeper into the earth, connecting it to the center of gravity of the earth. Above the crown we have this heaven connection, of primordial light, and above the feet we have an earth connection. So about a hand span below the feet of the earth connection which allows you to access center gravity of the Earth, and a hand span above your crown is a heaven connection which allows you to access primordial light. So you become sensitive to this whole stream from top to bottom all at the same time and just allow heaven and earth to manifest itself and bring light into all those layers of the mental, of the astral, of the physical – and down into the physical world.

Wherever you feel something, that is resistance. So, if your mind feels intensity, your astral feeling gets emotional or you feel heat, you feel any quality, any sensation, this means that you are resisting. It does not mean that you are achieving power, it means you are resisting power. So lubricate that resistance with Akasha and just allow the light to burn the karma away and 'clean house' – just allow light to pass through you and radiate into the environment. You never want to keep light inside your mental-astral-physical body, because it will try to ventilate itself. It is like a light bulb: if you wrap the light bulb with a cloth, the light bulb is going to overheat and it is going to burst. But if you remove the cloth, the light is going to radiate outwards until it touches something, gets absorbed by the environment. This primordial life should be treated in the same way, where you are a conductor of this light to move through you in thousands of different ways. It may be in the form of healing; maybe you radiate this light through your voice chords and express it as knowledge, maybe you express it through your feeling for an environment, or you may be expressing it as love.

Whatever your life's path is, you allow that light to radiate through that path and allow it to be a guiding light to your mental-astral-physical forms.

After several months of this practice, you are going to find that the mental-astral body will start to clear itself. So we need about a hundred hours or so to get a basic level of feeling clear. The dark light is just passing through you – you are not holding on to it or resisting it, you are just getting it out of the way and allowing it to do its thing.

Once you are at that point where you are allowing it to do its thing, you want to give it purpose and have a distinct quantitative awareness of how to fulfil that purpose – a quantitative field of the energy fulfilling that purpose. So qualitatively and quantitatively, you start directing that light towards different things. In the beginning, we just allow it to pass through and dissolve resistance. So you are a silent observer inside the Akasha as to how it is dissolving patterns of your mental body, how it is dissolving patterns in your astral body and how it is moving through the three physical bodies into the physical earth – you are a quiet observer to that process.

As it increases you can use intent to move it through, but when you use intent you are accessing subconscious belief structures and they will start overlaying on top of that light and forming personal truths. We are not really interested in personal truths; we are only interested in universal truths. So you have to be careful that the way you intend light, because intent is dualistic in nature. When it suddenly becomes dualistic, you will validate whatever you believe and this is a bit of a danger because what you believe may or may not be correct. So we want to observe that light passing through, we want to use the Akasha to dissolve duality and have no views: no view about what this light does, about any particular religion or about what the universal laws are – just allow that light to express itself.

Built into your spirit is your life purpose. As that light radiates through the mental-astral-physical form, and you have done so without intention, the highest part of your being will guide that in the correct way. If you start overlaying intent onto it too early, you will corrupt that process and you will not get a natural unfolding of that light and you will not see what your true life purpose is. It will be more of a product of fabrications of your ego and the books that you read, rather than what your spirit has already chosen to do before it came into this incarnation.

As you continue this process, you are going to find that each day you are going to create more space around you – more space in your awareness and your astral feeling, and physical form becomes emptier and emptier. As that happens, that light can penetrate through that empty feeling into those physical forms. The way you intend that light through those physical forms will have a very diverse effect upon those forms. So, in the beginning it is good to have qualities of love, well-being, health, success, having an easy life within as you practice and with how you think, feel and act, and give it a subtle intent. Because when light builds into something, you can end up with sunburn. It can cause overheating. Light can create all different types of effects, if you do not generate a clear concise effect that will manifest itself in accordance with your will. So we have this dichotomy. On one side, we do not want to allow any intent to corrupt our view, and on the other side we want to radiate the energy so that we can ensure that only positive outcomes arise from that energy.

Remember, uncreated light does not discriminate between good and evil; it does not say that everything has to be good. Evolution naturally wants to work towards the positive because that is what evolution does. But uncreated light put in the hands of a person who has very powerful concentration, without ethics, will manifest that light according to their beliefs and their will. So we need to have done a lot of work with a black-white mirror: we need to create our own precepts, ethics, code of conduct and living, and then charge that mental-astral-physical alignment to those precepts with light – so that they become a pillar of support, a type of safety net for how you think, feel and act, so you do not slip off the pathway.

A lot of these things might be common sense to most people who practice, but they are not emphasized enough by those people who see it as common sense. They know it, but they may not implement it enough. So, in these early stages, we have a balancing act between non-intention and no view and generally guarding the light to only have positive outcomes. So you are going to find yourself too, in qualitative sessions where you radiate light without intent and just allow it to unfold. And then you have quantitative sessions, where you generate light with some qualities of love and other effects and then you charge your environment with those effects – and from there, that is when the magic starts to happen. That is when life becomes very interesting and you can guide it through the sense gates to awaken different faculties; you can guide it through physical objects and charge those objects with different types of effects, and you can generate rituals for the light in the Akasha to create different types of manifestations and so forth. So all the magic comes from this platform exercise. Once we are at this point, then we can start expressing this light in a diverse range of ways and have all different types of effects.

Part 2

The Mental, Astral and Physical Streams of Practice

Preliminaries to Mind Stream Training

Introduction

One third of your training is the mind stream, one third of your training is the astral stream, and one third of the training is a physical stream. What we are looking to do is to synchronize these streams, to bring them all together and function together, in order to achieve a unified objective. This is super-important. Most people in life, they act in one way: they go to work, they have their job, they dream, "I really want this," and other things, and then their mind dwells on abstract stuff on television and the internet and so forth – so it is totally out of sync with the astral and physical action and desire. Then, they may go to church on Sunday and pray, and their spiritual direction has nothing to do with the way they think, feel and act.

What the initiation process is designed to do is to take your thinking, your feelings, and your actions and align them to a state of equilibrium. All parts of yourself share the same goal. With all parts of your being working together in alignment with your spiritual life, you will naturally achieve what you want to achieve in life. This synchronicity of the bodies generates success. How can you not succeed when every cell in your body has a directive to succeed in that one particular thing? Of course you are going to move towards it. The speed at which you move towards it is the amount of commitment you have on all those three levels towards that destination.

Meditation on the Hermetic path is not about relaxing – it is not guided meditation or something where a person just floats along to manage their stress. Hermetics is the path of a master. This is a path where you are peaking your spirit, your astral qualities and your body and you are taking yourselves to places other people simply cannot go or will not go for many life cycles. Not every person is capable of entering this path, because you have to face all of your flaws and all of the things hidden in your closet; all of the dark sides of your personality. You have to engage them, reveal them and manage to deal with them. Trust your higher self and all of the life circumstances that have brought you here. You've been brought to this book in part because you are most likely very capable of entering this path. Perhaps you are already on this path or have walked the path to your true nature before in a previous lifetime.

On Awakening the Spirit for Training

Right from the beginning of practice mental training is about training the spirit. The easiest way to invoke the spirit is to use a bucket of ice water and plunge your face into it. As soon as you have plunged your face into a bucket of ice water and hold it there for half of the extension of how long you can hold your breath, you will find that you will awaken the spirit to be very present, your feeling of your body will increase, your survival and strength will increase, and your spiritual presence will be there for practice.

That base feeling, you want to anchor it to cold water – you plunge your face into the bucket of ice, you feel that freezing feeling, you feel your spirit become aware. You will feel a deep calmness come through the body once the spirit is present; there is a spiritual presence and calmness with which you train. This is very important that you are training the right part of your mind. It is mental training, you are training your mental body. You are not training your astral ego or trying to sedate yourself into a lulled state of awareness. You are trying to heighten your state of awareness and increase your concentration.

Once you have done this exercise with ice water several times, then you can just splash ice water in your face. As you do that and you remember the feeling of plunging your face into a bucket of water, you bridge this feeling across, so ice water in your face stimulates your spirit. Once you have done that a dozen times, you imagine putting ice water on your face, imagine plunging your face into a bucket of water, and the spirit becomes present.

And before long, you do not need to use the ice water any more to make yourself very present in the moment for the mental training.

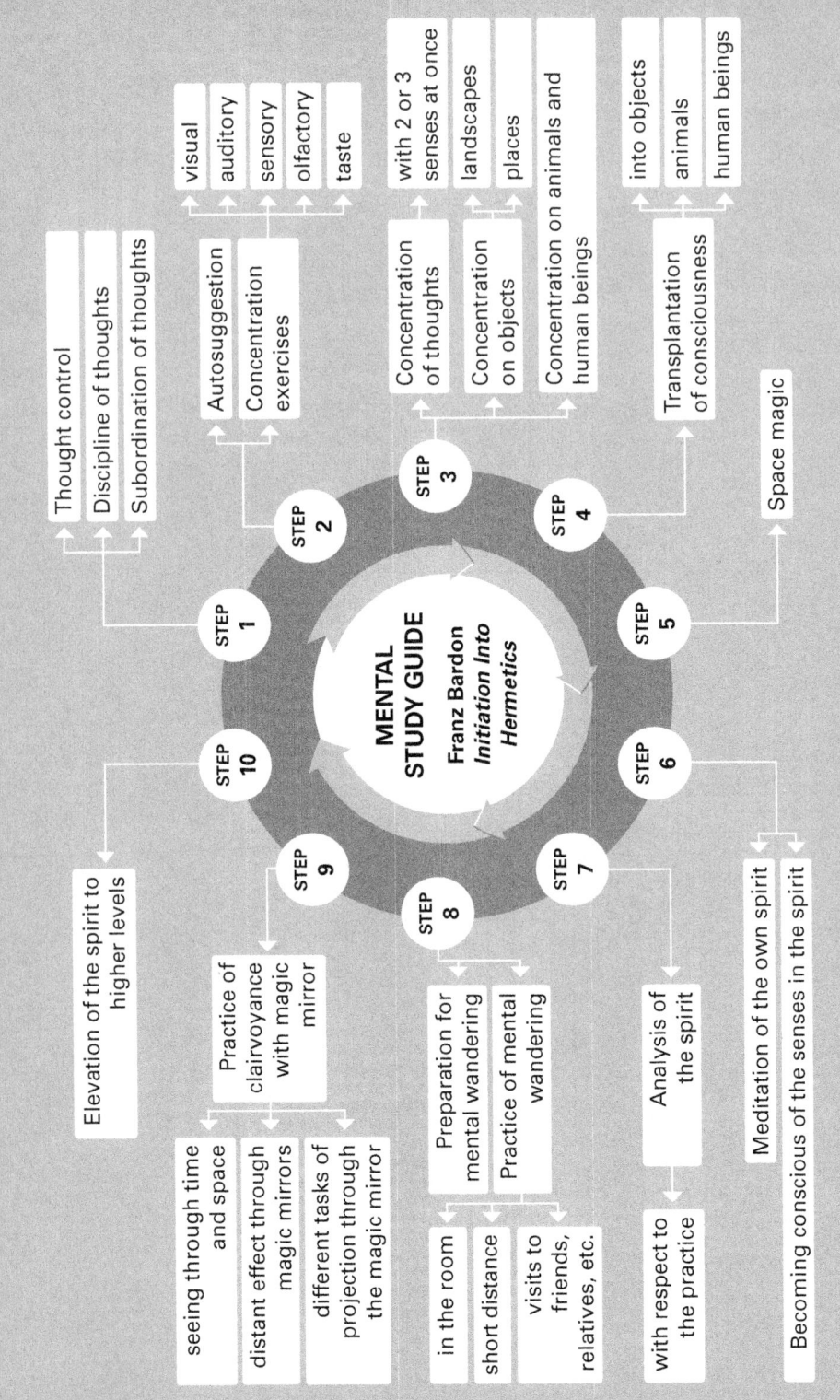

MENTAL STUDY GUIDE
Franz Bardon *Initiation Into Hermetics*

STEP 1
- Thought control
- Discipline of thoughts
- Subordination of thoughts

STEP 2
- Autosuggestion
- Concentration exercises
  - visual
  - auditory
  - sensory
  - olfactory
  - taste

STEP 3
- Concentration of thoughts — with 2 or 3 senses at once
- Concentration on objects
  - landscapes
  - places
- Concentration on animals and human beings

STEP 4
- Transplantation of consciousness
  - into objects
  - animals
  - human beings
- Space magic

STEP 5

STEP 6
- Meditation of the own spirit
- Becoming conscious of the senses in the spirit

STEP 7
- Analysis of the spirit with respect to the practice

STEP 8
- Preparation for mental wandering
- Practice of mental wandering
  - in the room
  - short distance
  - visits to friends, relatives, etc.

STEP 9
- Practice of clairvoyance with magic mirror
  - seeing through time and space
  - distant effect through magic mirrors
  - different tasks of projection through the magic mirror

STEP 10
- Elevation of the spirit to higher levels

Mental Stream Study Guide

Mental Stream

Step One

Bardon recommends observing the rising and falling away of thoughts as the basic introduction and the sixth sense gate of the mind. We want to train all six gates, not just one. When working with the mind itself, observe as the thoughts arise and do not touch them. Observe them from far away. Be a silent observer. As you silently observe, there will be more and more space that starts to arise between your awareness and the thoughts themselves. You recognize this space for its depth, its stillness, its distance. You give the space tangible measurements and you recognize your measurement system each time you practice that exercise, so that eventually forms a still space where thoughts can never reach you. You can sense the thoughts from very far away, but they cannot touch you.

Each time you practice, you have to write down the product of your experiences in your journal. You write down that there is an observer, this mental space, and thoughts which arise and fall away. Every now and then a highly charged emotional thought might come in and then your mind breaks concentration and your mind touches the thought. As soon as your mind touches the thought – it may be a stress, it may be a reminder to pay the bills – you will find yourself engaging in a story. That energy becomes creative and you start thinking and feeling that particular thought and you go into a creative cycle. All of a sudden you become aware that you are not allowed to touch the thoughts, that you are doing meditation, so you instead go into the destruction release cycle, where your mind steps back from the thought. Your mind goes, "Oops, okay … go into the emptiness, release it, let it go, let it go," and then you create more space between you and that thought form and the story dissolves – the story breaks apart.

We have just learned the creation cycle and the destruction release cycle, how to let go of stuff, and you write that down in your journal. You write down the thoughts that have a strong magnetic emotional charge as they are related to you. You also write down thoughts that belong to the environment that arise and fall away. These thoughts do not belong to you – you are not even in resonance with them. The space that you are in is in resonance with them. You write them down, then you write thoughts which you have resonance with, but have no emotional investment in. Just subtle background patterns which rise and fall away. Any pieces of information that relate to the black and white mirror you bring into the astral awareness, your black and white mirror. Write them down while doing this mental training exercise.

Once you have done the first mental training exercises, move into each of the six sense gates. So, you work with eye-consciousness, ear-consciousness, scent-consciousness, taste, feeling, and the mind. Have all six gates of the mind observing the rising and falling away. Each gate of the consciousness has a personality and each one of these personalities regulate your perception. Let us say that you hear a very loud sound when you are a child and a car drives by and beeps the horn and this gives you fear. That fear creates a blockage within your sound-consciousness. If you see something traumatic, eye-consciousness can become blocked. If you feel something traumatic, the feeling-consciousness becomes blocked, and so forth. What we want to do is create space between what we perceive – between the object and the consciousness. We then dissolve all the pre-conditions, the built reactions and blockages. We need to bring each of the six gates into equanimity, so that we do not touch anything. As we enter that stillness, we accumulate that stillness. The nature of this stillness is to dissolve; it will dissolve those blockages simply by being within the stillness. If you invite that stillness to dissolve even further, it will penetrate much farther as you surrender to the stillness. This way you get a profound sense of increased awareness as they reach the gates while that stillness deepens. Just that exercise alone is enough to awaken your psychic abilities.

Once you have done the six gates through observing the rising forms of thought, we move on to individual meditation objects through each gate. For the mind gate, you simply select a thought form. For the eye consciousness, you take a visual object. For the ear-consciousness, a sound, and so forth, to reach the gates. The difference between observing the rising form fall away is you are not selective – anything that is there, you observe it rise and fall away. When you are doing one point of concentration, you select a specific object, you block everything else out and there is one point to focus on that object. So you get this type of 'tunnel vision' between you and the object. You build a mental vacuum around you and your object.

There are two ways of doing this: one, you are unified with the object, you are that object that you concentrate on; and two, very similar to the first exercise, you just simply observe the object and you are separate to it. Both of these methods are very important. Whereas one method will allow you to discern things without any form of union with them – you are separate – the other will allow you to take on the object and see it from its perspective and get much deeper penetration into it, as you come into union with the object, that you are the frequency object. The flexibility of your mental body changes when you do this. So, your mental body will be able to take on frequencies with a lot more clarity and *vibrationally* match them. These base skills, you want to apply them in day-to-day life. So, you become more concentrated and mindful of the space around you while you work.

Franz Bardon recommends separating your personal life, your work life, from different categories of your life, different areas of your life, to become very one-pointed and focused within each category; thus, you are isolating all the other areas of your life. This trains a type of concentration which is very beneficial. We are basically training two invaluable skills. One is vipassana, observing the rising falling and away, as well as samadhi, one-pointed concentration in a balanced way in our day-to-day lives.

The fourth mental training exercise is mental vacuity – emptiness: entering the stillness and residing within that stillness. When we enter the stillness, it is a by-product of the earlier exercises. So, when you are observing the rising and falling away of thoughts, there is an accumulation of stillness, when you are entering samadhi and concentrate on a particular thought form – a visual object, and so forth – there is a sharper type of stillness. The sensory difference between these two, one is soft and one is sharp. Samadhi makes a very clear, shiny stillness. Vipassana, observing the rising fall away, makes a very soft stillness. These two different polarities of stillness need to be trained separately. When you are engaged in samadhi, you are engaged in one point of concentration. The stillness arises, then you move a meditation object into that stillness. You do the same as observing the rising and falling away of thoughts, where thoughts move further and further away from your mind, and your mind becomes very soft and empty. You move into the softness of that emptiness. You will have two different types of quality of experiences, one soft and one sharp. The vacuity within each one of these is very different. The amount of measurable vacuum within your perception, it is a different type of thing.

Samadhi has much more pressure in a small space from the vacuum. Vipassana has less pressure but a larger space. So, the degree of accumulated stillness may be identical, but the nature of the space containing it is different. Each method creates a different ability to release energy and control energy, and so forth. If you want to release energy use the vipassana approach of softening the stillness around a large space and dissolving. If you want to control energy through stillness, use a samadhi stillness to encapsulate and create a very strong vacuum around what you wish to control. Then you can control that energy. So these generate two very perceivable differences in types of stillness. They both will take you to the same place, but the sense of pressure, vacuity and sense of space within these two is notably different.

Step Two

Notice that we are not going to move into astral training yet – we are going into Step Two mental training instead. As we move into the second mental training exercise, we want to generate the exercise with objects that we are very emotionally invested in. If I want to hold a visual image in my mind, I want to hold a visual image that I have a deep connection to. So, let us say, you have lived in your home for 10 years and you have the same clock on the wall, or you have the same television sitting there, or the same couch that you sit on every day. If you pick that object – whether that is very familiar, that you have spent a lot of time with – and then you close your eyes and see that object, because so many hundreds of hours have passed with that object in your consciousness you will very easily be able to hold it within your mind. Choosing objects that are very familiar or which you are highly emotionally invested in will be much easier for imagination exercises than objects you are less invested in. We want to do this to all the six gates of the mind. Imagine what your favorite food tastes like, or how it feels when you are really hungry and then all of a sudden you eat your favorite food. Connect all these activities to things that you know you are going to be successful with, because they have passed through your consciousness thousands of times. These types of meditation objects generate success very quickly. They generate confidence and this allows you to approach more difficult meditation objects more easily.

If you have children, if you visualize the moment your child was born, there is a very strong emotional resonance with that, and it is very deep in your psyche. You can visualize that very easily. So, going to deep emotional investment that you have with other people and experiences, you will be able to reactivate those memories easily and hold them in your consciousness to develop your foundation for concentration. We want to do this through each of the six gates of the mind.

Additionally, we want to bring this into first person – it is you visualizing – second person – you are looking through someone else's eyes – and third person, the fly-on-the-wall perspective. So if there is a camera in the corner of a scene, what does that camera see? What is it here? Using this first, second and third person will give you enough spectrum within your consciousness to lay a foundation for clairvoyant work – to lay a foundation for mental wandering, mental projection, looking at environments, and so forth. We want to keep these training exercises in all three contexts. When you are creating a simple object, you are looking at something, someone else looking at it, or looking at it from a view from a distance. Be very creative with it. As you move into more complex meditation objects, it is important to compound your successes. Create scenarios where you know that you are going to succeed before attempting it. You will know what is difficult before you do something. So, incrementally use your intuition to choose successful things. Build your confidence, build the faith in what you are doing and continue to compound success.

Stopwatch Technique
If you hit a challenge where something is difficult, instead of using a timer to decide how long you are going to train for, use a stopwatch. Pick up the stopwatch, start it and then measure your success. Lock onto the object like

a pitbull. When you feel the mind starting to break, get your second wind, lock onto the object like a pitbull a bit stronger, and then by the time your attention starts to feather off – meaning that you know your mind is going to break – do not let it break. Hit the stopwatch before it breaks. You do not want to see any failure whatsoever. You hit your stopwatch, write down how many minutes of success you had, and then continue to compound that success. Every time that you practice, there is more and more success. By doing this you are teaching the subconscious mind to be successful. It would not matter if you are successful for four seconds – you have compounded four seconds of success, because you know the next time it is going to be five seconds, and then 10 seconds, then 20, and then 40, and then one minute, two minutes, and so forth. You are compounding success and building a substance within your mind that relates to success. This way you continually gain more and more success. This compounding of success is important. We do not want to measure our failures. This is a broken way of thinking. We need to measure our successes as growth thinking. How you structure the psychology of what you are doing is important.

Step Three

As we move into the next step, we start mixing the sense gates, imagining yourself doing living actions. So if you are into a particular sport, imagine yourself playing the sport. We start getting a dual function where you are developing your imagination skills and improving your ability to perform at that sport. You may decide to do some research on that sport, whether it is the biomechanics, the perfect way of executing a golf swing or swinging a tennis racket. Do your research and then feel it in your body, and then imagine it. As you imagine it, by having actually physically done the exercises first, the imagination will remember the feeling of the activity and when these three bridge across the activity to feeling into the mental body, the mental body can align that piece of information very easily because it has something to hold on to. There is a lot of research in different sports where visualization generates growth and skill development for the sport. In bodybuilding, you lift away and feel the sensations of lifting weight. Then you imagine yourself lifting the weight and as you hold the feeling, your muscles begin to grow. The physical activity of lifting the weights develops the muscle memory. You tune into the feeling of that muscle memory and as you imagine exercising, the muscle memory switches on, and your muscle begins to grow because it remembers the feeling – it is activating muscle memory which generates muscle growth, not the physical activity. This is an example of how everything is mind; where a person can produce results without the physical activity by just activating the mind and the mind's connection to the memory inside the muscles. You can use this to make things grow and develop.

Bridging the Sense Gates into Mental Wandering
We now get into more complex senses. We practice two senses, three senses, and then add all the sense gates together in our imagination skills. Because of the nature of this task, we want to be creative about how we do this – we want to make it fun, we want to see tangible changes within ourselves, within either the sport we are looking at or another activity. That activity could be playing a musical instrument, for example. Whatever it is, you want to be able to measure the reward of your effort, that you are actually getting better at that thing. Once you have gotten good at activating physical, physiological responses with your mind, then we can start moving into much more abstract things. For example, one could say to themselves, "Okay, I want to visit Vienna. I've never been there. What does it look like?" You could Google a few images of Vienna, then imagine those images, string them together as a stream, and then maybe all images of one location in Vienna. Then you put your mind there. You allow your mind to travel to that place in Vienna and hold those visualizations. As you string all these pictures together of that spot in Vienna, you will find that your mind will start filling the spaces between the pictures. It will start seeing the ground that you are mentally walking on, it will be looking up at the sky – all the things that are not in the pictures, your mind will see. These gaps between the pictures are very important, because this leads you into the feeling of mental wandering. In the beginning, we create two points and then as the mind moves from point A to point B, your mental body reaches out to Vienna, looks what is in-between these two places and it fills the gaps. From there, we can start developing mental wandering.

We create dots on a line and your mind draws a line between the dots. Each picture is a dot. We can get good at mental wandering very quickly by using these bridges – these support structures from the mind – to be flexible enough to start picking up this type of data. You want to start doing these types of exercises with a different emphasis on sensory gates, working on the visual gate, sound gate, feeling gate, scent gate, and taste gate.

One example, beginning with the scent gate, if you have ever been to a restaurant that just smells fantastic and you remember the scent, the temperature in the room when you walked in, how it felt to eat there and have the comfort of the chair, the sounds in the room, and so forth, once you've got all those anchor points through your memory, soften your mind back to that point in time and get up out of your chair, in your imagination, and have a walk around the restaurant. You have been there, your subconscious knows all the data, your astral body has assimilated it, and your mental body can go back there and have a walk around. Do it at that time that you were actually there. Walk around at that time and then, "Okay, I wonder what's happening there right now, in this time." Have a look at your watch, and at the same time in the evening or morning or lunch that you previously visited it, do the exercise. Take your mind to the restaurant – it might have been at 6:00 p.m. – so practice it at 6:00 p.m. Put your mind in the restaurant, walk through the door of the restaurant, wonder how many people are here, have a count, walk around the restaurant, get a feel for it, smell it, and get a sense for the environment in the restaurant at that moment. If it is convenient, bring your awareness back to your body and go back to that restaurant and have a physical look, take a smell, take a feel check how audible the music is, what volume people are talking at, and mark it up against your meditation experience. How close was it? Note the contrast between the two and release on it. So, next time you sit, release on what you remember, what you were creating, and you move towards what is, and you repeat this process.

From Creativity to Sensitivity
You can do this with lots of different environments. You might be walking down to the park and stop momentarily, close your eyes, and keep walking with your mind. You walk around the corner and inquire of what is there. You take note of the information, bring your awareness back into the body and then physically walk there and take note of the information. You will find that by requesting your subconscious mind to more accurately give you data and information, your subconscious will move from creativity to

sensitivity. Your mind will start to be sensitive to what is there as you move from the creative mind to the sensitive mind. Your spirit senses will start moving data through your astral body into your consciousness and you will be aware of what is happening in that place at that time. You are bridging between a physical experience, moving the mental body to that place, and then moving the physical body to that place; bridging, seeing the differences, and releasing them. You are also instructing your subconscious mind through journaling to increase the sensitivity of the spirit, activate the spirit senses, and reduce the amount of creativity in the mind.

You will feel the creativity to be an astral feeling where the spirit senses our separation of mind substance. The mind pulls across the layers, many layers and degrees of truth. When you pull everything apart, sensitivity to these layers is an exceedingly valuable skill. If you are healing people, you will be able to look into them and separate all the layers – their diseases, issues and emotional conditions. This will all become available to you, so that you are able to work with those as different energies.

Step Four

From there we choose a meditation object, then we feel the object, we go back to Step One mental training. There is a stillness, there is a meditation object – in this case a physical thing – and then there is a stillness around the object. When you engage in vipassana or samadhi, observing or concentrating, you will get this automatic memory of that when you concentrate on something, everything around it becomes still. We want to move that stillness under the object, so there is emptiness, and there is form – we want to differentiate these two.

The center of gravity of that object has a slightly lower pressure than the outside of the object – it is like emptiness always goes to center first and that emptiness in the center, we want to let our mind just soften onto the center of gravity of the object. This is very natural. Someone throws a ball to you and you catch it, you catch the whole ball, and you stick to its center of gravity so that you do not drop it. When you use an object like a sphere as your meditation object, you already have the subconscious ability, "I know the center gravity of the ball. I caught the ball hundreds of times." So the mind knows the center of gravity. When you use a sphere as your meditation object – perhaps a small crystal ball – you feel it in your hands as if you are catching the ball, give it a shake, feel the center gravity of that ball. Put your mind in the center and then go into that stillness within that center, which you have experienced in your earlier training.

Step Five

So that transfer into the center of gravity of the ball gives you a key to control. You put yourself into the center gravity of a disease within a person's body, and you are in control of the consciousness of the disease – you can influence it from there, you own that center. So to generate change within anything, you want to go to the center of gravity of the thing that you wish to create change within. Feel that through the stillness, engage it, unify with it, and then use the quadrapolar magnet.

You have your awareness – Air element – you have your cohesion – Water element – you unify, "I am the center of gravity of the object. I am this object," you have the Fire pillar, your will; you apply your willpower into the center gravity of the object in resonance with its vibration of the energy moving and your will begins to move that energy in resonance and you increase the will, you can change the frequency. The Earth element will naturally balance your perception, your Air, your cohesion, your oneness and connection with Water, your willpower, and you will have a type of persistence as they call it in Buddhism where the elements are balanced within your awareness and you can create change, transformation and movement between one state and another within that object.

When you start doing this with vital force or any type of energy in personality traits, for example, it is subject to laws of rhythm – it is in constant flux – so you can use your will to move that rhythm in one direction or another. It has mental transference into physical objects, into astral fields, into center of gravities, and people's consciousness, and so forth. This transfer allows for a powerful and rapid development when you work with the astral energies. While getting up to this point of your mental training and working it through as a stream, now when you begin astral training, you are a black and white mirror. You hold the sceptre of power. You can mentally transfer into the vibration of what you are looking at into the frequency of what you are looking at. You can move your awareness into the element and allow yourself to become that emotion, become that element. So, your black and white mirror will be far more profound.

It is suggested to first work through the mental exercises of the first half of the book before even starting the astral exercises. Align all the mental training exercises from Step One to Five, and then set a timer for two minutes. You might take a 10-15 second break between each round, splash some cold water on your face, and do the next round, and just stream through all those exercises of Step One to Five mental training.

As you repeat this a few dozen times, you are going to find that these exercises are going to take on a type of personality, because in every single one of these exercises you are compounding success. Your concentration is growing, your spirit is coming to the surface. Your spirit is becoming a part of your body, part of your astral feeling, a part of who you are as an individual. It is not an astral identity, as an ego substance, it is a concentrated part of you. This is a part of you that has higher awareness. So, we want to bring this up to the surface before we start astral training. The astral training is very easy when you have spent a few weeks doing Step One to Five, and if you have a lot of time you can knock this over in a few days, where you train all day in mental training.

You will be surprised by how invigorating iced water is and how long you can train with a bucket of ice water. You may even go as far as having a tub of ice and step into it between rounds. From just the thought of that you can imagine how invigorated you are going to be, and how enlivened your mind is going to be, and what type of mind-muscle-body memory you are going to have when you jump into a tub of water between every two minute round. When you are in there for 10 seconds, you jump out and then do your next exercise. You are so focused, so enlivened, that the only thing that can exist is success – failure is inconceivable. You are too present, too focused, too aware, and too powerful at that moment.

Step Six

In regards to developing the Akasha, there is a mental stream that needs to be in place before you can astrally manifest Akasha. The exercise of observing the arising and falling away of thoughts is necessary first. There is a point you reach where you feel this great distance between you – the observer

– and your thoughts. Thoughts will arise and fall from very far away. Once you have reached this state of awareness, you sense a stillness between you and the mental space upon which thoughts can arise. This stillness is the by-product of this observing process and is the beginning of an accumulation of Akasha and has a soft, vast, infinite quality to it.

In the second exercise, you select a thought-form and observe the thought-form, whether it is through your mind, through visual or auditory gates, or whatever your meditation object is, you will find yourself cocooning that meditation object with empty space in a way that everything else disappears – there is just a meditation object and empty space. If you are visually looking at something, you will find 'tunnel vision' forming where everything in the tunnel disappears, there is emptiness and the object in your eye-consciousness. If it is a thought-form, the emptiness accumulates around the thought-form. This type of emptiness is much sharper than the observing of the rising and falling away of thoughts – it is like a razor blade, a very sharp type of emptiness. The quality of it is very clean, clear and concise. It is a different form of emptiness compared to the first exercise which is generated as a by-product to the exercise.

These two types of emptiness need to be noted and incorporated into all the other exercises. In your mental training, you move the awareness to the stillness itself – the by-product of the first two exercises – and just enter that stillness. So here you end up entering two different types of stillness: one which is vast and infinite, and the other which has more of a sharp, clear and concise quality to it, a much more immediate quality. If we are to compare Buddhism to this, the first would be the emptiness arising from vipassana training, and the second would be emptiness arising from samadhi training. These two different types of emptiness are very distinguishably different. They need to be put in place and mastered before you begin Akasha work, because the mind needs to enter into that stillness and develop it. You will notice with every other mental exercise, when you fully engage your mind mentally into your different meditation objects, whether it will be visual exercises and so forth, there is a slightly different type of emptiness which arises in, around and underneath your meditation exercise. This emptiness, you want to bring it into the exercise as quickly as possible. So you recognize from the first Step One mental training exercises that empty space – that vacuum, that stillness – and you invite it into each extra exercise.

What this does is it brings you to mastery of the exercise much more quickly – it allows you to take two different directions to mastering something. One direction is you look at the mechanical process of the mental-astral-physical, engage it and just start practicing and building it. The other is you go to the emptiness underneath the skill – underneath the mastery – you invite the emptiness and then you allow the skill to express itself. So we have this yang approach of hitting it head-on; we have this yin approach where we engage the emptiness first and then we let the skill arise and practice the skill in a much more subtle, softer way, allowing it to come out of the empty space. This yin approach will naturally be much quicker and it is a by-product of having really looked at Step One mental training thoroughly and understanding that emptiness.

As you go through the first four steps, you end up with a range of different types of emptiness, which arises as a counterbalance to the concentration you are using. When we get to the fifth step and we are looking at space magic – going into the center of gravity of things – you will find that it is a slightly different type of emptiness. In the center of any object, there is a slight vacuum – it is like there is a lower pressure environment in the middle. When you enter into that lower pressure environment, it is as though you are getting sucked into a hole, into a space. This type of emptiness has a pressure differential. You will feel a distinct difference in pressure between the object on the outside and the center of gravity on the inside, and it is through this empty space where you can influence the object. So, going to the center of things and going into the infinite feeling of emptiness in the center of meditation objects: this particular quality allows you to measure the effect of Akasha on physical things.

When you are going into the low pressure area of an object within its center – you are sinking in and you have a sense that there is a physical form and then there is a center of that form – that pressure differential allows you to measure how much Akasha is present. Because Akasha, in and of itself, is empty – you cannot feel, sense or touch it because it does not have a form. What you can do is measure the difference between the form, the emptiness and the effect that is taking place. So we sense the effect and through the effect we know the emptiness. The stronger effect on form, the stronger the vacuum within the emptiness, and so forth. You sense Akashic substance as if it is a form, but what you are actually sensing is the effect that the Akasha is having upon form. This is very important to recognize from the beginning, because if your mind adheres to the effect of Akasha on the form, then you are not really controlling the Akasha – you are creating effects that Akasha has, but you go on a different tangent. We have our own way of measuring the Akasha.

This concept of vacuums and pressure differentials allows you to generate a gauge, a type of measurement within your perception. When you are breathing Akasha and you get a sense of how it is affecting your mental space, your astral space, your physical body, your environment, the room you are in, and so forth, you can get a sense of measurement of how much Akasha has been accumulated or how deep you have sent your awareness into Akasha.

Each one of these steps leading up to the building of Akasha allow you to penetrate deeper into that stillness and then manifest that stillness to affect form in the astral training. Akasha, when it is viewed clairvoyantly, is dark violet in color. So we just naturally take that dark violet color, we associate it with Akasha. When you have been doing the mental training exercise and you recognize that the vacuity in that emptiness and the pressure difference between Akasha and form, you associate dark violet color to it, and you remember each of your experiences with Akasha with that color and you anchor them. So that all you need to do is breathe that dark violet feeling in, with a sense of timelessness, release space, breathe out, go into the infinity quality, and very quickly you will be anchored into Akasha by simply pore breathing in the dark violet color. An emptiness simply arises.

When you are breathing Akasha into your astral body, it has a much more profound effect on form. The general side effects are a sense of drunkenness, a sense of separation or swaying of the body, the mind slipping in and out of normal consciousness, getting pulled into a vacuum, and so forth. Some people say that they feel stoned. Generally it is the side effect of the three bodies separating slightly. If the mental body separates from the astral, there is this disconnect from the physical world and you end up in a different type of mental or astral space. As you begin the Akasha breathing exercises, you will find that there are a few things which will be dependent on your success or failure. If you are training as an independent practitioner – meaning that you are not working in a group – your success with Akasha will be dependent upon how profoundly deep your samadhi is. You have to have extreme concentration to generate extreme Akasha.

Samadhi produces Akasha as a counterbalance, the stillness underneath the concentration. So, if you are doing this on your own, you really have to master these various forms of concentration, so that the Akasha – which is a counterbalance to the concentration – arises. If you have a teacher who has already worked with Akasha for many years, they can simply breathe that into you and guide you through the process of breathing timelessness and breathing spacelessness out, connecting to the infinity quality with the dark violet color as you pore breathe, and they can lead you to the Akashic quality that they have already developed. So they can give you a taste of it. As soon as you have got a taste of it, you anchor it into that same breathing process and before long you are training Akasha without having to have done many years of hard concentration work.

If you have already done the hard concentration work in other systems and then you encounter someone who has developed Akasha for a long time and they give you that energetic quality, your willpower automatically 'tune in' and you will rapidly take ownership of that Akasha. If you are new to practicing and you are given the Akasha feeling – the Akasha quality – by a teacher, then you will have to take ownership of that quickly and practice it every day until it roots in and becomes a part of your psyche. If you do not practice it every day or do the practice without serious focus, those energies will not be able to manifest correctly within your field of consciousness due to the lack of samadhi and support structure for that to happen. We need to look at the process and as soon as you receive a transmission from a teacher, repeat the process in order to take ownership of it in your own time. If you only train with the teacher, you will not be able to have ownership because you will be riding the teacher's energy unconsciously. It will be so much easier just to cruise with the teacher's words rather than focus your will upon the energies that are there. So you need to do more training than what you do with your teacher in order to take ownership of what he or she gives you.

Once you have started the process of breathing timelessness and spacelessness out, associating a dark violet color, and then entering into that deep stillness with a vacuum, you will notice that the side effects will start to arise, and then after a few weeks the side effects will start to diminish. The drunken feeling and the disorientation will disappear, the feeling of being stoned will disappear, but you will feel an increased space between the three bodies. That remains forever. Your mental, astral and physical bodies have a larger gap between them and this empty space is underneath your mental, astral and physical bodies and forms a type of gateway. So, if you are pore breathing, you go into Akashic trance and pore breathe, you draw vital force directly out of the Akasha. You can draw astral force directly out of the Akasha and mental force directly out of the Akasha. So you can pull these energies out of the Akasha. To do this, produce that space in your mental-astral matrix, in and around and under each of the energy bodies. Doing this will give you access to create a door from the Akasha.

A lot of this type of work is highly intuitive. Remember that in his book Bardon only talks about less than one percent of your learning. When you do the exercise, you generate the experience and then you have the "A-ha" moments of how it works and it is nothing like it is written in the book. If you intellectually read the book and get a picture, it is the wrong picture, because that picture is arising out of your ego – it is not arising from the direct experience of doing each exercise. So we really need to take this into consideration that we are not generating any self-fulfilling prophecy from the beginning like, "This is what I expect to get, that's what I'm going to get when I do this exercise," because it will be incorrect from the beginning. You have to guard against these types of expectations. If you are doing high quality journaling with each exercise and you are looking at what you are doing – not only academically, but intuitively as you read your journal – you will find that you will get a deep insight into how these processes function, how the whole initiation process mind maps and weaves together, and how you develop Akasha.

In Taoism's *Tao De Ching*, Lao Tzu states that, "the Tao that can be named is not the true Tao." This statement is an Akashic parable, that you cannot label an experience, you cannot make sense of an Akashic experience. The Akasha is outside of time and space and your brain is inside of time and space. When you are having these experiences, you journal them but you journal them in such a way that you can go back to those same frequencies, to those same places, and continue developing them. You are not trying to understand the Akasha in an intellectual way because that cannot be done. A brain inside of time-space cannot comprehend something outside of time and space. The consciousness just has to accept Akashic experiences, to simply remain within the Akasha. So more of our time is spent on developing the process of how to enter and exit Akasha, and how to use Akasha to draw energies in and out, and how to be a creative being. You do not need to understand what Akasha is. If you put too much time into that, it will trap you and you will find that you have lost a decade of your time trying to figure it out, when there is no need to figure it out.

When you are inside that Akashic space, there is this intuitive intellect that simply understands the experience. When you move back into a normal body consciousness, just allow that information to stay where it is within your Akashic memory, in that inner knowing, and you will get much more benefit out of the practice.

Step Seven

When we are working with the mental body we recognize that the mental plane has no edges – it is an infinite space, but it does have a mind substance, and this mind substance can be perceived as a form. There is a viewing lens, there is consciousness. Mental consciousness has a substance that appears to be similar to the astral, but it is very different. The mind of most people has a form, but at an essential level it does not. The only form that the mind has are the attachments of the astral which are stuck to it. In Buddhism, these are called mental effluents – **the Samsaric energies which stick to the mind, the karma that sticks to the mind, which delude our perception.**

When we are working with developing awareness of the mental body, first we have to recognize that any perceptions, thought forms, fabric of consciousness, any perception of itself is an attachment – it is something which is dirty: it is making our vision dirty. We have to move into the Akashic quality of infinity and allow that infinity to pervade the mental body, if you understand what the mental body is (when) connected to pure spirit. Because we are incarnated in a physical body and the mental body has karma, it has a center of gravity. Pure spirit does not have a center of gravity, because it is infinite in all directions. A spirit that has karma has contaminants. Those contaminants are that Samsaric force which pulls you from one incarnation to the next. This Samsaric force has a center of gravity and that center gravity is detectable; it tends to both gravitate and pull itself in the physical body and into the pineal gland.

When we are working with the mental body and we do Akashic breathing, we enter into the Akasha and the attachments of the mental body naturally dissolve away. They do not dissolve away permanently, but they are compartmentalized and move away from the consciousness so that you have access to the essence of your spirit – to pure spirit. This essence or pure spirit is an aspect of the universal mind, just like a vibrational match in the microcosm to the macrocosm. This pure spirit could only be accessed through Akashic trance. So, when you have been doing a lot of Akasha work, your mental body takes on this infinity quality of the mental plane and you become sensitive to your Samsaric contaminants – what holds your mental body in a state of reincarnation. These contaminants that form a center of gravity, that form a body that reincarnates, that we want to mingle with the Akasha and dissolve. We want to get rid of that perception of self, we want to get rid of that center of gravity and dissolve it into pure mind. Once that has been done, the concept of entering Nirvana becomes accessible. By working with Akasha, you can work to the highest level.

Through this intermingling of Akashic trance and Akasha viewing your own spirit, looking at the qualities of your own spirit from within Akasha, the contaminants begin to dissolve and fall away. Initially they compartmentalize – they fall away, but do not stay permanently away. As your mind is equalized with Akasha, they begin to dissolve and this is a way of managing your own karma.

When we get to the essence of that mental body there is a light, and because we are in a human form, that light will have a center of gravity attached to the body. If we are outside of human form, that light will be equal in all places throughout our mental body, which will have a human shape. If we equalize this with non-dual light, then there will be no shape there. There will just be simply vast consciousness and that consciousness appears wherever you concentrate yourself. So there will be a center of gravity that will present itself because that is your point of concentration. But if your mind spreads, the center of gravity disappears, and your mind becomes vast and open. This is an experience that can only be understood by working through Akasha, recognizing the essence of the mental body, recognizing that non-dual light, and dwelling within it for several hundred hours until that insight arises: that this is the spirit of the microcosm, this is a spirit of the macrocosm, and it is Akasha which opens that door.

Fire
There is a range of spirit qualities which arise through these universal qualities. These are a reflection of the form of the elements. So the form reflection of the Fire element is a type of omnipotence, a type of very strong power of concentration – a very focused mind. When you draw this down from the non-dual light, then through the Akasha back into the spirit, the spirit will seek to express itself through the astral-physical body with an immovable mind. The mind will be extremely concentrated. In the Air element, there is a qualitative type of understanding, insight – it is a frequency that simply looks at things and has answers, not questions. This insight of the mind is the pinnacle of the Air element and again, it is only accessible through Akasha, going to the essence of the mental body, and allowing that essence to reflect back into the mental body to see those insight qualities, those very deep levels of understanding. The Water element reflects through the Akasha as a type of universal love, a type of understanding without judgment – a type of connection to the environment that nurtures and cares for the environment. The Earth element has a type of omnipresence, a deeper sense of connection than the Water element. This element has a balance of all the elements: it has the will of the Fire, the insight of the Air, the love of the Water to be unified and have a unified consciousness, with your physical environment, your social circles, your connection and ethical responsibilities to the planet, the solar system, the Akasha, and the top of the universal consciousness connection.

When you come into the center of gravity of the sun, the essence of the center of gravity of the sun is the same as all the other suns, so your awareness spreads through them as well and you get a universal consciousness experience. It reflects back through the Akasha and then you see all the other forms of consciousness, from the black holes to a vast range of other universal intelligences that exist outside of our current understanding of the universe. These resonances generate a type of universal consciousness which makes you feel connected to everything that exists. This connection gives you a sense for everything that has existed and everything that is going to exist in the future at the same time. The human brain is simply not capable of comprehending something like that, but the spirit is able to absorb that quality, because the universe is mind, the universe is spirit, and this omnipresence quality becomes accessible within the spirit. Again, when you have these experiences, you leave them within their home within the Akasha, within the spirit, and you do not try to pull them back into the body because the body cannot make any sense of them – it will all just go into a state of chaos because each body has different rules of time and space. Each of the learnings needs to be left within the space of where that learning resides; if brought into another space, too much chaos will arise.

As we go through this process of recognizing the qualities of the spirit, we want to bring these qualities of the spirit down through the mental body, into the astral body, and make them functional, make them improve the quality of our experience in this incarnation. As the qualities of omnipotence, of extreme willpower, come down to the astral, then the astral body becomes very wilful. It becomes very strong and starts to pervade through the physical and there is a yearning to conquer your body, so that the physical body cannot rule how you feel, think and act, but your spirit will rule how you think, feel and act. This will cross over into a need to practice asceticism for your will of the spirit to be greater than the desires of the astral and physical bodies. This type of training will automatically begin conquering your physical form as you begin stimulating it.

Water
When the Water element comes from a universal level or through the spirit and into the astral body, we get an overwhelming sense of compassion which arises. This compassion is different to universal love – it is more of a reaction to love. Compassion stimulates action. It stimulates your desire to heal others and stimulates your ability to connect to people, generate networks, be supportive of your community and environment, protect the planet, and raise the frequency of the planet. Because of the nature of compassion, it urges you to do so – it pulls out of you to raise the frequency of the group consciousness, because you have compassion arising within you. It is a side effect of touching the universal consciousness through Akasha. That compassion naturally arises. This is reflected in the path of light, where you bring your awareness into an incarnation and choose to be of service – to teach, heal and raise the frequency of the planet. It may be in an isolated cave in the Himalayas or you may simply charge energy in the mental-astral plane that elevates group consciousness, or it may be in the form of a writer, teacher, healer, or guide or mentor for other people around you. It may also

be in the way that you walk down the street and smile at people, raising their frequency as your energy emanates outwards in your day-to-day life.

Whatever form you choose to express, it will be unique to you. It does not have to be in a state of a high grade teacher that has thousands of followers. You may choose to be a bricklayer and charge every brick with love, compassion and healing – you would put in these qualities and build a person's home. As their dream home forms they have a house that is surrounded with love; it brings them into a state of harmony for their environment and their spirit rises because of the house that you contributed towards building. These different paths in how compassion expresses itself are unique to the individual. Whatever your path is, recognize it and do your best with it, give one hundred percent of yourself. The energy which allows you to do that is free energy – it is the desire and passion you have to initiate which powers you. Compassion is fuel for action.

If you have to push yourself to do something, it is not free energy coming out of compassion – it is coming from willpower. This compassion is a free energy which just drives you to get things done. You can invoke that and use free energy to motivate yourself in what you are doing.

Air
The Air element will stimulate a desire for learning in the astral body. As it comes from the mental to the astral, you will want to study, learn and educate yourself. Your intuition by now is already being stimulated and you are having a wide range of experiences that you simply cannot understand.

As you educate yourself, you will find the physical sciences will allow for "A-ha" moments to happen within the spiritual senses. "I understand how this works now," either literally through the physical sciences or metaphorically. It will just reflect as a metaphor into your psyche. For example, if you've studied engineering, you may come to an understanding that vital force has a hydraulic pressure affect to it. When you store vital energy by putting it into a battery, it increases hydraulic pressure. If this hydraulic pressure is not assimilated into the body, your body will overheat from the side effects. So you will get these "A-ha" moments because of your understanding of mechanical sciences, physics, quantum physics, etc. This desire to study natural and theoretical sciences kicks in and you'll want to learn how the world functions scientifically.

If you are channelling a high level of knowledge from the universal mind – from higher deities and spirits – if your brain simply cannot comprehend it, it will not make any sense to you. You will be able to feel it, but you cannot manifest it as a physical technology. Of course we all want to manifest these technologies as physical things to help the planet develop, evolve, ease suffering, and increase evolution. Education is a big part of the spiritual path. You want to educate yourself so that you can develop more efficient processes either for spiritual development or within the scientific fields to evolve the group consciousness.

Earth
When you bring the Earth element down from the mental to the astral, there is a profound sense of sensitivity to your physical space – you put your hand on the ground and you feel around the forest that you are in, around the space that you are in, you can feel the vibration of the earth, the earth speaks to you: it is called consciousness. You can feel people walking on the ground hundreds of meters away, you can feel cars drive by a kilometer away, you get a sense of "I can feel the earth and feel the animals. I can feel the insects crawling. I can feel life," and this sense of extension of your consciousness eventually becomes your consciousness that you are the forest, the planet, the earth. This omnipresence which moves through your astral being allows you to be connected to all these energy circles. The group consciousness of your family, social circles, a community, your hobbies and interests, chat groups on the internet – you will get a sense of all these different types of group consciousness. When you engage them, you are them. You identify, "I am this group," and you understand the frequency of the vibration of the group.

When you are the group, you can raise the frequency of it. You can breathe light and breathe Akasha and you can raise and ascend that group consciousness, whether it is a micro-group or a macro-group. This becomes the type of yearning within the spirit to do this, because everything is about evolution. In order for the universe to expand as a macrocosm, the individual has to expand as a microcosm. As you expand microcosmically, the universe is expanding macrocosmically, and these two are dependent upon each other. That is all about evolution, rising frequency.

This yearning to evolve ourselves – to expand the mind, the astral, the physical sciences, to make everything grow – is what the universe is essentially doing: it is growing. We are mimicking that within our microcosm, mentally, astrally and physically. When we understand that, we can become sensitive to the expansion of the universe and ride that energy to expand our microcosm; to allow streams of universal knowledge that flow through the mental body, to interpret those in the astral, and then develop training systems and express them physically through teaching and developing new sciences, technologies, paradigms of consciousness and so forth.

So this last aspect of the Earth element – omnipresence – allows us to make everything we have learned functional; to make physical things that can be physically expressed, and they will regulate all the other elements and decide on how successful each of the elements are within their expression.

Step Eight

What most people call astral travel is actually mental wandering, with the mental body exploring the astral kingdom.

Mental wandering
The deciding factor in the ability to mental wander is your Akasha ability. If you are able to enter into Akashic trance, then you find yourself instantly able to demagnetize your mental matrix and allow your mental body to leave your astral-physical bodies behind to enter wherever it wishes.

If you have been doing all your mental training exercises, all the sensory imagination exercises and have developed the spirit senses, when your mental body leaves the astral-physical, you will be in a feedback loop in which you will be able to see, feel and hear the experience. If your feeling is highly developed when your mental body separates, your spirit senses will give a feedback loop of feeling. You extend your mental body out across the street and connect to a person, you mentally transfer into that person and you will be able to feel them. If your clairvoyance is developed, you will be able to see their past, present and future through the Akasha. If your clairaudience is developed, you will be able to hear their thinking, their memories, their future, and so forth.

So the mental training exercises will regulate the effectiveness of the experience. Akasha will regulate your ability to separate the mental body and move your mental body into any point of focus you wish, whether it is in the astral realm, mental realm or an Akashic space. You can access wherever your point of concentration is, providing you demagnetize the mental matrix. The best time to begin this training is in the afternoon. Try this exercise around mid-afternoon, between 2:30 p.m. and 3:00 p.m. A lot of people like to have a catnap. Lay down on a daybed, have your back at about a 45 degree angle, with a pillow tucked under your knees, so that you are very comfortable and settled in. From there, simply start Akasha breathing and increasing the space around you. As you Akasha breathe, increase the space around you, move into Akashic trance and then move your awareness up through your crown chakra and just slip out through the crown. Make yourself suspend from above, increase the space a bit more, and then release the space.

It does not matter where you go – moving through the crown will ensure you go up in a high frequency space. Just let yourself go wherever the energy pulls you and quietly do Step One mental training. Observe the rising-falling away of the experience. Do not touch anything, do not control anything, just be a silent observer to this mental wandering. It is wandering, you are not controlling anything – you are just allowing the energies that be to move, and you are silently observing them, monitoring the rising-falling away of the experience. As you observe this arising and falling of experience, the amount of Akasha that you used to dissolve your mental matrix when you initially released will have a tightening of that mental matrix to pull you back to your body. This experience may last a few minutes to several hours. As your mental matrix becomes magnetized again, your mind gets pulled back into the body.

If there is a loud sound, a noise, a sudden intensity of energy being knocked at the door of your consciousness, your mental matrix would receive a shock. Your physical body would electrically stimulate the nervous system creating a magnetic fluid, which energizes your mental matrix and would pull your mental body back to your astral-physical form. This is part of our survival instinct. So, to reduce this ensure that you are in a place where it is quiet, with no disturbances – so that Akashic accumulation through the mental matrix raised up through the crown has no energies that are going to pull you back to the body; so nothing can increase the magnetic fluid in your mental matrix, and you can develop this further.

Because you are laying on a daybed and have a pillow supporting under your knees, and your body is set at a 45 degree angle, it would be very comfortable just falling into these pillows, as there is nothing in your physical body to pull you back into form. Be completely relaxed and release your body's form. You are just floating on a cloud.

You have learned how to exit through the crown chakra and enter into these levels, and you have been practicing observing the rising-falling away of the experience without touching the experience, without putting any intentions on your mental body. If you intend on your mental body it can be linked through the mental matrix, through the silver cord which energizes it and sucks you back to your astral form, which you do not want. Your mastery of observing the rising and falling away when you are entering into mental wandering is critical. You need to have this skill well mastered. You just observe the experience, do not apply your will to anything, do not ask any questions or project any thoughts – just quietly, mentally wander.

As soon as that has been established and becomes stable, your will can move like a feather – like blowing a feather very softly – and you move your will to wander in a direction that you wish, without getting pulled back to your body. Remember that our unconscious habit for the will is physiological and astral. We normally express our will through the will of the body, where we are now expressing through the will of the spirit. When you express the will of the body, it creates a magnetic fluid. Your mental matrix can suck you back into the body. We do not want this to be an imagination exercise, we want this to be mental wandering. So how you express your will of the spirit is very different to how you express the will of the body. We need to move intent very softly like a feather, so that it does not generate any magnetism to pull the mental body back into form.

With steering of the experience, we create mental space in one direction or another to get your experience to go in the direction that you want – it is almost opposite to the will of the body. It is like creating a vacuum of direction that gently moves you as your awareness remains in stillness. Your awareness is like a feather and if you take a feather and move a feather through the air it is like a vacuum behind the feather. This vacuum pulls the air along. That pulls your experience. It is a type of will opposite to the normal quality of will.

Once you have established this moving of the vacuum to pull your mental body in the direction that you wish to guide your mental wandering, then your skill becomes deeper with mental wandering. You are able to do the same with the other pillars. The Air pillar, to create space in the mental body – remember that the mental bodies are not subject to space, so you have got to create this openness in order to receive information, to understand something. You have got to create this openness in order for the Water element to create cohesion and connection to things without getting stuck back in your astral body. To connect and influence things mentally, astrally and physically with your spirit to utilize the Earth element, the will has to create this openness of space, which allows the spirit to express itself through not having space. So this is very counter-intuitive. It doesn't make sense from a physical perspective. But when you look at how space opens in your mental body through the elements, you also see that you have the keys to mastering the universal qualities, the elements within the spirit. You have the master keys to mental wandering, and how to control those experiences and allow your mental body to go wherever you desire by controlling the qualities of infinity through Akasha, to take you where you want to go. Practice allows this and higher levels of insight and understanding to arise.

Step Nine

Let us take a look at the magic mirror work. The magic mirror is a crystal ball. A crystal ball or anything larger than your fist will work. You want to come and look at the ball, to be able to visualize images into it. So, we start off with all the Kabbalistic letters, pick up Franz Bardon's third book *Key to the True Kabbalah* (KTQ). You can chart out each of the colors of the Kabbalah – there are 27 colors. Then you place the crystal ball in front of you and go to your peripheral vision. This peripheral vision takes in the space around the ball, and then you start up with 'A', a light blue color, visualize that, and so forth. You can move through all the Kabbalistic letters of the KTQ book. As short as one minute rounds for each letter is fine. Hold the color over the ball of the sphere, so that you make the whole sphere that particular color and set your timer to one minute, and systematically go through. You can have a 10 second break, if you like, between rounds to douse yourself with ice water and splash your face.

 I have tried jumping under a cold shower during my 10 second break and stepping out, to do my next round, and that worked fantastically. You can jump into a cold body of water, whichever works for you. The most important thing is that you are super-present, and that you really force your body to the present moment. Once you have worked through all the colors and the one minute round and extend to the crown, if you like, then we look at associating the element from Kabbalah into that particular color. So we are not really looking at Kabbalah in a classical sense of frequency or the effects and so forth – we just want to bring the color and an element feeling into it, into place and work it as a feeling exercise, visual exercise and then we add the sound exercise into it and taste and scent exercises that we did at the beginning of the training. We want to add this into the crystal ball work.

Once you have taken the color, you take the elements related to it, so a light blue for letter 'A', and you breathe the Air element into a light blue color in the ball, and you put your hands over it to hold energy around it – you breathe that element in. Get used to charging energy into the ball. From there, go through all the different color and element relationships until you have covered them all.

This preliminary training is very important because it is the opening of the three bodies, and a mental transference into the ball and the energy you put into it, which allows you to get enough separation from the bodies for information to flow through you. Each of the sense gates that you are wanting to use with the mirror work, with the crystal ball work, you have to spread that sense gate open. When you pull eye-consciousness open, you will see all the resistance, stress and anxiety around our consciousness and barriers that have arisen every time. Dissolve resistance within your eye-consciousness – then you will be able to get in there and start releasing and using Akasha techniques, light techniques, and so forth.

This fundamental training can dictate your success and failure, so make sure that you are able to visualize color clearly, feelings clearly, and pull everything apart. We want to have a clear information stream to look out through the ball, so we are going to get everything open. If you want to have the exercises where you go through different sounds, tastes and scents, you can take the exercise that we did in the early mental training and then transplant them into the ball. So you mentally transfer it into the ball and then you pull everything open, you practice that same exercise with your mind inside the space of the ball. The reason why I prefer a ball over a mirror is that a ball is of three-dimensional space. So when I enter my mind into the ball, I am in a white room that is spherical and inside that sphere, that is my office: I store all the data there, I store all my rituals there; this is where I go to practice.

Whether you have a physical sphere in which you move your mind into, which is heavily charged with energy to practice, develop communication with other deities and so forth, or whether you charge a space up in the ocean of light, is up to you. With a physical sphere, you are able to produce a lot more electromagnetic charge through the elements, through Akasha, through light into it, so you can use that as a battery for all different types of functions, as well as for an awareness development tool.

Once you have done your basic mental training exercises inside the ball – you have got through all the colors and the element feeling in relation to colors – then you can decide how are you going to charge this ball of energy, how are you going to load it so that it becomes functional. We want to look at the vibrational scale of the chakras for that. The root chakra is Earth element, so you start charging more with Earth. You move up to Water for sacral, the solar plexus with Fire, the heart with Air, the throat with Akasha, third eye with light, and then the crown chakra with prayer, universal consciousness. Charging the ball with that spectrum of energy will give a nice battery effect to the ball, so it will stabilize your consciousness when you are inside of it. Before you put those elements in, you have a very clear and concise understanding of what the function of that ball is, and what you can use it for. Are you going to have a crystal ball as a battery for elemental beings? You can use crystal balls for clairvoyant work, you can use them for doing readings for people, or you can use a ball to commune with deities. You decide that first, because when you put these elements in, you want to build the element with that outcome in mind as you build it. So the information inside the element – how the element is expressing itself – is already pre-set. When all the elements have the same goal in mind then you get a far greater outcome.

Once you have gone through the process – you have decided what this crystal ball is going to be used for, and charged all the elements in – you charge the ball with the Akasha, light and prayer. You hold that prayer at a crown chakra level. If you were a Buddhist, you could bring a deity through a prayer, bring the deity into a crystal ball, and make that the space in which you practiced your deity yoga with that deity. If you belong to another religion, when you get to the crown chakra prayer level of charging the ball you look at the deity of your religion and invoke that deity into the ball.

When you do this type of work, you should have a certain level of altruism in your intent. You should be working with that ball for the benefit of others. If you want to awaken clairvoyance skills in yourself, the intent is that you are opening that clairvoyance to be a better reader to help other people, or to be better at your job as a teacher or healer. Whatever your role is, that clairvoyance is not for you – it is for the benefit of the people you are in service to. This merit that you generate by placing that ideal in place will open the clairvoyance, will pull the sense gates open as a side effect. Be very sensitive to the seeds of why you do this type of training. When you dedicate a crystal ball towards a particular function, then we really have to very clearly look at your motive. The higher the motive, the faster the development. The more egocentric the motive, the slower the development. This rule holds true.

So we go through the process of deciding. As an example, we are going to use a crystal ball for clairvoyant work. We have charged the elements into the ball with the frequency of clairvoyance, and we have done all the preliminary visualization work and all transference in the ball, spending time and looking at it as a television set, and so forth. From there, we start looking at how to get the peripheral vision correct. You want to look at the ball without focal vision and start expanding your peripheral vision a few inches around the ball. Just start breathing with your eyes. We want to breathe white light for the eyes while we are doing this. Then inch-by-inch we expand the peripheral vision a bit further out from the ball, while we are doing white light breathing.

The white light breathing exercise consists of raising up to universal light, streaming light through the crown, and letting the stream run through the three bodies, down through the feet. We want to stream that out through the eyes. Once we run that frequency, we can breathe through the eyes, breathe through the pores. So, eye-consciousness, the connection of the physical eyes to the pineal gland and that part of the consciousness which sees, will breathe like that part of the consciousness. It is not necessary to connect that stream into a new streaming light through the eyes, you can just go into natural breathing.

The reason why natural breathing works so well is as you are breathing it, there is a slight flux between electric and magnetic energy in your eye-consciousness. If you slow the flux down, it will bring you into the frequencies in which you see. Initially you will move through the frequencies, where you can see too quickly. You have got to slow the breath right down and become sensitive to where these images are appearing and disappearing.

You expand your awareness out around the ball, inch by inch, and expand your peripheral vision, breathing light, you start tuning into these areas of the eye-consciousness where you can see information appear. You slow down and fine tune the feeling. So each incremental movement of sight one inch away from the ball is expanding your peripheral vision. While each incremental movement is not an exact measurement, it is a refined enough way of determining when to slow down, pause or when to expand our awareness out one inch of space. In summary, you make very small increments in peripheral vision and then tune your awareness to a point where you are seeing information arrive through your awareness.

Whatever information is flying through, look at it without any labelling, identification or thought. Since information arrives when you are falling away in your consciousness, hold it in anyway – do not try to capture it or analyze it, just watch it and keep those layers of the mental-astral-physical all separate and apart. Use the Akasha to neutralize it, allowing all matrices to be floating. As all these layers are pulled apart and you are looking through the ball, you will get an expansion of consciousness state as a reflection of seeing.

As soon as you see something clairvoyantly – even though your peripheral vision is stretched out to a certain amount – your spirit will become enlivened and expand. Be sensitive to that expansion because we are going to want to do a little work with that and activating your spirit senses with that expansion and refining them. When your spirit is engaged in something like clairvoyance, it becomes very stimulated and generates a type of 'hype' – some people call it 'rapture'. During rapture, some people will have tears running down their eyes, some people will have a feeling of incredible joy or freedom, and so forth. But when the spirit senses come into play and you tune them, rapture is a natural side effect. Be aware when these side effects rise and fall away, and then always leading through that bliss back into equanimity, and continue your training. You do not want to be getting distracted by the rapture and bliss that the spirit is feeling once you have freed it up inside. So, it is about coming into your true self.

Once you have your stream of visions through the ball and you have seen different bits of information coming through, there is a skill of mentally noting the information. So you have the information stream and there is a part of the observer that puts markers on the information. This inner dialogue may speak like, "This is important, that's important, that's important." At the end of the session you closed, pick up your journal and write out the key points immediately. When you write them down, you want to be in the same frequency and headspace as when you experience them. This will give you a different frequency of consciousness – it will give you different grammar, and everything will take on a whole different flavor. When you have written it down while being inside that frequency, the next time you go back to the crystal ball and train, you read the journal and continue at the peak frequency where you left off. That opens up that particular frequency. Always remember to write down where you are when you practiced, if you change location, because Akashically, everything is locked in the Akasha in the place where it happened. If you go back to the place, either physically or mentally, you can much more easily access that Akasha information. Remember to write down the location or anything you discover that helps access that state. Another thing worth mentioning is that moon cycles have a big impact upon people's abilities. Some people wonder why they succeeded the last time, but they cannot do it this time. The moon phase has a strong pool in the astral body; a strong rhythm in the astral realm. We want to be very sensitive to that and recognize how it is affecting our practice. We want to have a sense of what practices are being affected by different moon phases.

So, you have gone through the process, filled out your journal, written down what you felt. You want to have a deep sense of humility in regards to the experience. You want to have a very deep sense of devotion to your spiritual path in relation to the experience. You want to have a deep sense of reverence in relation to that experience, and then a deep sense of sacredness in relation to that experience. As we move up from the base chakra, the humility, the devotion, solar plexus, the reverence, and sacredness in the heart, and then we move up to your throat – the Akasha. The Akasha has a deep stillness, so your gratitude for what you just experienced pulls up that vibrational scale all the way through light into prayer, to have profound thanks for what you just experienced. When you recognize the vibrational quality of the prayer working up to the crown chakra, you seal that into your journal as a closing act of the exercise. The counter-force in the Akasha happens when you open that channel up again next time – it sucks you back into that place, like a vacuum. Picture this – imagine a giant slingshot pulls you back and through elasticity, shoots you out to the distant horizon. Accessing your previous practice through your journal accelerates you forward from your last state of practice.

When you draw a slingshot, that rock flies a hundred meters. We want to really take advantage of this power of prayer of gratitude in closing of any experience that you want more of. The prayer of gratitude is an accelerator: it induces power. In Biblical phrasing, "The meek shall inherit the Earth," has nothing to do with the meek, it has something to do with these qualities of humility – the devotion, reverence and sacredness in relation to your spiritual path. That is not meek, it is power. With this slingshot effect, we want to take advantage of it between every cycle of the practice.

Once you have charged a crystal ball for a particular function and been using it for that function for a while, if you want to change its function, it is best to demagnetize it and start again. To demagnetize it, put it in salt water overnight, and put it on a windowsill at the moonlight, put prayer over it, and ask the spirit of the Water element to demagnetize the energy out of the crystal ball. Then you can start again. It is a good idea to do that with any new crystal ball that you get as well, to demagnetize it. If you get something new – whether it is a crystal ball, amulet or any tool for practice – you want to put it in the salt water, if it is appropriate. As soon as you pull it out of salt water, give thanks to the spirit of the Water element for the purification. Once it is done, connect up to your highest connection of universal light, and load it with light so nothing else sneaks in.

Once you have loaded it with light, from there you can have some sort of dedication ceremony that you dedicate towards a special process, person or outcome. You may dedicate it to your past, present or future students for their benefit, or whatever it is for. The dedication that you do when you get these new implements and new tools, it generates a condition inside of a self-fulfilling prophecy, allowing energy to affect that. All of the other stuff you are doing on top of that is generating expansion and pulling you from the open, connecting you to the path of your dedication.

For example, let us say that we have decided we want to use the crystal ball as a storage device and we want to put a large amount of energy into it. You want to pick the crystal ball up and put it in your hands. If it is a very large ball – like bowling ball size – you can physically cradle and touch the ball and feel the weight of the ball under your hands. The reason why we do that is to feel the weight of the ball. When you relax and release your muscles, the fascia stretches its elasticity under the ball. When you tune your life force into the ball and physically hold it, your body is conducting energy naturally into the physical realm. When the ball is there, your hands are there, and you are breathing, it is just outside the physical. When the ball is in your hand and you feel your fascia in the stretch and you have tuned the fascia to life force, you have been breathing into it, it has a very physical battery effect on the ball – where that energy is affecting your physical environment, affecting the emotions of every person who walks in the environment, and having a profound physical effect upon you.

When you want your crystal ball to be a battery, charge it while you are holding it, feeling the weight of the ball, the mass of the ball; it stretches your fascia, and the physical energy moved into the physical state stays on that physical edge. It is very different to putting your hands around something and not touching it, charging energy in. That would pull it closer into the astral layers and an actual physical layer of ball. You have the crystal ball in your hand and you hold it in your left hand, right hand on top, or you cradle it with both hands, like you are holding a ball. Then you want to move the vibrational scale through the elements, same as we did before. But the feeling of the energy is much more physical. If you want it to be a battery, you want to keep it as close to the physical world as possible, so that the energies you were charging it with can affect the physical-astral realms. If you are working with a large ball, do not lift it off the stand – just feel the weight of it as you are breathing into it. You may only be supporting 10% of the weight and the stand is holding the rest of the weight, because it is very large. So this phase is very important.

With the crystal ball in your hands, move up through a vibrational scale. Have a clear intent as you move to the Earth element and do the same with Water, Fire, Air, Akasha, light, and move onto prayer. Make sure that the prayer is aligning to the greater good for everyone; everything involved in its function is to be for service. There is a certain degree of holiness inside your field of consciousness when you start to work with that ball. If you treat it truly like a sacred object – like this device is for communing with divinity, for service and the benefit of the next generation – that relationship you have to divinity and your outcome of wanting this tool, this device, for the betterment of the next generation, you are connecting divinity to the next generation.

That dedication of merit and that attitude of opening the ball automatically connects all the people that this energy is going to influence in the future and it starts radiating light before you have even done anything. You take the silk cloth off and might say to yourself, "Wow, this ball is full of light." It is some natural and physical reaction from having the right attitude. We have a dedication to merit, entering into doing the holy work. Then you get a reaction in the light between the light realms and the physical realm of you holding it and the light starts to radiate physically. This is when interesting things happen, when what people call 'miracles' start to happen – where these higher Akasha light realms interact with the physical realm due to a person's sense of sacredness in their practice. Their clairvoyance accelerates, their practice accelerates, everything starts to pick up speed and momentum. It is very important that we recognize the effect of the state of your consciousness when you engage in any practice. When you start the practice it generates a continuity of momentum through the session. So, when you have a session where you open the session with the right mindset, you know the rest of that session is going to get better. If you open a session feeling out of sync slightly or not being in a good place, you have to reset it, start again. You basically close off the session, wash your face with ice water to reactivate and practice again.

If you are applying the initiation text to your work, passions or teachings, there is a sense of sacredness to be followed. For example, if you are taking the initiation text and overlaying it on tennis coaching and you want to use it for a blueprint of how you teach tennis – how to teach the psychology, how you teach the energetics of moving, and so forth – a lot of that sacredness is going to be dissolved out of the equation. Very few people will look at any sport as a sacred act of communing with God. It will naturally take on a different personality when you overlay that blueprint onto different activities. For yourself, you should always look at the blueprint of the highest first and then overlay it onto lower frequency functions later. If you established habits that are too sports-oriented, then you want to move into the more higher sacred frequencies of light, you are going to find that it would be much more difficult. But if you go into a sacred space first and then go to the lower frequency, it will be much easier to get the results that you are looking for.

So there are a lot of different areas in which one can use the mirror or crystal ball. What we are going to look at now is mirror projection into different realms. This crystal ball is an excellent doorway. Your primary charge is going to be Akasha. You are going to be using Akasha at a very intense, deep level to get those portals to open. Using the formula E-U in Kabbalah works incredibly well. Use dark violet and a shiny black color to get those portals to open. It is best to have a crystal ball, to pre-build one portal for one destination. You do not want to have an open end and say, "Well, today I'm going to go here or there," and change venues with this particular one.

If you have several different places that you want to go to, you have to build the crystal ball to go to those places and nowhere else. You might have a crystal ball to visit all planetary spheres – the portal to each planetary sphere in one ball – but you would not want to be putting in more entry points, because too many other things can start passing through your ball. Remember that it is a two-way door, in and out. Remember to wrap the ball and soak it after you finish practice and keep it properly insulated – keep it in a good space, have a box for it, where you can seal the box. Use the E-N formula to blanket those objects that are valuable for your practice.

Once you have gone over the Akasha, whatever your Akashic training is, the self-fulfilling prophecy you generate is going to connect you to a place. When you enter the ball, you transfer yourself into the Akasha of the ball. Now you have a self-fulfilling prophecy, then this takes you to the sun sphere, the moon sphere, before you enter into that Akasha – so you have already set up the destination. Then you drop into the Akashic trance and put yourself into the ball. Some like to spend a moment in the Akasha and equalize to that Akashic environment. What that does, it demagnetizes the mental body and takes away all the 'stickiness' of the physical and astral bodies. By bathing in that Akasha for a few minutes before entering the sun sphere, it is kind of like a cleaning process. It allows one to have a much more profound clean-clear effect, an experience of moving into the sun sphere.

Once you are in the Akasha, in trance, inside the ball, you feel demagnetized, you feel equalized with Akasha, then you move your awareness to center gravity of the sun. Once you are in the center of gravity of the sun – the control point of the sun – you just start to relax your awareness up to the feeling of the core frequency of the sun. From that whole frequency, all of the other frequencies arise. This same rule applies to all the other realms of planetary spheres if you are using it as the gates to move those spheres. If you are moving it as a gate to a place you have already been to – let us say, if you have worked in the spirit realm or may have been sitting in a cave somewhere and had a spirit visit you, which led you into an interesting experience – you can build that door back to that place in your crystal ball, so that you can go back to that place again in the future.

When mental wandering using a crystal ball as a gateway, it is very handy to charge your mental body with your greatest good in the highest of light before you enter into each realm. Any being that is there identifies you by the frequency of light, and they will treat you accordingly. If you have not cleared yourself and then you charge yourself with light before you enter a realm, they will treat you with hostility, rudeness and so forth. But if your density of light and your spirit is greater than the beings you are connecting to, or the realm you are entering, they will recognize that. Their eyes will burn; they will bow their heads down so that their eyes don't get burned. They will pay respect to you and ask how they can help you. It is a totally different type of interaction if you are used to going to a place and getting mistreated. Beings, when they see another being that has a much higher intensity of light in themselves, their natural reaction to this type of hierarchical thinking is respect, friendship and wishing to help you.

This type of reaction allows very interesting streams of knowledge. William Cook Edward's advice was to be very humble, no matter what density of light you have, and say you are a student of the path, who wishes to learn. As you use that type of humility, there is a type of reflection of your spirit in relation to what your learning needs are. Those beings will see that, accommodate that learning need and reflect the information that is pertinent to your spiritual growth. Because they recognize that there are a lot of people who are incarnated on a very high light frequency, that do not know them. They have no self-awareness of who they actually are in their spiritual achievements. They only recognize what their ego has been through incarnating that body. But these beings see your spiritual signature for what it is and they know that to have a friend of a high frequency has huge value. On a conscious and unconscious level they seek to help you. So, charge yourself with light before entering into any realm.

When you are going through the Akasha and raising your awareness into a particular realm – let us say if we look at the Earth realm, you need to equalize your mental body with Earth. So you need to fill your mental body with the Earth element – actually fill all three bodies with Earth element so each body can generate separate equilibriums that are independent from each other. This way, your mind can move out without anything pulling it back. Then add the light into it. So, you would have the frequency of the realm that you are going to and the universal light to make that element or that frequency glow on a high level. So that you would be perceived as royalty or a very high level entity. This approach to mental wandering is important. You ensure a much higher quality experience result when you take the time to set up the transference of the spirit into that particular place.

In Bardon's book *Initiation into Hermetics*, he uses all different types of clairvoyance with the crystal ball – from prophetic visions, to seeing the things happening in the present moment, same timelines, for future projections of things, same causation patterns within your practices. In short, there are many different areas that you can develop. Most of those areas are obvious and intuitive. You look at it and break it down and say, "This is easy. I can do this." The belief structure of ease – that self assurance of "This is easy. I can do this," – needs to be in place for everything, because that is your destination. You want to do everything with ease, you are going to be doing it naturally. You want to have a belief structure that stems from the confident notion that states, "I can do this!" The subconscious mind can work through the human bodies' fascia as a syncing process, it moves information from the unconscious to the consciousness how to do things and vice versa. Your spirit already knows how to do all this. We just need to transfer it down into the subconscious and the body consciousness, align the three bodies to the spiritual process you are going through, so it becomes cognitive and then you connect it out. Then you can translate your experience to be beneficial for yourself and those processes and systems that are beneficial for others.

Step Ten

Once we have gone through the process of mental wandering and experienced the freedom of the spirit by creating emptiness around consciousness and the consciousness moves through the emptiness, there is a deep-seated desire to go into the essence of the spirit – to go to the essence of consciousness – where you basically collapse in on your own consciousness, to go into the essence of light of consciousness. So you want to go to the essence of the microcosm to touch the essence of the macrocosm. This will naturally happen as a side effect of pressure differentials.

So, you have mind and you have infinity – when they touch each other, things collapse into themselves. When the mind collapses into itself, we have Step Five mental training with the mind becoming smaller, where the Akashic trance starts to form. But when we go to the essence of our own mind, we go to divine light on a microcosmic level; and when we touch this divine light on a microcosmic level, we come into resonance with a divine light on a macrocosmic level. This is something that exists on the other side of Akasha. So you need to have been working with Akashic trance for an extended period of time. You need to practice separating your mental body for an extended period of time in order to really get a deep handle on divine light – both at the essence of our spirit and at the essence of the universal mind.

Once we get used to this touching of divine light, we recognize that underneath everything there is divine light. Underneath every bit of Akasha is divine light; under every bit of form there is divine light as universal mind. And this divine light is non-dual – it is seeking to come into form, waiting for the conditions to be right, to move through the Akasha into singular form, into a dual form and generate through the creative process. This yearning that happens to touch divine light exists within every living creature. Every religion is established because of that yearning, because on some level everybody wants to connect back to this divine light and complete the cycle of creation, the cycle of evolution. The only way to enter it is to be still. Through stillness, awareness arises that your vibrational match the universal mind. As the saying goes, "Be still and know that I am God."

The process of stillness in relation to consciousness makes consciousness collapse in on itself. At the end of that collapsing is light. As you enter into that light, everything that exists is light from microcosm to macrocosm, and you touch universal mind. Once you have touched universal mind, you recognize that there is a type of vibrational scale within this non-dual light. You have touched the outside of it, but you have not touched the center of it. When your mind begins to touch the outside of it and it reflects back, there is a huge contrast between you and what you are touching – it generates what some people call 'epiphanies', where information and insight will reflect through the mental-astral-physical bodies and you will have these amazing 'A-ha' moments. These are the superficial energy flares that are coming out of this divine light. It is something for the ego to cling to, so that you can do the work.

These divine light levels are so subtle that as you penetrate deeper into these levels of divine light, without these epiphanies – these astral flares that come through – you would have nothing to hold onto and could not develop off these energies. So we need these energies to shoot through the ego, to say, "Hey, you're on the right track. Keep going." If we did not have them we simply could not continue to develop because the ego would distract us too much – our physical and astral forms would take us in a different direction. So we hold on to these epiphanies and these experiences as the ego perceives them, which of course, is incorrect. It is not a pure experience once the ego touches it – it is an interpretation – but nevertheless it gives us the impetus to continue following the process to re-access this light through the Akasha.

As we develop this connection both to and within divine light, we develop the awareness that the light is everywhere, all the time, always waiting to come into form. When we touch it, the place where it chooses to enter into our body is the crown chakra, because we have a vibrational scale built into our body. The physical center of gravity is subject of time and space. When we release time, we are in the astral center of gravity. When we release space we are in the mental center of gravity. When we release the quality of time-space which is moving towards infinity, the crown chakra opens, which gives us access to a vibrational scale which connects us to the universal mind. So the first place on this vibrational scale is a divine light that seeks to express itself through the crown chakra. When we make a prayer and invite that light down into the crown chakra, it will naturally radiate through the three bodies. It will fill the mental body with light, it will fill the astral body with light, and it will begin opening up into the physical body and radiating light. We want this light to pass through us as a movement to generate flow. If you pour water into a cup, a cup gets full, and the only way to put more water into it is put it under pressure. When you put it under pressure, it becomes uncomfortable and it begins to press outwards. This means that the mind will overheat and become chaotic, the astral body will overheat and become chaotic and unstable, and the physical body will seek to release this energy in some way.

If we let this light simply flow through the three bodies, it will demagnetize negative energy states, the mental authority of the mind and unneeded emotions, and it will pull toxicity out of the physical body. So if you let it pass through you, it will clean at a rate in which you feel harmonized, balanced and healthy. If you overload the system in order to try and accelerate the development, we will go through extreme levels of chaos. It is not that this chaos is negative, it is just uncomfortable mentally, astrally and physically because you will be feeling like you are on a ship in a hurricane out in the ocean and it is just not fun. So the best way to enter into this practice is to let this divine light stream through you and pass through you into the ground. When it passes through you into the ground, you are giving your highest level of awareness and connectivity to divine light, to the earth – so in essence you are healing the earth. The earth is absorbing this and the group consciousness of the earth is rising. Even just bringing these lights through you into the earth is a life well spent, because of the benefit that the earth is getting from this transmission of light.

If you bring this light through by working into a mental plane of a group consciousness, into a particular teaching, into the astral plane of a group consciousness, raising people with ethics or into the physical plane, it is a life well spent. Simply by passing this light through, every one of these levels of consciousness is evolving and raising in frequency. We can see many ascetics in the Himalayas, living in caves and mountains, and hermits practicing raising energy and all these inner levels act as a benefit to the group consciousness. It is nullifying the calm of the group consciousness, it is raising the thinking, feeling and action as group consciousness, and it is nurturing the planet as a whole.

How you choose to channel these lights through and what type of consciousness you choose to feed this light into, of course, is fully up to you. Your spirit in this incarnation is gifted with a unique yearning, a desire to nurture whatever part of humanity you wish to help evolve through your choices and your own intuition. Your own inner guidance will lead that light through your thinking, feeling and action to develop whatever area that you feel inclined to do.

A lot of people think that there is this mission that you have to achieve something – that you have a hierarchy above you saying, "you must do this, you must do that." This is a half-truth. When you look at everything as unified consciousness – that everything is connected – if there is healing needed within the consciousness to raise it's frequency, it is natural for part of the whole to produce that healing. It is the same as if you have a cut, your body heals itself – the cut naturally heals. This happens within the group consciousness. It is not a command from one part of the group consciousness to another part of the group consciousness commanding you to do something. When you come into your spiritual wholeness, you act, think and feel in a certain way, and that is almost always inside a path of service. If it is not inside a path for service, it may be that a larger part of the real consciousness is affecting a small part of your consciousness to create a rhythmic contrast for a balancing to happen. But only a Buddha can understand these karmic actions completely; it is better not to give too much thought to them. Rather than focusing on connecting to universal divine light and allowing that light to express itself through you, there will just be a natural desire to serve, balance, harmonize, and evolve group consciousness when that light radiates through you.

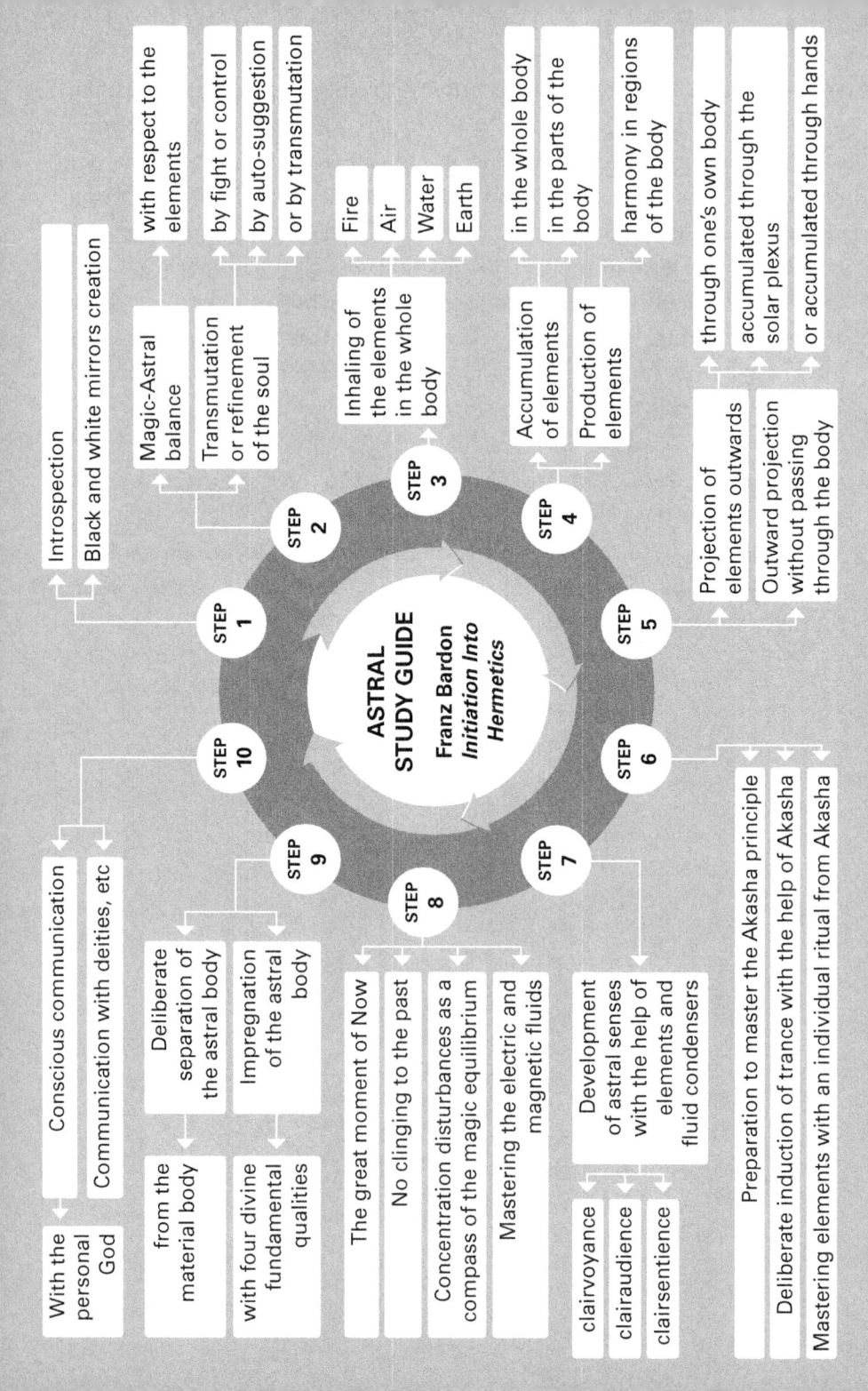

ASTRAL STUDY GUIDE
Franz Bardon *Initiation Into Hermetics*

STEP 1
- Introspection
- Black and white mirrors creation

STEP 2
- Magic-Astral balance — with respect to the elements
  - by fight or control
  - by auto-suggestion
  - or by transmutation
- Transmutation or refinement of the soul

STEP 3
- Inhaling of the elements in the whole body
  - Fire
  - Air
  - Water
  - Earth

STEP 4
- Accumulation of elements
  - in the whole body
  - in the parts of the body
- Production of elements — harmony in regions of the body

STEP 5
- Projection of elements outwards
  - through one's own body
  - accumulated through the solar plexus
  - or accumulated through hands
- Outward projection without passing through the body

STEP 6
- Development of astral senses with the help of elements and fluid condensers
  - clairvoyance
  - clairaudience
  - clairsentience
- Preparation to master the Akasha principle
- Deliberate induction of trance with the help of Akasha
- Mastering elements with an individual ritual from Akasha

STEP 7
- Mastering the electric and magnetic fluids

STEP 8
- The great moment of Now
- No clinging to the past
- Concentration disturbances as a compass of the magic equilibrium

STEP 9
- Deliberate separation of the astral body — from the material body
- Impregnation of the astral body — with four divine fundamental qualities

STEP 10
- Conscious communication
  - With the personal God
- Communication with deities, etc

Astral Stream Study Guide

Astral Stream: Steps One through Ten

Steps One to Three

Step One, Step Two and Step Three astral training cannot really be separated – they are intertwined. They are all about identifying the astral body. You are already affecting how the astral body fully vibrates, the direction that stream is flowing, and the future. So, the astral stream pulls the training into the astral training exercises, if you recognise that as a current full of energy. That is critically important for engaging the initiation text. Everything is moving forward. If you allow anything to stop, progress will obviously become slowed down.

The whole initiation process flows from one path to one path, by keeping the stream flowing where it is strongest, holding up parts that are pushed or pulled – so it is a difficult exercise. It will become easier as you train in the exercises that are moving. This psychology is intrinsically important to your success.

At first it may seem counterintuitive to ignore what your weaknesses are. But if you do work at it slowly, ignoring your weaknesses and focusing upon your strengths, your strength will permeate through these personality streams. It is a self-image thing. If you believe in what you are doing – that whatever you are working on is easy – it gets easier when you believe the process will be faster. So build confidence and self-belief and get your self-image on track to be a master of what you are doing. This is your fabric of future development. If you do not believe in yourself, you simply will not get success in this type of work.

The Astral Black and White Soul Mirror

Take the Personality Plus test and test the 20 positive and 20 negative qualities for each other. Do not worry about the test itself – it is just a list of your personality traits. Go to the first row and then contemplate what each word means, so every word will be animated. Start with the word 'animated' – what does the word mean, to be animated? You recognize this idea in your mind, then generate that quality of being animated within you – breathe the intent of the word, stimulate it and generate it for about one to two minutes of extreme animation. Use your body to animate, make gestures, and you will feel what it feels like to be an animated person. Then release that element out, release that quality out of your system and then look out and ask, "How animated am I?" and then rate it from 1 to 10. If it does not relate to you at all, it might be down at 0 or 1; if you are a very animated person, completely comfortable in your element to be like that, then you will give it a 10. And it goes for every trait on the test.

This is like a starting point because you have a very rough guide as to your elemental balance once you have gone through all 80 positives and 80 negatives – it is within the text. From there, keep a notebook on you at all times in your day-to-day life – just a small pocket notebook– and every time you notice there is a behaviour pattern that is strong, write it down. Get to know what the triggers of that behaviour pattern are, what environment does it come up in, was it associated with certain food, people, places, and so forth. The personality trait that showed was strong enough for you to notice the pattern. If you like, you can ask your friends to profile you. You let them express their own way first, and then break it down into the elements for yourself. It explains the basic psychology of the elements. You do this so that you can get a better insight.

From there, once you have gone through the process of generating these qualities continuously, and having gone through contemplation in day-to-day life asking your friends, we put it all together and make a picture. We transcribe the picture of your personality, contemplate it, and really look at it – this will give us an idea of ourselves. We start to see the root of everybody's personality traits, where they came from. This is in a stream. This astral personality has a stream of the past, or where the personality trait started, and to the present. A word is a combination of where energies take you. A word is a stream going to the future – it has a projection. As you do the astral breathing exercises, slow down time and tune it to this astral stream, you will start to see predictable outcomes in your black and white mirror. Those predictable outcomes, there you can change them – you can change the astral stream in any direction that you want. This section of this book is about generating those changes. By being able to see them, just simply perception, you are already changing the outcome. By perceiving something you can engage and reinforce it, or you can pull it apart and steer it in different ways – just through seeing, feeling, knowing. You know something when you have changed it, changed your relationship to it and energy starts to shift.

This black and white mirror exercise generates the foundation of your practice and it does so for several reasons. The first is that the first half of the Initiation text is about equanimity. The black and white mirror allows you to have an internal training environment where equanimity is possible. If you do not have that introspection – you do not know it – equanimity is simply not possible. Equalize your body and mind, finding the center of gravity for the mental, astral and physical bodies. This way, you compartmentalize certain parts of your personality and shut them down before you are even entering it. This will work to temporarily overcome deep personality flaws; a person will change greatly that moment. To illustrate this point, there are some Buddhist Arhats in Thailand who are completely addicted to smoking. However, these arhats can compartmentalise their cravings to the body temporarily, enter into samadhi, enter into equanimity, and they will not be disturbed by that craving to smoke. And then when they come out of their samadhi back into the body, the body craving arises again. You can put these astral settings aside for a short period of time, but it only lasts for a short period of time. This is a possible way to get profound results even with severe personality flaws. You can compartmentalize things you are not ready to let go of. You can do this to maintain progress, but you will still have these limitations. These are cravings you can let go of in the future.

As we go forward with the exercises, we want to do contemplation exercises. We recognise the depth of that stream. These contemplation exercises start with vital breathing and once we are connected to the vital fluid of the magnetic force, we can adhere our mind to a universal quality – you just slow down the astral body, then you do the whole astral breathing, and now you can breathe into the stream. As you release on that stream, release on where it is going. We can magnetise that stream. So you can see within our astral stream that we develop a willpower. We can magnetise that in the stream. So the stream is pulled towards the idea. As it gets pulled towards the idea, our cravings will have that idea, our feelings will have to engage that body, that craving will support the direction of that stream. So you get a lot of peripheral benefits from magnetising a particular element or vibrational stream. And you want to do that for all the elemental variations.

Fire element	Samadhi
Air element	Vipassassana awareness
Water element	Love
Earth element	Interconnectedness to all things

So we look at the personality being transformed into the element and into the stream. It can magnetise the future, so the stream goes in a particular direction. By magnetising this future direction, we will find that things will shape us as a magnet to the personality towards developing those qualities.

Once we have magnetised the stream, broken it down into its universal elemental qualities, done the astral breathing exercises, taken control of the astral body, identified the direction of each of the elemental streams, once we have established that direction then we have to stream from the flow of that direction. In doing so, let us say, you are doing the Fire element – you will select an exercise and challenge your physical limitations; you will measure your heart rates, try to maintain the same workload, and you train. You may say, "Okay, I want to go on a run for 20 minutes and see how many steps I can take." And every day you challenge yourself to do more. So you use your will on your body. And when you use your will on your body, you will find it very easy to use your will on your astral and mental bodies, because they are all regulated first by your physical body.

By first mastering your physical body, the astral body and the mind streams touch the spirit so that it can fully express itself in your being. It could be practices of asceticism, where you are either restricting your intake or being of greater service to others; so you are producing something, or preventing something, or releasing something. So if you are hungry, release the craving for food, release the hunger. Once the hunger is overcome, then you can eat. Doing this changes your decision making process. Once the astral mind goes out of the way, the higher mind comes in and you will begin craving healthier, more nutritious foods. So practicing asceticism on each craving that arises moves the decision-making process from the lowest aspect of being, to the ego, to the higher aspect of the spirit.

As you go through this process of practicing asceticism, your ego is going to protect itself. Your senses are going to be in areas that you seem to overlook. Any area that you seem to overlook is your ego protecting itself – it is trying to survive, it wants to stay invisible. You do not want to look at some paths of your personality. So you mistakenly leave back doors open. We need to look at these back doors, close them, and then investigate every aspect of your astral body.

So when you went through the physical cravings and released something before engaging the astral cravings, release on them before engaging and then the mental cravings and then release on them. Mental craving is something as simple as desire to understand. Do you have a need to understand things? And of course, we all do. This need to understand is often rooted in the need for control or the need for acknowledgment from our peers. On occasion it is rooted in the need for security. When we look at the roots of each of these qualities, we get a better understanding of the black and white mirror. So the black and white mirror is a never-ending process of getting to know yourself, unlocking and releasing different qualities that are hidden over time. So the mental asceticism is restricting the input to your mind. Astral asceticism is releasing on all the emotional inputs, and then the physical asceticism is releasing on all your physical requirements. This hands control over to the spirit – this puts the spirit in charge – and when the spirit is in charge we get much more profound results in our practice.

Step Four: Astral Training

Straighten the spine, the whole body pore breathing. Once you have built the feeling of life force throughout the hands and your whole body, then we move the awareness purely to the hands. Place the hands in front of you as if you are holding the ball, draw the vital energy into the hands and out of the hands and focus on the space between your hands. Once you have that magnetic feeling in the hands, then we move to the left forearm, vital breathing in and out of the left forearm until you feel that the quality of life force – that magnetic fluid – very clearly. Move to the right forearm, vital breathing in and out until the feeling is clear, and then the upper arm on the left and upper arm on the right, breathing into the shoulders left and then right, and then breathing into the whole spine.

What I want you to do next is to put an anatomy chart up in front of you and then go through each of the organs. Find the liver, breathe in and out of the liver. You can charge the liver up for nine breaths and then release for nine breaths or just breathing out, washing the energy through the liver. Then go through each set of organs on that chart: kidneys, intestines, genitals, stomach, liver, lungs, larynx and so forth. The only organs of the body that you do not breathe directly into independently of the area around it are the heart and the brain. But go through the whole body, going through each organ, each system, through the bones, through each leg and so forth until you have covered each body part individually. Breathing in, breathing out, charging energy in for up to nine breaths, releasing energy out for nine breaths, and so forth. Once you have got accustomed to this feeling of density within each organ, within each body part, then you can move on to the next exercise.

Next, we breathe into the regions and when we breathe into each region we want to increase the element within that region. The leg region represents the Earth element, including the hips, buttocks, groin and all the way down to the feet. Begin with vital breathing into that region. Once the vital energy is accumulated, move the awareness to gravity – the feeling of heaviness, density and form – continue breathing the Earth element, swinging the life force into the Earth element, slowing it down, condensing it within the legs.

After about nine breaths or when you feel that your legs are full and dense, meditate on the Earth element coming into perfect equanimity from within the legs and affecting the rest of the body. We are alternately doing this in order to generate a stillness and equanimity within the region of the body.

Then move up to the Water region. The Water region overlaps from the groin with the Earth region and then the abdominals up to the solar plexus and breathing the Water element in. With the Water element, we gently pull the joints open, same as the magnetic fluid practices, and we have a feeling of coolness and a feeling of contraction. Everything is pulling in and condensing together. To get this in the astral, just look at two drops of water next to each other and then bring them closer and closer and feel the power of attraction of when those two drops of water pull together to become one drop. There is this cohesion – cohesiveness – within the water that has an attractive force that just pulls the surface tension of those two drops together.

This is a feeling you want to have in the Water breathing as you breathe the Water element in. Then you put this right into the Water region, condense for nine breaths, and then meditate on the equanimity of the Water element for the next nine breaths. This is very good for balancing emotions and harmonizing any stresses that are in your system, any emotional stresses.

Next, we move on to the Air region from the solar plexus up to the throat through your Adam's apple. There is an overlap of the Fire region above which includes the top of the shoulder blades, the trapezius muscles – they are part of the Fire element, so the Air and the Fire overlap there. If you feel stress and tension in the shoulder blades and the trapezius muscles from the Fire, relax and release that tension. Breathe into the whole Air region a light-sky blue color, having the feeling of floating upwards. Very gently stretch the fascia, move your center of balance up into the chest so that you are falling upwards and charge that area for nine breaths with the Air element. Once you have put nine breaths in and got an adequate charge, so your center of gravity is centered in the chest and you stretch into a slightly upward float with your posture, then meditate on the Air element coming to perfect equanimity, balance.

You are harmonizing the Air element through the rest of the body by breathing into the Air region and moving on to the head region – the Fire element. Breathe the Fire element with a blazing red color, feeling the heat and expansion and power, and then nine breaths bring calm and equanimity into the Fire element throughout the whole body.

Once you have done this through each of the regions, then scan through each of those regions, bringing each of those areas into harmony and sit in stillness for a few minutes. You will notice that the solar plexus area has the deepest level of stillness because the active elements above the solar plexus, the passive elements below the solar plexus, are meeting at this point, so there is a deep stillness. But the next area of training in the mental body – moving into the solar plexus – will develop this skill further.

Working with the Elements and Fundamentals

When you are working with the elements of Fire, Air, Water and Earth, the easiest way to begin this training is with vital breathing. With the vital breathing exercises we have already covered, you are breathing in through the pores and floating your body like a balloon, focusing your willpower on the breath and stretching the fascia of the body, so that the feeling of energy arises by stretching the outside of the skin throughout the whole body to create that feeling of inflation, which activates the fascia, and there is an expansion of your joints.

This vital breathing process we want to separate into yin-yang – into electric and magnetic, or Fire and Water. For Water, we pull the joints open and those key parts of the body that we want to pull open to amplify this magnetic feeling. The first key part is the hollow of the palm. You will notice when you are vital breathing, if you stretch the hollow of the palm out and push it out, the energy becomes more electric – it is like the hands are repelling each other. When you hollow the palm and create a slight pulling action on the hand, the energy melts into the hollow of the palm and the center of the palm is much more soft and jelly-like. The tension disappears for the most part. This is the first point.

When we move to the wrist – the magnetic – the wrist is pulling open. Imagine you grab something and pull on it and use that pull to open the wrist, the elbow and the shoulder and open the joints up so that there is a tensile force on the outside. You grab that force and pull on it and use that to pull your joints open. If that object was not there, you would use the same muscles to pull, and you will get a magnetic effect in your body providing that your mind is on the frequency of vital energy. The vital energy would move from an electromagnetic state towards the magnetic state. If you touch your wrist and pull the wrist open, you will find that there is a hollowing of the center of the wrist. As the wrist pulls open, you get a jelly-ness in the wrist. You put your finger on the center of your palm and pull the palm open, there is a jelly-ness on the center of your palm. If you put your finger on the center of the elbow joint, on the top halfway between the cubital of the crease on two ends of the elbow, and you put your finger on the inside of that tendon and pull the joint open, the tendon will rise; you slip it to the side, and keep pulling, then there will be a softness in that space.

Same thing with the shoulder and all the joints of the body, that when you pull the joint open – even though you are using a tensile force to pull the joint open – there is a melting quality on the inside of the joint. You can physically push your finger on to those points, find them, and feel how they melt when you produce a magnetic state in your body.

The life force, you are swinging it towards the magnetic, or if you do the reverse and expand the hollow of the palm, you expand the wrist from the center of the wrist, you expand from the center of the elbow, it is like that same point that melted during the magnetic phase now fills and bulges during the electric phase. You are creating a melting in the center of your joint as you pull the joint open for magnetic, and you are creating an expansion in the joint when you move into the electric phase. This moves the vital force into the energetic states of Fire (pushing) and Water (pulling) elements.

These two exercises are simple. We can apply them to a pushing-pulling action where we expand the joints and push the vital energy out and stream it out several meters in front of us, and then we grab that object that we are streaming the energy towards, pull and melt the joints and pull everything open as we go into the magnetic state, as we sink into that magnetic field, pulling everything towards our core. We can push and pull, reversing the polarity between electric and magnetic.

If you just build one polarity – let us say just electric or just magnetic – the contrast is not there for the sensitivity. When there is contrast, you feel more. So, producing the contrast, the switching between electric and magnetic, you feel the energy more clearly so that when you have longer extended periods of electric – Fire element – or magnetic – Water element – it is clear and concise, what you are building, because you already have experienced that contrast.

In the early stage as you are building in energy, use that law of polarity to go from one extreme of the polarity to the other, so that you have the contrast and you can differentiate what energy you are working with. Once you have established those base frequencies – electric and magnetic, Fire and Water – then you can build pure Water element or pure Fire element for an extended period of time.

Initially we start with a one breath rhythm: electric, one breath; magnetic, one breath. The electric, three breaths; magnetic, three breaths. Then go to nine breaths, one minute or so of electric, one minute or so of magnetic, and so forth until you are doing 10, 15, 20, 30 minutes of one phase and then switch to the opposite phase. Those time periods are up to you. I like to use two minute, 12 minute and 45 minute platforms for you to sit from 45 minutes and you stretch up to three hours.

You will find that once you sit on a two minute platform you can extend beyond two minutes. Once you have stabilized a 12 minute platform, it will be easy to reach out to 45 minutes. Once you stabilize the 45 minute platform, it will be easy to reach up to three hours. Each of those platforms, stabilize it, get your mind solid within that time period, then extend to the next.

For the Air element, we want to stretch upwards. If you are sitting in a chair and vital breathing and you are about to get out of the chair, lean a little bit forward with your chest in order to bring your chest to your center of gravity. From the stretch in your chest, push down onto the ground and stretch your chest upwards to move your center of gravity up to get out of the chair. There is this loading of your weight into the legs and propelling your way up into the chest and the upward stretch – a movement of your mind, your center of gravity, and of energy to get out of the chair.

If you were to do this in slow motion, you would not be able to use momentum to move your weight up to the chest fast enough – it is going to be much more difficult to get out of the chair. We have this normal elastic speed at which the fascia conducts body weight, where we rock our body weight forward, drop it into the legs, send it up to the chest, and use momentum to stand up. What we want to do is take a body weight and use momentum and stretch it up to the top of the joint. We are vital breathing, we turn our palms up and stretch everything up to our chest and the top of the joints will feel light. That feeling of stretch, we hold it there.

Even though our body weight will stabilize back through the rest of the body, we use momentum to raise everything up, so that our center of gravity is in the chest, all the joints, the energies are on the top of the joint, sort of like a string connected to a puppet – strings connected to the wrist and plucking your energy up; connected to the elbow plucking up, to the shoulders, the crown, all the joints, and the string is suspending and floating your energy and body upwards.

This buoyant feeling of when you stretch the fascia upwards – as if you are about to get up out of the chair – this feeling, you put your lifeforce into that feeling. The whole body becomes lighter. When your body is in this feeling of the Air element and everything is light, you are able to cultivate and build the Air element. We take the life force, the electromagnetic fluid and mechanically drop our weight down into our legs which is Earth, stretch it up into the chest which is Air, and suspend all the joints and breathe in a light feeling. We keep the feeling that we are just about to get up, like we are floating. The life force in the body will naturally swing towards this Air element and then we drop the energy back down into the legs and in the chair and we rock from the chair onto our legs and then pop our body weight up, and we do it again.

We hold that. Initially we are only holding this for about three second rounds, floating and then we drop the body weight back onto the chair and onto our legs, and we repeat the process.

You will find after a few repetitions that you can throw your body way up to activate that Air fascia because you cannot just open your joints and activate Air, because it is holding in Earth – it is holding gravity. So we need to reset the muscles. Having a light throwing action, we throw our body weight up, create the feeling, and then hold the feeling we can maintain the Air state. Even though the weight which was gently thrown up drops back down again, we have activated the Air fascia and can sit within the Air element for longer and longer periods of time.

Again, use the platform of two minutes, 12 minutes, 45 minutes, and three hours. Each platform will make it easier to achieve the next. Two minutes is very important because that is roughly how long it takes for your chemistry to reset. If you concentrate on one frequency for two minutes, the chemistry of the body aligns to that frequency, aligns to that feeling. So a bodily reset takes place within two minutes. Really master every exercise in the program for two minutes first and then move to the 12 minute mark.

Okay, for the Earth element, we have the contrast of the Air. When we were dropping our body weight into our legs and then throwing the body weight up into the Air, feeling of rising, now we feel gravity acting on our body while we vital breathe and we just drop – you drop the body weight down, you feel the sit bones, you stretch the spine, you feel your feet on the ground as you sit in the chair, and turn your palms to face down.

As you vital breathe, allow gravity and life force to synchronize through feeling. As both gravity and life force sync, your mental, astral and physical bodies, the protective chi increases because the electromagnetic fluid which forms the binding between the three bodies increases. That means your body becomes more protected. Your mental space becomes smaller, your vital field becomes denser, the 'armor' around your body becomes stronger, and you feel more protected from viruses, external influences and so forth, when you are in this Earth state. Everything has its barriers up, protective chi is more active, when you are within the Earth element. You are in a defensive type of mode, condensing all your energy into a smaller space.

This feeling of heaviness while you vital breathe – the feeling of sinking, hanging all the muscles of the body, dropping the joints down, letting the fascia take over so that the whole body is one connected unit – you are relaxing, switching main muscles off, so that everything is heavy, dropping and sinking.

Once you have established this feeling of gravity passing through the life force, you can extend this feeling for longer periods of time – you can switch between the Earth and Air in order to generate the contrast, to establish the two feelings. Rock your body weight forward as if you are about to get out of the chair, turn your palms up and then flick your body weight up and push it all up to your chest; activate the Air feeling, float the whole body for a few seconds up to two minutes, and then drop and let everything sink, aligned to gravity, allowing the life force to sync with gravity, let everything become heavy. Stretch the spine out, feel the sit bones on the chair, and align to that feeling of protection and the increased electric and magnetic fluid on your life force which binds the three bodies together. You become less influenceable.

By being less influenceable you are also less sensitive as protective chi increases. When you are in the Air state of the mental body being more open and you flick the joints up, your intellect is more open to ideas, you are more flexible, ideas are correlating to the information that you need, and you get an inspired way of thinking when you are in this Air state. While you are in that Air state and this inspired way of thinking, you are also more vulnerable to external energies coming in with that openness – so it is a trade-off.

When you are working with the four elements vitally, we use the body mechanics, we use the feeling mechanics, and we attune the mind to these four qualities: the Fire being the feeling of expansion, heat from the joints; the Water being the feeling of magnetism and melting into the center joint, to pull the joint open and everything will ultimately be pulling back to your core; the Air element being a feeling of lightness, of rising, like you are getting out of the chair, and throwing your body weight up. As you throw your body weight up the fascia activates for rising with the Air element and you vital breathe into that feeling, and then for the Earth element you drop all the joints, hang and move into that heavy Earth feeling.

This opens the door for the elements. To move this energy from the vital to the astral level, we need to release time. We do this with the electromagnetic energy. You vital breathe in and out, you breathe in and then pause, enter stillness, no breathing in, no breathing out, let the mind become quiet, and enter that stillness. In that stillness there is no time or space – there is the infinite void. The first quality we want to incorporate from that infinite void is the release of time, so that they are slowing down the energy.

As we move back into the breath cycle, we breathe that slowness in with the vital energy until we get to the other end of the breath cycle, then we pause again. We stop, enter the stillness, identify the feeling of timelessness, and then breathe that timelessness in. We mix that with the life force. After three or so breaths you will notice the life force will begin to slow down. After nine or so breaths the life force would become thick, and that thick heavy fluidic feeling is your astral body.

Once you have done this a few times, you can instantly put your mind in your astral body and begin pore breathing and the energy will thicken automatically from the vital field to the astral field. Or you can begin working with astral energy immediately, depending on what your objective is. If you are strengthening the astral body, you draw vital energy from the environment – from the forest, from the trees – you breathe it in, release time, and condense it in the astral body with a particular purpose. It may be increased motivation, focus, it may be to perform a particular skill – whatever you want to charge that astral energy with, on the out-breath you put the information into the astral energy with it.

Once we have achieved this thick astral feeling, then we take the element breathing exercise which we have already done. We build the Air element vitally and then release time and work it in the astral. We will repeat all the elements in the same way on a slower rhythm, so that we have the astral elements being cultivated. You will release time and begin working with the astral elements. It will be easy to breathe these elements for 45 minutes. When you are working with them vitally – where your mind and body are more restricted by time – you will find shorter time periods will hold you. But astrally longer time periods would be easy. This is how we easily develop the elements of Fire, Air, Water, and Earth.

Step Five

Connect your mind to the Fire element, then whole body pore breathe the Fire element, condensing the Fire element throughout the whole body. Here we are paying special attention to generating heat. To generate heat, you really need to slow the energy down, slow the breath down. You breathe Fire element in, you pause into the stillness, release time, and as you release time you are breathing out, slowing the energy down. This energy, as it slides down, will condense both heat and pressure. It generates the type of effect of applying pressure to energy, and applying this pressure to energy through releasing time increases the density, meaning that it will generate the feeling of heat – so it is the releasing of time which allows the heat to build up.

You can measure that increase of heat through simply feeling your body coming to a high temperature, or placing a thermometer in the room and then filling the room from the solar plexus with the Fire element and increasing the temperature in the room. We are after a one to two degree increase in temperature, to master this exercise and move on. The reason why we are only looking for one to two degree temperature increase is that is how much the Fire element affects your physiology. If you were to get very angry and your face would go red and you would be in a state of extreme Fire element, your body temperature would rise by about one degree. Your face would be showing that through the color of the skin, and we want to develop that amount of the element so that you can master your astral body and bring it under control and bring it into equanimity, so you can work with Akasha. We do not need to generate Fire. We do not need to do very high level Fire element work – we just need to be raising it through our astral bodies. This is how much we want to develop this element.

Once you have released the energy through the solar plexus into the room and filled the room, dissolve that energy and move on to the next element – the Air element. When you do the Air element, again, you stretch the fascia upward and make your body feel light, move your center of gravity up to the chest as if you are about to sit up or take a step. Upward stretch with the astral breathing will generate a lightness within your body. With that lightness, again, slow the energy down, release time to condense the lightness, condense the idea to bring it into the form of the body that your body feels genuinely light and blend.

Once you have released the Air element out of the room, then move on to the Water element. The Water element – blue-green ocean color, feeling a coolness – again, gently pull the joints open and nine breaths, condensing the Water element into the body, feeling your body getting cooler and slow the energy down to get that density; release time so that magnetic fluid becomes an obvious part of your feeling and it is so dense and magnetic that you can feel an attractive power in and around you.

Once you have done that, release it through the solar plexus out into the room in a sudden burst and fill the whole room with that nine breaths of Water element that you have condensed within yourself. Each time you practice this, you want to fill the energy faster through the solar plexus and let it release outwards at an increasingly greater speed.

Then continue with the Earth element. With the Earth element we want to create a feeling of heaviness – of gravity – throughout the whole body. Again, release time, slow the energy down to generate that level of density and as the energy becomes denser and heavier, on each breath monitor how heavy it is and then increase that heaviness. So, you have a critical mass that takes place with energy, rolling down the hill, getting heavier with each breath, and you generate momentum inside of that, inside that cycle.

The same principles of rhythm applies to all the elements. Once you feel that acceleration of the energy in the direction you want to go, use a lot of rhythm to amplify it further and keep it going. Once you have got that density that you are happy with inside the body and you keep it within for nine breaths, then release it through the solar plexus, fill the whole room with that created heaviness throughout the room. You want to feel like anyone who enters that room has a lead blanket thrown over their body that is heavy – gravity increases, and they feel pressured into the ground. The Earth element has a strong increase of the feeling of gravity. You want to generate an immunity to that feeling within yourself so that when you put it into a room everyone else experiences it except you.

The next exercise is to create a ball of the element in front of the solar plexus. With this, we breathe the Fire element in, accumulate a high density of Fire element within your body and then put it inside the solar plexus. You condense all that element that is in your body into a golf ball inside your solar plexus, then you move it one foot from your body in front of you – in front of the solar plexus – and you hold it there. This accumulating of a sphere of heat, like a radiating sun, is an important part of training.

At this stage we keep it in the shape of a ball, but later we will move it into the shapes of seagulls, drawings, images, and so forth – we will put it to more work. For the moment, hold it as a very intense sphere and then when you dissolve it, you can explode it or empty it into the Akasha, depending on what your skill set is. Emptying something into the Akasha is a valuable skill because if you see or feel the Fire element accumulated inside of a person that generates heat, it is a sign of a liver problem, overheating problem; could be a cancer or a tumor that is overheating – it is an excess of electrical fluid, of a type of radiation in their body. Being able to dissolve it into the Akasha is a valuable skill.

Building spheres of energy and then dissolving them into the Akasha gets you familiar and comfortable with the ability to do that at a moment's notice – to walk into the room, feel a negative energy, open the Akasha and dissolve that negative energy straight into the Akasha. When you have that sphere of heat in front of the solar plexus, then instantaneously dissolve it.

From there we work with each of the elements. Do the same with a sphere of the Air element: build it in the body, accumulate in the solar plexus and move it out in front of you – it is a sphere of sky-blue color that is light, and then when you dissolve it, let it fly upwards and dissolve into the Akasha or explode outwards. Repeat with the Water element: Water element throughout the whole body, accumulate in the solar plexus, move it out in front of you, and then dissolve it. Same with the Earth element: accumulate the Earth element throughout the whole body, accumulate as a golf ball sized sphere in the solar plexus, move it out in front of you and dissolve it.

This dissolving process is important. This accumulation into shapes is very important. You can start off with simple shapes like spheres, cubes, cones, spirals, and so forth and go into more complex shapes as needed. If you are a student of sacred geometry, you will put it into those sacred geometry shapes. If this is your interest, get a chart of each of the shapes – the shapes of quartz and different minerals. Start with the mineral kingdom, going to the outlines of those shapes and then build the energy in those shapes and dissolve them. Just put a chart in front of you, of what is the shape of a crystal of quartz, and then build it up and release it and then move through various crystals. By the time you have gone through the mineral kingdom, you will have an unconscious resonance to move into the plant kingdom, which will bring you into the animal kingdom. The sacred geometry will intuitively start to make sense and that will reorganize your intuition and you will understand what sacred geometry is, from working from the mineral to the plant and animal kingdoms. From there, you move on to the planetary levels – from the Earth, the moon, you go through the spheres mentioned in Practical Magical Evocation (PMO) and then you go to cosmic patterns. This continuity of the sacred geometry is very important. You find the microcosm and the macrocosm meet and that is when the sacredness becomes obvious.

Once you have practiced doing the various shapes, we want to build the energy in the body, put it into the shape and the solar plexus, put the shape in front of us, and then allow the shape to release and fill the room. We can put a sphere of Fire element in front of us and then release it into the room, so that the whole room becomes Fire element. As it occupies more space, we expand our will through that Fire element to generate more heat to accommodate that room. Repeat the same with all the elements.

These exercises will generate a type of flexibility within your mental and astral bodies, and this creative cycle that comes through not only amplifies your intuition but also your functionality within various forms of magic. If you are working with sigil magic it will become obvious: sacred geometry and patterning and how those patterns are antennas for energy when you visualize the pattern; the pattern itself by its very nature attracts life force. Like the Fibonacci spiral, you can simply visualize the pattern, vital breathe energy into the pattern, and you will get more vital energy going in with less effort than if you are putting energy into normal space.

Once you have worked through those elements and through developing various intuitive creative ways of working with the patterns of the elements, sacred geometry of the elements, and filling rooms with energy, then we move on to enlivening people. Have a person stand up in front of you, gently touch their forearms, and with your fingertips feel their fascia – squeeze the fascia of their body. Length stretch their arms down so that it creates a stretch to the shoulder and connects you to the person's feet through their fascial web, the fascia connection. Breathe into your partner with life force and enliven the whole body with life force. As soon as you have done this for nine breaths, your partner is going to start to float and lose their balance and then the exercise is achieved. Once you can enliven that person's health with vitality and their balance is obviously being affected, you will find more ways of using this energy – including for healing and so forth – from this point on.

Step Six

6.1

In the first part of the training we learned how to observe the rising and flowing away of thoughts. There was a type of stillness which accompanied that observation. That stillness created the space between the thoughts that were rising in the observer, as if the thoughts were coming from afar – a softer type of stillness.

You need one-pointed concentration to be focused on a meditation object – the type of stillness that accumulates a 'tunnel vision' between you and the object, until the object starts to flicker and disappear. After that, we paid attention to the stillness itself and dwelled within that empty space. This is all Step One mental training. When you got on to balancing the elements, there was a very distinct sense of quietude that happened when you balanced the elements in each of the four regions.

From there we looked at every exercise and the stillness and the residue of emptiness that accompanied each exercise. All these training processes are developing a platform to do this next exercise of Akasha. With Akasha work the first thing to do is release time, slow everything down. You can do this through your normal pore breathing: pore breathing in, pore breathing out, and as you release time you find yourself in your astral body. Energy thickens and becomes slow and dense.

As you release space, you recognize that everything is mind substance, then you go into the mental body –there is a spacelessness. We want to take this timelessness and spacelessness together and breathe infinite equanimity in. When you invite this deep stillness and quietude to lead you into the infinite, there is no top or bottom, left or right, or dimensional space – just a deep profound stillness.

All the preliminary training exercises brought you to this space, to this exercise. The first half of Bardon's book is really about getting you ready for entering the Akashic trance. When you are breathing both the timeless and spaceless feeling of infinity in and out, there is a qualitative color to it. Akasha, it is a dark black-violet color. Pore breathe that in and pore breathe that out. As you pore breathe it, I want you to breathe it directly into the blood.

Why? because when you breathe it into the blood, it permeates physiology and releases the physiology of form, so that your mind lets go of the body, the astral and the mental and it goes into infinite space. We want to permeate Akasha inside the blood through pore breathing. So, timelessness in, spacelessness out, infinity in, infinity out, until you are sitting in infinite space. As you sit in this infinite space, you are going to find that there is a clear and concise part of the mind that just knows things that you place your awareness upon.

When you are in Akashic trance and you look at something, there is a clarity of knowing the object you are looking at. It is like you see the causal chain of events which led up to the manifestation and the state that that particular object is in. Each time you enter into Akashic trance, let your awareness occupy a huge amount of infinite space while knowing the nature of what you are looking at; whether the time is released and you see the past, present and future of the object; whether you see the inner nature of the object or whether you see the maturity – spiritual maturity – of the object. Whatever it is, it is allowed to rise and fall away and begin viewing things from the Akasha.

6.2

Continuing with Akasha and the elements: enter into Akashic trance, the same as before, draw the Akasha in through the pores, breathing it into the blood, and you will begin to realize that Akasha is being accumulated. But in reality it is the opposite of accumulation – it is as if you are accumulating a vacuum underneath your form. When you breathe the Akasha in, there is this vacuous space. As we breathe out, we want to invoke the element that we are working on out of the Akasha.

If it is the Fire element, we expand our joints ever-so-slightly and connect into the feeling of heat, power and expansion. As we breathe out, we invoke the Fire element out of the Akasha to fill the Akashic space – the vacuum which we created inside of us. You breathe the Akasha into the blood. As you breathe out of the blood, you breathe out of that Akasha and the feeling of the Fire element and you create the mechanical environment that you did when you built the Fire element for the resonance, so that Fire element can come into form.

Akasha in, everything soft, limp, your body is very jelly-like, your mind is occupying infinite space as you condense that empty space inside the body, then you move your awareness to the Fire element. You breathe out and invoke the Fire from the Akasha into the body and the body becomes warm, feels powerful and emanates the Fire element.

We repeat this with each of the elements and you can also do this with vital energy.

Akasha on the in-breath, amplify vitality on the out-breath.

Akasha on the in-breath, amplify the Fire element on the out-breath – remembering to maintain the body mechanics of the Fire element.

Akasha on the in-breath, pull the joints open slightly, generate the Water element.

Akasha on the in-breath, stretch everything upwards, become light and buoyant, produce the Air element.

So you are mechanically and astrally creating a condition in which the element you are working with can arise out of the Akasha and fill the space. You cannot produce the element out the Akasha if you do not create the mental-astral alignment for that resonance to manifest itself. You are going to create pre-conditions for it to arise.

And then you do the same with the Earth element as well. Until it is comfortable, Akasha on the in-breath, you might breathe directly into a space and then you mentally and astrally prepare that space for the element you wish to produce out of the Akasha to vibrate, and then with your will – mentally, astrally and physically – you produce that particular feeling of the elements within that space.

6.3

Now that we have started to manifest energy out of the Akasha, you got the feeling of how when you produce Akasha in the blood your form becomes vacuous and wants to be filled with something. We realize that we should never leave Akasha in the body, as it always has to be equalized – otherwise there will be problems with your health and mental-astral-physical balance. We also realize that this is a very powerful tool for the black and white mirror.

Now we are at a point where we can penetrate much deeper into our mental, astral and physical body alignment, into our *karma* and begin balancing things out.

This next exercise is to revisit your black and white mirror, it means swinging the pendulum. If you find yourself irritable at times, breathe Akasha into the irritability, fill it with Fire and redirect it to focused will, concentrated mind, stability of the mind. Choose a universal quality that is in resonance with your path and swing the pendulum for each character trait that is still influencing you – that is still affecting your personality. We want to do this with, first of all, the major personality quirks, and then move down to the lesser ones, so that you are using Akasha to increase the stability of your black and white mirror.

If you do not address this at this time, your Akashic work will actually strengthen those weaknesses. We want to get this out of the way as early in the process as possible.

6.4

Our next stage is assigning rituals to working with the elements out of Akasha. A simple process used by many traditions is for you to place your hand on your body with your thumb up and pinky finger down, and then look at the element relationship with the chakras. Your pinky on the bottom is the base chakra, Earth element; your ring finger is the Water element; your middle finger is the Fire element, and your index finger is the Air element. The thumb, of course, is Akasha.

These four element relationships, you will find to be very effective because so many different traditions in India and the Buddhist Vajrayana-Mahayana traditions use this alignment. If you wish to generate a visualization with the finger ritual and a sound, you would have the whole body and mind aligned and you could produce personal rituals. [1]

All you need to do is activate the ritual or you practice the Akasha on the in-breath and the element production on the out-breath and anchor them

---

1 Bardon's personal instructions about element attributes for fingers is different. Do what works best for you.

together. Eventually you just produce the ritual and you do not need to do the Akasha breath and the out-breath of the element to produce the effect. But there is this transition on building the effect, moving from intent to non-intent, that the trigger for the intent for things to happen is the ritual itself.

Step Seven: Sense Gates

Sight
Whatever skill you wish to develop, we need to look at what are the physical mechanics to support the skill. What are the astral qualities of that skill? How do they present themselves? What are the mental body laws of that skill? What and where are the space and timing of that particular skill?

We have three bodies that need to be considered for every particular type of skill. Let us take, for instance, that you wanted to develop clairvoyance and wanted the skill of clairvoyance. If the clairvoyance was a physical type of clairvoyance – where you wanted to see vital energy, to see life force – this type of clairvoyance would be very simple. You would simply stretch the hands and stretch the fascia of the body to activate your normal feelings of life force and then connect the eyes to that feeling and stretch the muscles in the eyes, from the eyes back to the pineal gland, have a slight magnetic backwards pull, go into peripheral vision, and begin breathing through the eyes.

As you breathe through the eyes you will get a separation between intent and what you are observing. The observer, the intender and the observed will all pull apart. We need to separate these different qualities. Once we have separated them – and to quite a large degree this has already been done through Step One mental training – we will get a sense of these qualities: that this is the observer, this is the intender, and this is the observed. The mind is moving in and out of the frequency of life force the whole time. Our whole body is breathing in and out, and we are concentrating that life force in and out of the eyes, so that the peripheral vision of the eyes will tune itself to the feeling of the life force. Soon you will begin to see the life force.

The life force will initially present itself around trees, plants and people. This is a one to two inch coating of energy like a haze around living things. Non-living things also have this haze but it is a slightly different frequency. Rocks have a life force emanation, but it is not a living life force – it is a life force that has a different type of living mind in it, but does not have breath.

When something is breathing, like a plant or an animal, the life force that emanates out of it is different to the spirit life of rock. A rock still has life force in it but it is a different type because everything that exists is mind.

When you have mind inside of a gravitational field, it starts generating life, such is a fact of evolution. Rocks are changing their crystalline structure over millions of years, they are evolving and growing. The mind substance is changing, universal energies are moving through those rocks, they are radiating and are on an evolutionary curve. When something comes into a biological state of life, the type of life force emanation is different. Depending upon the type of life force you wish to work with, you need to tune your mind to that particular frequency, feel it – as it is much easier than seeing – and then start directing that particular feeling to the peripheral receptors of the eyes.

We look at what is the body mechanic, tune the fascia of the body to feel, tune the eyes to feel. We stretch from the eyes back to the pineal gland, there is a stretch from the eyes through, we tune that stretch to the feeling of life force and then that feeling into the astral body builds. We just stretch and feel. You will start to see the life force through your astral vision. There must be an overlap between the vital astral bodies as the energy reticulates through the eye-consciousness: you keep an open enough space, separate the observer, the intender and the observed, and let the life force move between these three components, and you will naturally begin to see life force.

This skill is very clear: the mental space, the astral quality and the physical quality. Any skill you wish to develop, you have to break down these three bodies and the function of each of the three bodies in order for that particular skill to arise. As you move through the initiation text, this becomes obvious.

Sound

Clairaudience is dependent upon two frequencies: the development of Akasha and the development of the Air element. Let us begin with Akasha. Enter into Akashic trance, accumulate the Akasha through your mental, astral and physical bodies. Saturate yourself within it. Test the boundaries of your mental matrix by lightly rocking your body forwards and backwards to allow your body to dissolve the edges of your matrices. Rock your body to dissolve the edges of the mental matrix. Perhaps, if you will, slowly rocking left and right and get that Akashic feeling.

From there, accumulate the Akasha in your eardrums. As you accumulate in your eardrums, you are looking at the physical organ through breathing into your physical ears and breathing out. From there, we begin washing the Akasha through your sense of hearing, through the sound consciousness, and you are mixing between the organ and sound consciousness – blending and building a bridge in this Akashic breathing. Next, we move into sounds. You have sounds coming from your environment, breathe through the organ, through sound-consciousness into the information where the sound is coming in and reticulate the Akasha, building a bridge. From there, bring the Akasha in the organ through the consciousness, to the information, to the mind substance of what is sending the information.

So, if you hear a bird outside you are connecting to the spirit of the bird – not the physical body but the spirit of the bird, the physical sound it is making which has astral sounds with it, and the information coming to sound consciousness and the organ itself. So, you reticulate the organ, sound consciousness, the sounds, and then the spirit, and the mind substance that is sending the sounds. You continually reticulate that backwards and forwards, blending and bridging these three qualities together. This will clear the lines between the mind substance you connect to and what you are building to hear within the spirit through the Akashic doorway, to access a flow of information.

Next is the Air element. It is basically the same process: you breathe the Air element into your eardrum, into sound consciousness, into the information coming through the sound consciousness, and then into the mind substance of what is sending the sound. So, it is the same in the Akasha and the Air element.

Next, practice sound-consciousness. Do the three transformations. Raise it up to light, up to the crown. Do this by taking a few Akasha breaths, saturate the Akasha, open the crown chakra, filling the Akasha through the crown, and make a prayer "May the path of light guide and protect," let your awareness rise up into light. Inside that light make a prayer to invoke clairaudience for the benefit of all sentient beings, so it aligns with your path of service, and then invite that light of clairaudience back down through the crown into the astral body, into the physical. Let it saturate your ears – on the physical let it saturate your ears, in the astral let it saturate your ears, and in the mental let it saturate sound consciousness physically, astrally and mentally and let information flow in physically, astrally and mentally. Let it connect to the spirit of information coming through so that you build a bridge with that light. This is how you develop clairaudience.

Feeling
Breathing the Akasha into the pores, bring the feeling into the skin and increase the Akasha inside of the skin organ. Then moving to the consciousness feeling, saturate the Akasha and the consciousness feeling. From there we move into the information that the consciousness is picking up, and then we saturate and bind the mind substance that is sending that information for you to feel. So, the same process that we did in clairaudience, clairvoyance and also in feeling (clairsentience) – they are all the same. You can apply the same training principle to the other sense gates.

Taste
Taste is the same process as the others again, but we use the Water element in the Akasha. Begin with Akasha and clean your sense of taste. Saturate your tongue with Akasha. Saturate your consciousness of taste with Akasha. Saturate the information flow you have coming into your sense of taste with Akasha, and then connect with the mind substance where that information started. If you are eating an apple, you not only connect to the mind substance of the apple but to the tree which the apple came from – you have reached that Akashic substance right through. Once you have completed the Akasha, repeat the same exercise with the Water element.

Smell
To increase your psychic sense of smell, we start with Akasha, same as with the other gates. Connect to the organ of smell and saturate it with Akasha. When we move to the consciousness itself, saturate the Akasha in, then move the information that is moving into the scent, saturate Akasha, and then go to the mind substance, into the source of that information. From there we build a bridge with Akasha and increase and connect the Akashic link we have; from the organ to consciousness to the information to the consciousness that is sending out – wherever you send that bridge. From there, senses are controlled by the Air element. You repeat the same process with the Air element. Breath the Air element into the organ, into consciousness,

into the information, and then into the source – the mind substance of consciousness where the information is coming from, to build a bridge, and this will increase your sense of smell intuitively.

Step Eight: The Electric and Magnetic Fluid

The Great Moment of Now
In this stage of training, we move the length of concentration up. We started with two minutes of concentration, now we want to get this extended to 15 minutes. Considering the various depth of skills that you have been developing, a lot of people think that you have to meditate for 45 minutes, one hour, two hours, three hours – that naturally comes. However, information psychically appears in a fraction of a second, so you really only need to enter equanimity for a fraction of a second in order to get that psychic compression. You maintain that equanimity to translate that information. That is more like sprinting than marathon running.

Your concentration has to be very intense, very perfect for a short amount of time. We gradually want to lengthen that time. So, revise all your sense gates and measure how long you can concentrate on the following: through visual concentration, auditory concentration, feeling concentration, scent, taste, your mind gate of observing thought as it arises, your ability to concentrate on a train of thought, and the vacancy of thought in your mind.

Revise the six gates of the mind and ensure that you can hold that concentration for at least 15 minutes.

With the mind gate, you are holding concepts, ideas, knowledge, wisdom, and complex combinations of things. It is not just an individual gate, it is a combination of all the gates for the type of inner knowing of something – when you have an inner knowing or inner feeling in relation to how something functions as a blending of the gates and translating the information. Get creative on how you concentrate with the mind gate.

Living in the moment of being mindful of how you think, feel and act, and neutralizing unbeneficial thoughts, feelings and behaviors should be a constant part of your life. This is a just a normal part of your life. The black and white mirror work we did in the beginning pointed out whether you have more of one element or another, and allowed you to reach equanimity more quickly. Do a self-check to make sure that you are on track.

Our next area with living in the great moment of now on the elements and the balance, is the feeling of equanimity as a constant underlying the consciousness. Yes, your mind needs to function and think and can be active, you need to have feelings about what you are doing – but it is the continual awareness of equanimity underlying that. It is like you are thinking and you feel equanimity simultaneously. This quality needs to be developed so that you only pay attention to equanimity and equanimity arises, that it is always there underneath, that you are never far from it.

This quality allows you to develop yourself to a higher level. Without that quality it can be very difficult.

The Electric and the Magnetic
Even though Bardon presents the electrical-magnetic fluids very late in the *Initiation into Hermetics* text, it can be practiced in the first week of training with a partner. Through partner training, one can approach it in a physical, mechanical way of pushing the joints open for electric, and pulling the joints for electric while vital breathing, and then releasing time astrally. Then Akashically breathe while doing that to create volts. I like to do this very quickly because it can give students incredibly fast growth rates for getting breakthroughs, for pushing through barriers, for getting the will to use the akasha through an electric volt to break through and create a rhythmic arc that shatters barriers to progress.

Inward Electric Fluid
With the inward electric fluid, we transfer the mind into a volcano, into the molten lava. Of course it is only the mental idea the mind is coming into resonance with. As you astrally pore breathe the molten lava – the frequency of electric fluid – in, it supports your imagination to tune the mental body into the idea of electric fluid. You pore breathe that in, imagining that molten lava around you, so that the pressure is outside yourself, and you invite it in. You breathe it astrally into your astral body and you pressurize your astral body until your astral body is equal to that amount of pressure of electric fluid that is around you in a volcano. Your astral body is not moving out into a volcano – it is on your mental body to give you the resonance with the electric fluid as you astrally breathe it.

You quickly realize that whatever your mind comes into resonance with, you can astrally breathe it in and out and produce that within your own astral body, sitting in your physical body.

We pressurize the astral body to a point where the electric fluid is bubbling, expanding and highly pressurized. This is on the border of physical pain. It should hurt a little bit when you are doing this – that you are putting that much intent in that you feel like you are going to explode. Hold it in your body for a minute or so and then release the idea of being inside the molten lava volcano, and then pore breathe that energy out and dissipate it out into the environment.

Keep repeating this so that you can hold that energy for longer and longer periods, so you get a type of electric fluid tenacity in your astral body. This generates a whole range of types of immunity to different types of effects. It dramatically increases the active elements of Fire and Air and increases your willpower, your ability to break through barriers and achieve whatever you need to achieve.

Step Nine: Astral Travel and Leaving the Physical Body Matrix

When separating the astral body there is a very high risk of death, and to reduce this risk you need to master vital breathing into your asana or into your meditation posture. When you breathe into your meditation posture with vital energy and you super stretch your body into your asana, there is a point at which the body consciousness takes over the stretch and the opening of your spine and joints and generates vitality. This is essential for separating the astral body.

If you have not achieved that, when your astral body starts to separate your physical body will just collapse, which essentially means that you can only do it when you are lying down. If you are lying down, you do not have that energetic stretch – you will not have the vital force being generated for protection and which is required to nurture your physical form, and your vulnerability is increased. Mastering your vital breathing into the fascia is essential because as that separation starts to take place, you do not want any collapsing of your physical form – you want your body to be straight, radiant and protected.

You have mastered the vital breathing and your asana, and you are able to do all your meditation exercises, mental wandering and so forth without your physical body collapsing – now we move from the vital breathing to the astral breathing. Do the whole body astral pore breathing exercise and generate a sensitivity to your astral body. Once you have that sensitivity to your astral body, generate a sensitivity to your astral matrix – the magnetic fluid which holds the astral body to your physical.

This magnetic fluid can be neutralized – not completely, but it can be softened. As you are sensitive to your astral body and your astral matrix, you soften that matrix, you are able to either rise up through the crown or what I like to do is to practice standing up. Because I practice sitting in a chair – my physical body sitting in the chair – and then as the astral body rises I simply stand my astral body up. As you begin to stand up, there is an initiation of will to move the astral body without your physical body. This magnetic vacuum of space that wants to pull on your physical body, it will give you a clear, clean and concise release of that astral matrix. You will have to soften and neutralize that magnetic hold.

Once you have practiced standing up, then sit your astral body back down to your physical. So you can rise and stretch directly up and float yourself above your crown, or simply practice standing with your astral body.

Standing up with the astral body gives you a much clearer, concise experience. It dissolves any sense of you imagining doing something because of the magnetic pull you have on your physical body when you stand up. This gives you a clear line that differentiates: this is the astral, this is the physical, this is the astral matrix, and you can neutralize the astral matrix.

Once you are at the stage where you can stand up and sit down, then take a couple of steps and move back into your astral body. Here is a very interesting part of your development. The habits that you instill, they are going to be your limitations. If you make yourself dependent upon stepping, moving of the astral body, it will be more difficult to fly because your astral body will be subject to your physical limitations – because an astral form is an extension of that. So, float forward and float back. This urge to be restricted by a physical body can be quite overwhelming, because that is your physical body habit and your astral body is conditioned to follow this habit.

These exercises, again, have a high risk of death. If someone touches your physical body when you are astrally separated, you are going to have a heart attack and your physical body is going to die. Make sure that you have locked the room and have proper security, because your physical body will look like it is dead: your heart rate slows down to nothing and your whole body goes into this morbid state. Someone who sees you is going to come over and they are going to grab your body and shake you to try and wake you up, because you look like you are dead – people intercepting your practice is what will kill you. Do not trust that no one's going to touch you when you do this, because you will not look like you do normally.

From there, we move on to moving around the room that you are in and coming back to the body. This law of rhythm of time is important: each time you practice, just gradually increase the amount of time you are out of the body. Make a very momentary back in and out. Mastering the astral matrix is the key. Doing a little bit of Akasha into your astral matrix will soften it and allow your astral body to separate.

Once you are at this point, move on to the next part of the astral training, which is impregnating universal qualities into your astral body. With this, we move into the Akasha principle, soften into Akashic trance, connect your mind to the universal quality of will. Then, through prayer, invite and breathe that into your astral body – start charging your astral body with that quality. Once that is charged, step your astral body out of your physical and back in again. We do the astral separation while in resonance with the universal quality and then move to wisdom and in the Akasha tune in, repeat the same process.

When you go into the Water element, you have two qualities – love and immortality. They are very different qualities and they are connected, but the astral expressions are different. Do those two individual qualities within the Water element separately. When you move to omnipresence, omnipresence is a strong feeling of unification with the environment – that you are your physical environment, that you are the astral plane. It is also connected to your immortality. When you practice the Earth element this way, if you are searching for physical immortality then work that quality and the omnipresence has two separate vibrations.

As you are imprinting these divine qualities from the Akasha into your astral body and then stepping out of your astral body, and doing that – you just need to stand your astral body up. There is no need to move around while your physical body is sitting. What happens is you get a type of pure transfer of energy through the astral.

Once you are at this stage, I suggest that you leave the room that you are in with your astral body. The reason why is that your astral body will be much stronger and less susceptible to the tricks of beings within the astral plane. They will see those divine qualities and give you respect accordingly. I do not suggest you go wandering in the astral planes as a beginner of this skill. Practice impregnating universal qualities. By this time of your training you will have spiritual support – you will be sensitive to the various spiritual beings that are there to help you on your spiritual path. When you separate your astral body they will move with you, so the risks decrease: you are not alone.

You have a huge spectrum of different types of effects and techniques that you can practice from the astral plane, but it is my recommendation to just practice stepping out of the physical body into the astral and then meditate on the divine qualities from the Akasha through prayer and invoke them into your astral body. As you move further from your physical body to your astral form, your connection to those divine qualities should be quite strong.

Step Ten: Astral Training Paths of Self Realization

There are four fundamental methods of connecting to universal consciousness. These four paths have a strong connection to the elements. The first method is the *saintly path*. The saintly path is a system where it is precept-dependent. You establish your precepts – like in Buddhism and all other religious systems – and you put high amounts of light, prayer and energy through those precepts. Your astral body becomes a type of superconductor for light.

When you do a lot of prayer and you are following this saintly path, those precepts become tuning forks – they become superconductors, and these superconductors generate a bridge between the physical body, their actions, the astral body, the belief structures, feelings and emotional relationship to the environment, the mental body on a lower level within the intellect and view and on the higher aspect within the spirit, essence and fabric. This permeates into the Akasha. Prayer bonds these aspects together to connect you to universal consciousness. The saintly path is about building precepts and tuning forks. Very high frequency deities can conduct energy directly from Akasha during prayer through the three bodies to produce miracles for those following the saintly path. It is a profound path. Not many people can follow this path. It is the most difficult path to follow out of these four methods.

The next path is more akin to the Fire element – it is the **deity invocation path**. With deity invocation it is more based upon mental transference into the frequency of the deity in front of an altar – in front of a sacred place – and going into union with the deity. As you tune your awareness – your mental body – to the deity, you open your heart astrally to the deity, and you are in a physical space where that deity's energy is accumulated. You get a union of the three bodies with the deity. Because this is a method for touching God, touching universal mind, this does not apply to dualistic deities. This only applies to deities that have achieved Nirvana or are Nirvanic by nature but have not gone into parinirvana by dissolving into Nirvanic substance.

They still have a bridge open. They are still in the path of service, but they have already achieved the highest. These deities, they connect you to universal consciousness – to God. The deity yoga method is mental transference mentally, astrally and physically into the deity as a concentration method. By having the image of the deity and visualizing the deity and so forth, you can get all these qualities. If we are looking at Buddhist methods, you sit in front of the image of the deity, you have the mudra which connects the deity, the mantra which is the frequency of connection, and the visualization image. You have body, speech and mind and you use those to invoke the deity. Through that connection to the deity, the deity connects you to universal consciousness.

This **insight path** is an Air element path of touching divinity – it is a continual observing of the mechanistic nature of karma and how things function. You observe, you create space. You go into your Akasha, observe, create space. This causal chain of how creation unfolds, you are reverse-engineering that and going to the essence of creation. This is the Air element method. Both the saintly path, the Water method and the *samadhi* concentration, the Fire method approach, these are both accumulating Akasha in a type of prayer that accompanies the meditations. As the Akasha accumulates, it fluxes. It is going to flux more into a qualitative awareness state of the Air element where you have a clear insight into what you are looking at and what in Buddhism is called the intellectual path – where you look at causation, you understand this is how it functions. Through the understanding of how it functions, there is a reflection inside the universal consciousness to bring you closer to divinity, because it is a continual opening of the awareness to truth. Through that frequency of insight and truth that you rise closer to God. In Buddhism, you are rising closer to the door of Nirvana.

The **Earth element method** is much more solid, concrete, physical, and is similar to the Fire method, but it is more of the body. This method requires you to be very intense. When you invite the deity into your body, you are the deity, you physically look like the deity, are in resonance with the deity, and the deity speaks through you – it is very mediumistic. You are taking on the identity of the deity and allowing it to become you, whereas in the Fire method of the will coming into vibrational match with the deity, you are allowing the deity to make adjustments to you, to pull you up to connect to universal consciousness.

In this Earth method, you take universal consciousness through the deity and bring it into your body in this present moment, so that as this happens, this body is enlightened. Your DNA is enlightened, your astral nature is enlightened, and your spirit is enlightened, and everything comes into union with God in a physical body. This is the most magical, where you can express the most physical healing, you can produce miracles and so forth because of the nature of you becoming the deity, and the deity speaks through you, and God speaks through you, until you have broken away all of your defilements and you are God.

This covers the four methods. There is a type of elemental logic in it. When you feel the elements, you can see how you can touch divinity through each of the elements.

Using the elements metaphorically allows you to access the psychology of the non-dual nature of the elements and bridges from the physical, astral and mental up into spiritual worlds. For beings of the Water element, they are going to use the saintly path to touch God. Beings of the Fire element are going to use the *samadhi* concentration path to touch God. Beings of the Air element are going to use insight to touch God, and beings of the Earth element are going to have deity invocation methods in the physical form to touch God.

Each one of these paths are important because the path you use to touch God is the return path in which God works through you. The way the causal chain of energy reacts back in physical form is important. How you attain matters, because that is your path of service and how energy optimally reflects back into form.

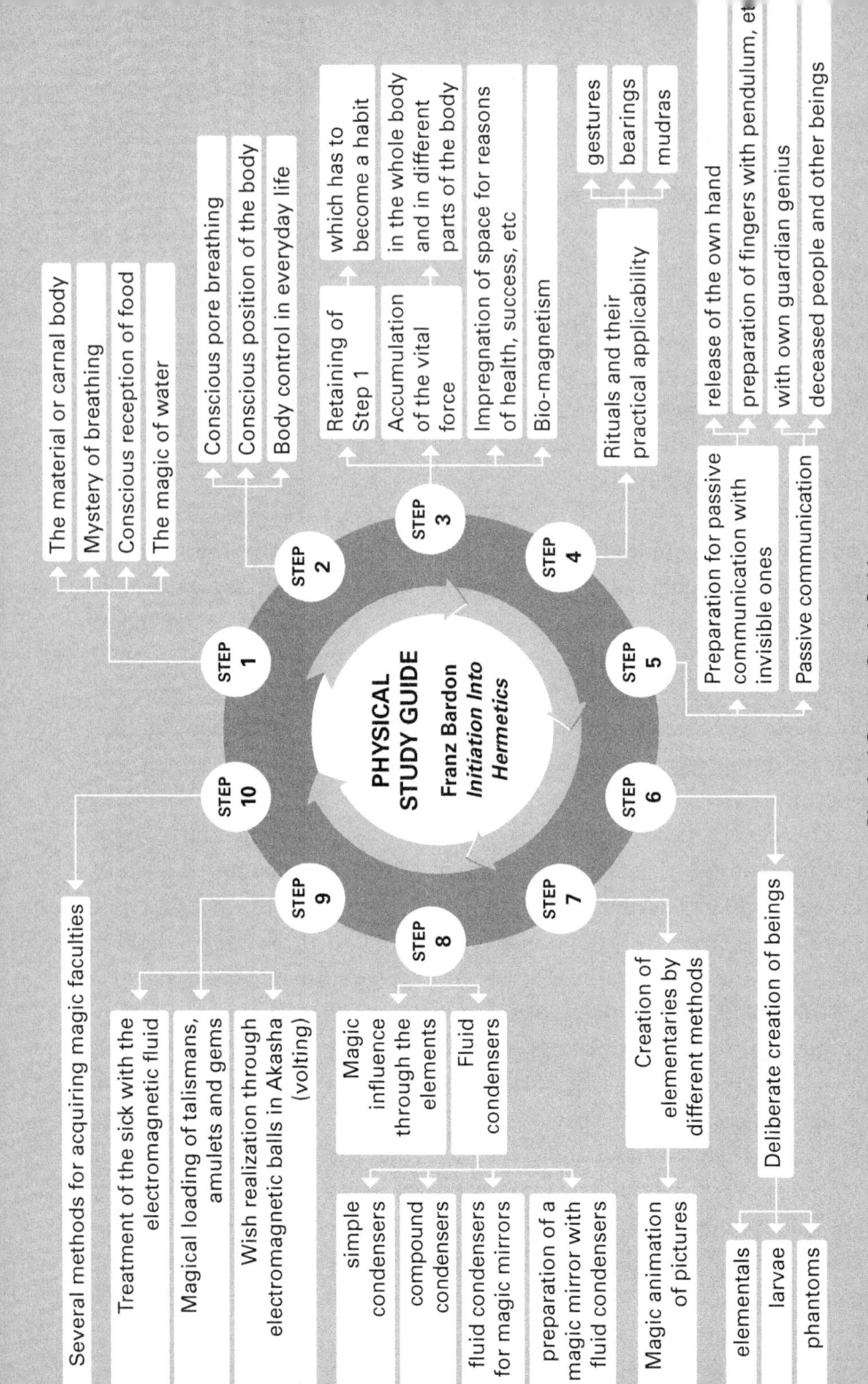

PHYSICAL STUDY GUIDE
Franz Bardon *Initiation Into Hermetics*

Physical Stream Study Guide

STEP 1
- The material or carnal body
- Mystery of breathing
- Conscious reception of food
- The magic of water

STEP 2
- Conscious pore breathing
- Conscious position of the body
- Body control in everyday life

STEP 3
- Retaining of Step 1 — which has to become a habit in the whole body and in different parts of the body
- Accumulation of the vital force
- Impregnation of space for reasons of health, success, etc
- Bio-magnetism

STEP 4
- Rituals and their practical applicability
  - gestures
  - bearings
  - mudras

STEP 5
- Preparation for passive communication with invisible ones
- Passive communication
  - release of the own hand
  - preparation of fingers with pendulum, etc
  - with own guardian genius
  - deceased people and other beings

STEP 6
- Creation of elementaries by different methods
- Deliberate creation of beings
  - elementals
  - larvae
  - phantoms

STEP 7
- Magic animation of pictures

STEP 8
- Magic influence through the elements
- Fluid condensers
  - simple condensers
  - compound condensers
  - fluid condensers for magic mirrors
  - preparation of a magic mirror with fluid condensers

STEP 9
- Several methods for acquiring magic faculties

STEP 10
- Treatment of the sick with the electromagnetic fluid
- Magical loading of talismans, amulets and gems
- Wish realization through electromagnetic balls in Akasha (volting)

Physical Stream: Steps One through Ten

Step One

As there are the mental and astral streams, so there is a physical stream. Each exercise needs to be connected together – synchronized mentally – so that you feel continuity within your mental training, your astral training and your physical training. Physical training starts off with asceticism. All the cravings of the body – thirst, hunger, sexual, desire, money, social connection – whatever your desire is, you need to identify when the desire of the body is arising, take a step back from it, so that your mind, your spirit, your will separates itself from the desire and observes it and starts releasing the control it has over your astral and mental forms.

This ascetic practice has to apply to every desire which arises of the body and needs to be practiced daily until you have mastered the skill. Practicing asceticism does not mean that you are taking anything away – it just means that you are changing the decision-making process before you indulge. So, if you like a particular food, you release on that food before you eat. The amount you eat, whether you actually choose that food or not, and so forth, changes because the decision is made by a higher part of your consciousness rather than a lower part which craves. This ascetic practice forms the fabric of being a *practitioner*. It does not need to go to the extremes like you see in India, but it does need to be in place so that your spirit is master of your ego and body. The only way to achieve that is by going through this ascetic release process, to transcend the body being in control.

With the whole body pore breathing Step One practice, we have the same idea. This pore breathing is simply breathing in an idea, which – say, you breathe a wish into your body and take it into the pores and then out of the pores and whatever that wish is, you want to be pulling it into your cells, into your bloodstream. So it might be for health, abundance or synchronicity within your thinking, feeling, actions. Whatever that wish is, you breathe it in, breathe it out, and you get into the routine of reinforcing a synchronicity between your breathing, goals, actions, and feelings. All the three bodies are synchronized together by breathing ideas into your cells. Of course when you have reached the point where you have learned how to pore breathe, you will automatically do this with pore breathing, with life force – because life force will further synchronize, activate and connect your ideas and the three bodies that you wish to place them. When we will go through the physical training, even though vital breathing comes into the later steps, you want to get into it as quickly as possible. This is so the earlier steps become easy.

Conscious reception of food – now, there are a few ways to work with this practice. My favorite is the Buddhist method, where you are practicing asceticism. You simply take a bite of the food, see how your body responds to it, you respond to the taste, you may respond to the food, "Ah, this is nice. This is not nice." You make judgments and watch yourself go through that process and then you pull the three bodies apart, so that the mental body occupies more space; notice the astral feelings, notice that space and then the body, the reaction to the food, and watch how each body responds to the food – there are different responses. Your physical body will be taking in nourishment and it will be guided by simple tastes. Your astral body will be guided by conditioning – so, you like this, you don't like that; you come across research which says this is good or that is bad, and you will have all these judgments and decisions you've made in the past about that particular type of food. And then the mental body, which occupies more space again, will be in tune with the spiritual nourishment of that food. How is it connected to the group consciousness? How is it connected to the energetic web?

Garden of Eden Diet
This is where the Garden of Eden diet comes into play, where – if you pick fruit from a tree and then eat the fruit and share gratitude to the fruit, your

mental body connects to the consciousness of the tree or trees and network, the orchard – your spirit gets nurtured by the tree you are giving thanks to. So when the plant that your food comes from is still alive and you show gratitude and make a prayer towards the source of the food, your mental body becomes unified with the power of that farm, of that place where the food came from. If it is organic and has been alive, it has been taken care of and the farmers nurtured the tree in which that food has come from, then there is a transmission of power that happens from the spirit – your spirit gets nourishment. If you were to eat a dead animal there would be no nourishment for the spirit. The spirit would have a sense of contractions, viable instinct, death, and that would not be nourished. Your astral body also does not experience any love, compassion or higher frequencies through consuming that food.

So only a physical body can be nourished through eating a dead animal, whereas in order for the mental-astral body to be nourished it has to be higher frequencies that are involved in the food chain. So, with the Garden of Eden diet you are always looking at how the food reached your plate and the consciousness of the food and the consciousness of the mother of the food, the plant that it came from. That awareness generates a nourishment for your mental body when you pray and show gratitude for that particular food. This is an important part of practice.

Now, when you are drinking water, there is the spirit of Water. You have the oceans, lakes and rivers – the water on the entire planet has consciousness. Before you take water into your body, if you show gratitude to the spirit of Water, before you drink water, this gratitude brings you into resonance with the water and consciousness of the entire planet. This nurtures your spirit. Your body is for the most part composed of water. The body gets nourished, the astral substance gets nourished, and the spirit also is nourished. By having a profound gratitude for water before you bring it into your body, it becomes an amplifier of the qualities of water that are within you. This brings good health to your body. Try having this process of gratitude to the consciousness of Water and apply it to bathing as well. When you have a shower, connect to the consciousness of Water and make a prayer to make this water purify the mind, purify the astral ego, and purify the body. As you shower, that water demagnetizes the three bodies and removes contaminants mentally, astrally and physically. The depth of that prayer creates a vacuum which amplifies the demagnetizing of negative qualities during bathing. So, this is also an accelerator of your practice.

If you do this on a daily basis, within a few weeks you will notice a change in your thinking patterns – there is less static, you are more grounded and centered, you feel connected to your environment, and the water element in your body is not jumping around as 'monkey mind'. The water element in your body is in a state of stability, and you can have profound results from your practice. All of this arises from simple gratitude and respect to a spirit of Water, because most of you essentially is water.

When we put all this into vital breathing and charging energy into your food, your water, air, your activities and goals – this whole body pore breathing process – you can generate strong electromagnetic charges within the food, water and air, in the space you are sitting in to synchronize your three bodies with your goals. The synchronicity not only works within you, but it works in your environment. Let us say that you want to purchase a new electronic device and you think, "Yes, I need to get this." By breathing that idea into your mental, astral and physical bodies, you will synchronize with the environment so that the person, the place, the sale – whatever it is – will present itself to you. "Ah, here's the item I need," because you are synchronized on the astral plane with that particular item, within that particular charge. So charging your food, water and air with things you need, or with your goals, generates the synchronicity between your astral body in the astral field, between your body consciousness, and the consciousness of your physical environment. And the same with your mental body and the mental plane.

This unconscious synchronicity aligns your goals to your reality – so the two come together and as that synchronizes, everything slipstreams. Some people call this good luck, but in reality it is synchronicity between you and your environment. Some people will randomly synchronize momentarily and win the lottery, but these people who win the lotto are usually broke within a few years, because they go out of synchronicity. When something synchronizes momentarily, yes, that can be called luck. But when you do whole body pore breathing, charging your food and water with particular ideas, you are in a continuous state of synchronicity – you are in a continuous state of luck because your astral, physical and mental worlds are in synchronicity with your ideas and they are continually manifesting with ease, within your experience. So this makes a lot of things very easy.

This first stage of training and connecting these lifestyle principles together generates the fabric of what it means to be a *practitioner*. It makes life straightforward and things just happen. There is a strange type of faith which accumulates when you start entering into this way of thinking. You know that everything is synchronized and everything is going to align and manifest itself as it should. This faith speeds everything up and harmonizes synchronicity, so everything aligns correctly.

Step Two: Asanas

The conscious pore breathing exercise is really the fabric of the asana training. We need to stream through the first few steps straight away, so that you can do the first steps more efficiently by having done the second or third step. A conscious position of the body is about mastering your asanas, sitting postures, the way you walk and talk, your speech patterns and dress, how people perceive you, your image, and so forth. You have all of these different aspects of your public persona on the outside and you are in a physical environment on the inside – how do you relax within your body and outwards through your image? These two need to be taken care of because we live in a society. We need to blend into whatever society we are in and function within it. So being a yogi and dressing like a yogi works very well in India, because that is the accepted social norm of that society for someone who is a yogi. But being a yogi does not work in Western culture. If you dress and act like a yogi in Western culture, you will likely be considered a lower class person, maybe a social outcast – most parts of society will reject you and make fun of you. So, blending into the society through correct dress, speech, manners, and so forth is important.

As a *practitioner*, if you should teach people, you have to put yourself into a physical situation where that is possible – and it is not possible if you put yourself in a situation where you try to act and dress like a yogi in a Western culture. You have to live in the culture you are in and make it comfortable for people to come to you and learn in order for you to successfully teach.

Choose whatever asana or meditation posture you are used to working with. You may have been practicing in a chair with your knees generally pulled together, perhaps with your knees apart in an Earth grounding posture, standing postures, cross leg postures, kneeling postures, and so forth.

You might use an ergonomic chair. Whichever postures you choose, you need to be able to be comfortable sitting within that posture for an extended period of time. The key to success is the stretch. When you vital breathe, there is a stretch in your joints. You open your joints up so that life force begins to radiate. When you are working any particular sitting or standing posture, you need to open the joints and stretch so that the whole body is open. The whole body is radiating life force as you hold that posture. That posture will then become self-supporting. The energy of the stretch and the energy of that outward radiation automatically both supports and allows you to remain in posture for as long as you wish. This is because the energy is holding the position through the stretch, through the openness to the joints, and through that peak feeling of life force.

This is equivalent to the Taoist practice of standing, where you stand in a posture and generate energy. You can sit in any posture, tune the whole body to life force and radiate that life force through whatever posture you wish. It is the same fundamental practice.

When it comes down to a walking practice, you learn to control your body. You learn to walk in a particular way, generate a particular energetic emanation. When you are talking, you learn how to talk in a particular way, emanate energy through your voice chords. It is only a very gentle stretch of your vocal chords, which enlightens the energy in your vocal chords to magnetize the sound, so that when people hear it, it gets their attention. Some people have this naturally – when they speak, everyone turns and listens. If you wish to generate this yourself, you need to gently pull the vocal chords down and stretch your neck up as you speak to tune the fascia of the vocal chords to life force, so that the sound you are making has more life force conducting through it. The same way that you stretch your fingers when you build energy between your hands, to peak the life force, you stretch your vocal chords and throat and neck muscles to open energy and radiate energy through speech. These exercises need to be practiced.

Step Three: Accumulating Vital Power

In the beginning, we actually do not want to accumulate power – we want to build it and release it. So when you do seven to nine breaths of accumulating, seven to nine breaths of releasing, we are not holding it – we are just building up a charge and then we discharge it. You will find that within a few sessions, you do not need to have the same amount of breaths out as in to release the energy – even two or three breaths you will release the energy and have another two or three breaths to clean up and release the residual tension that is there. Of course you do not want to breathe that back out through your pores and waste the energy – you would put it into a bottle of water or into an amulet or an object to charge that object with a particular intent, because that energy is useful and functional. You do not go to work and make money and then just throw the money away – you put the money in the bank. Energy, money, it is the same thing – you store it.

As your practice reaches higher frequencies, money or energy becomes more accessible. It is easier for you to get energy and then the storage aspect of it, you store in the Akashic space underneath your body or underneath your center of gravity or under the center of the bone marrow. So you feel the central access to the marrow of a bone and you relax life force into that Akashic space under the marrow. It makes it accessible so that your body can release energy out of that Akashic space when you need to use it. It depends upon your level of skill, as to how you store energy or how you would put money in the bank for later use.

As you become more proficient at vital breathing, you will find that the way you relax the muscles, open the joints and stretch the fascia peaks out that vital force. We have this process of relaxing the muscles, letting them hang, gently open the joints, stretch the fascia, and there is a peak within that stretch where the life force radiates. We need to look at how we get to that peak, how we relax and release the muscle so that it hangs; that the stretch is open and the stretch is radiating energy. This becomes the platform of pore breathing and the accumulation of power, whole body breathing and so forth – they are all overlapping skills. Practice the opening of the joints, relaxing and hanging of the muscles, and generating a stretch throughout your whole field to make everything radiate. This is one of the major platforms of training.

If you want to build a particular element, you need to have this stage mastered. You cannot build the Fire element until you can get the fascia to open. You cannot build the Water element until you get the fascia to open and the muscles to release. So this is a critical part of training, tuning the whole body, fascia the whole body to radiating life force, getting your stretch correct.

When breathing life force into parts of the body, you will get a sense of how much you accumulate through a type of gauge of pressure. When you pressurize a particular body part, it will start to feel like you are inflating a balloon. It might be your forearm and your forearm will feel inflated. You will find that as you inflate the forearm, that energy will just naturally leak and dissipate before you reach a full pressure. This sense of energy leaking needs to be closed up, so that the energy coming in is staying and the pressure is building. This way you truly can pressurize a space of your body. While being able to pressurize each part of your body, you get a resistance, resilience to that amount of pressure externally. If you do nine breaths with a very high amount of pressure into your forearm, that becomes a natural immunity level, a natural resistance level to energy within your forearm. You will find that you will automatically be able to have a natural resistance level simply by pressurizing and depressurizing the body. If something bumps your arm, the unconscious mind will release energy and instantaneously put a type of counter-pressure into that part of your body where you are being bumped. So you get this natural ruggedness, natural toughness, natural resilience to cold and heat, the environment, flu and colds – all these things cannot touch you because of that pressurization of the fascia and life force. Your body remembers. It can summon energy instantly through that memory. So it is important that when you pressurize a part of your body and at the end of this you release that pressure – release that pressure into the etheric blueprint, into your Akashic body. That puts the money in the bank and it becomes accessible for later, when needed. You just need to relax and implant that energy into your etheric body, then it is available for later. So you pull it out of the Akasha into the body and then you drop it back into the Akasha. There is an in-out cyclical type of training that will make large reservoirs of energy accessible to you when needed. Your body consciousness will also be able to have access to those energy reservoirs when it needs strength, power, resilience, and so forth. Accessing these reservoirs happens even if you are not conscious of it.

In the same way that we pressurize parts of our own body or whole body, we also pressurize space. So in the room that you are practicing in you may vital breathe into it with a quality of relaxation, a quality of release, a quality of intuitive ability that is amplifying, and so forth. And you can put whatever qualities into that space you want because this energy has two phases – it has qualitative and quantitative. Quantitative is how much energy and qualitative, what is the patterning or function of that energy? What does it do? The qualitative training and the quantitative training need to be harmonized. The mental body training tends to gravitate towards qualitative. The physical body training gravitates towards quantitative and in the astral body, qualitative and quantitative mix to generate the conditions that you want. So the alchemical melting pot is the astral plane. The qualitative transformation and changes in the mental, and the quantitative in physical. And we want to bring these together astrally to generate different types of conditions.

When you are breathing into a room, you will find that you will have the scale of pressure. So, let us say, you want to breathe happiness into a room and you pressurize the room with happiness. You will first notice as you pressurize that it is depressurizing – energy is leaking. So the way you seal the room so that the energy stays in it is a skill unto itself. Learn to develop your way of keeping energy inside of a space without any loss. Open windows or moving air will naturally pull energy out of the room, so you might want to close the doors and windows when you start practicing this, in order to maintain that energetic pressure more easily. The type of ideas that you are pressurizing with the energy into the room also control how well that actually stays in a space. If the thoughts and feelings are very conducive to the environment, to your practice, then those energies will naturally want to stay there. If they are thoughts and energies that are not conducive to your development, those energies will dissipate at a much faster rate. So you will notice that the nature of the energy you are storing in a space plays a huge part in whether it will stay there or not, and what its dissipation rates are.

When people walk into that space, you can choose whether that person is immediately affected by the energy or whether it is buffered, so that another person does not notice it. So you may choose to charge a room with spiritual light and that anyone who is in resonance with spiritual light, their life will automatically become brighter when they walk into the room. But people who live a mundane lifestyle will not even notice. They will walk into the room and their spiritual light will not activate. Whereas people who are in touch with their spiritual light naturally raise up, their head will be suspended, the crown will open and they will begin to radiate light. Brothers and sisters who are walking the path of light will automatically feel that this is a special place that I'm walking into, whereas normal people, who live a normal life, they will be completely unaware as to what had just taken place.

This vital breathing can be used for healing. You can touch a person's body while placing a slight amount of pressure. You touch their root, their connection to the ground, their connection to gravity. You engage the field of gravity that is acting upon them, increase the pressure of that gravitational action on them and then depressurize to pull the pressure off, thereby increasing the space. The three bodies will open slightly. When the mental matrix opens, then you can breathe vital energy through that gap and revitalize their energy system. If you just breathe vital energy into a normal person without that door being opened, they will tend to reject it or saturate it very slowly. But if you pressurize and depressurize the system to pop the balance out of the body – to open the door, to get the mental matrix to spread – and then you put that energetic charge through that door, through that gap, and feel their energy filled up, they will accept that energy instantly. The way you metabolize that energy into this system so that it becomes functional energy is to relax and release it into their immune system. So you float them, compress the body, decompress, create space, the mental matrix opens up, you breathe into it, and then you relax and release it into their immune system. Relax and release it into their bones, strengthen their bones, relax and release it into their muscles to generate a faster recovery for any type of training. Whatever the need is, you need to relax the energy into a state in which the body can resolve and use that energy. If you just create pressure of life force in someone's body they will feel irritable, because their body will be rejecting it, because it is not in resonance with them. You need to relax that life force into their resonance and this takes a particular feeling quality of relaxing into them, while you are putting electromagnetic charge of life force through that relaxation. The relaxation is conducted through into their body to fulfil a particular purpose.

In the same way, you can charge space to create all these types of electromagnetic effects for healing, different types of thinking, inspiration. Let us say you belong to a poetry society and the society meets in a particular hall or place each week and people present their poetry. So you may breathe into that room the astral frequencies of poetry and how this is activated through speech, so that each person who walks into the room, that inner genius that is connected to poetry automatically begins to express itself – anyone who walks into that room is a poetic genius. Activating these particular frequencies, you can be very selective about who activates the energy and who comes in resonance with it. General people who are not interested in poetry may not be touched at all by the energy. But someone who seeks inspiration within poetry will automatically be touched and the energy will go more towards the people who will benefit from it and less to the people who will not benefit from it.

Step Four

When we are moving into rituals and the mechanics of how they function, we need to look at what we are energetically releasing through ritual. To do this, we need to store energy in our etheric body. We need to align that energy through our mental body, through our astral body, and through our physical body into the function of the ritual. So we need to perform the function in which the ritual is going to act first; we need to have an energetic patterning in place for that particular ritual to fulfill its function. Let us say that you were playing with tai chi and working with 'bouncing' people, like rebounding force in tai chi. You would normally touch their bridge, their body, and feel their base connection. You would then put in a little bit of electric energy to compress them you would pull back to open the three bodies and once that gap forms and they are open, you would relax under through the gap and then you would extend and stretch the life force through that person's center of mass, through their tension, through their balance, and you give them a balance. And you would create a pattern. So there would be a process: a step one, two three, four, five, six, and seven that would have been taking place to balance the person.

Once you have that pattern – that repetitive loop – you would run the energy through that loop with less and less intention, but you would still be getting the same result. And then you anchor that loop to a particular ritual. For example, the ritual might be to have a push gesture of your tai chi form, where you put your hands on someone, drop your hip, stretch your spine, and open up the energy. That would be the ritual for producing this rebounding force energy. Every time that you touch someone – drop into them, stretch into their spine – you activate the ritual. The energy cycles through the vertical circles, they lose their balance, energy flows through the gap, there is a pulse and you give the person their balance. It is removed of your intent – you simply do the movement, the energy moves and they balance. With this type of ritual you build it up through repetition until the energy pattern does not require intent anymore – it just requires you to push the button to activate the ritual for that particular issue all to take effect. So it has to be built, repeated, manifested, and brought into reality, before you start to hit that button. If you have not charged into the four bodies correctly – etherically, astrally, mentally, and physically – then it is simply not going to work. We want to look at the metaphysical rules which are in place for it to work. We use those rules to make it work and then release the intent of making it work into the ritual.

Gestures are similar to rituals, but we mostly use gestures for controlling our internal states. If we place a hand on our body with the pinky on the bottom and our thumb on the top, let us place it on our chest. The pinky, we connect that to the base chakra and that is the Earth element. And then the next finger – the ring finger – is the Water element, connect that to the navel chakra; the middle finger connects the solar plexus and that is the Fire finger; index finger is the Air element, the heart, and the thumb is the Akasha. So we have this vibrational scale from the bottom to the top, the small thing into the sum that matches our chakra system. These are element relationships to the fingers. Let us say, if you wanted to build the Fire element, you place your thumb on your Fire element finger, do Akasha breath and then do the Fire element breath, and draw the Fire element from the Akasha while holding that gesture, and pull that in. You can make slight adjustments to the gesture by rotating your thumb and finger around each other to different angles, in order to produce different effects. If you wanted to make yourself feel happy and joyful, you would breathe the elements in, pull your mind in a happy joyful state and then hit the ritual when you are at the peak of that feeling of joy, and then repeat that process over and over and then remove the intent of building the energy and hit the ritual and feel a smile coming your face – feel a sense of bliss and joy overwhelm your body. This becomes very handy for when you encounter a state of sadness and you need to switch it to a state of joy – you get your ritual and your physiology changes state instantly. It is also very convenient for activating things like clairvoyance, clairaudience and various intuitive skills, where you activate the ritual for that skill to awaken and then you reverse the ritual for that skill to close.

The reason that we do not want to have these skills open all the time is because it is a risk to our mental health. It is not good to hear, feel or see the spiritual world all the time – there is a time and a place for these skills to be active. We want to completely control when those skills are awake, when they are working and when they are not. This allows us to maintain groundedness. Groundedness allows for good health, it allows you to function in the physical world. It allows you keep a separation between the physical and spiritual worlds when you need to function in the physical. If you open these doors up too much, you will not be able to properly function in the spiritual or in the physical world when your mind is in the spiritual-astral world at the same time – they do not cross over very well. As an example, you may open up Akashic trance while you are walking down the street, you will suddenly stop and you may be there standing in that posture for several minutes, several hours, dwelling in the Akasha, and then you come back to your physical body or snap out of it and continue walking as if nothing happens. Now that may not be socially acceptable in a lot of societies. Perhaps in India it would be acceptable for someone simply to stop where they are standing and practice, but in Western society it is not. So you need to consider when you open and close these skills and what rituals, gestures and so forth you use for those particular skills to function.

Step Five

When you are working with spiritual entities you can use a pendulum – a type of wand, which is basically just a handle with a wire on it and a small weight on the end, a wrapper, a small crystal and so forth on the end of the wire – and hold the handle. So you have a handle, a wire extending out, and a crystal. That tip of the crystal is bouncing around, it is moving left-right, up-down, circles, just by micro-movements of moving the handle. This type of pendulum allows you to get yes-no answers easily without any muscle intervention. You will notice with the pendulum, even when you try to hold the pendulum still, that it is very easy for muscle intervention to control the pendulum using the handle, the wires, the small crystal on the end – you will notice that it is far easier to separate your intent from the movement. Simply allow your body consciousness to communicate with you. This method works very well for connecting to body consciousness and also opening up your matrices and allowing spirit to work through your hand and give you answers to various questions.

Remember that the spiritual world just above the physical knows nothing more about reality than you do. The adjacent spirit worlds are not filled with supernatural answers to questions that may be on your mind. They have a slightly different view of the physical world because there is more overlap in the spiritual and physical worlds, but for the most part they are just as ignorant as normal people. So they are not the people you want to go to for higher spiritual answers – you want to go to higher spiritual beings to get higher spiritual answers.

When you are working with the realms of nature, it is more of an equalization process, learning about the construction of things, how things are built, and the intelligences that exist in the realm, and what level these intelligences are at. You do not go to a tree or to a low level spirit to find out about the ultimate reality – you go to an Akashic being or high level deity to understand that. So when you are starting off working with spirits, whether using a pendulum or wand as I just described to connect and communicate with them, get good at the process of communication, but do not worry too much about what the questions and answers are – they will come later. You will be working with much higher level spiritual consciousness, much higher level deities, and they are the ones you look to for guidance and advice about your learning process.

When you vital breathe into your hands, you will find that there is a certain accumulation of vital energy where your bones float. We call it floating the bones because the life force accumulates to a point where there is an electromagnetic charge in the life force. It makes your hands feel like they are empty in light and floating in a fluid. When you get to this point where the bones are floating through, let us say, building the ball exercise, then you simply put your hands on the table and breathe into your hands. Begin charging them up with energy and then lift your mental hand an inch above your physical, and then pull the astral hand an inch above your physical, and feel the magnetic connection between your astral and physical hand. There is a pulling on your physical hand – it is like a magnet wanting to lift your hand up. We start from the tips of the fingers and float the mental-astral up after we have learnt how to float the bones, and then your finger will just start to float by itself. Then you extend that to your whole hand, hinging off the wrist, and then your arm, hinging off the elbow, and the whole arm, hinging off the shoulder. You will find that by floating the bones and then moving the mental body up, the astral body becomes sensitive to the electromagnetic connection between the astral and physical bodies. Then float the bones to the point where that electromagnetic connection becomes stronger than gravity, and you can float your arm up.

By doing this and then taking that skill and transferring it back into the use of a pendulum or the wire handle wand, you will find that you will be able to bring spiritual beings into your hand very easily and then ask them questions – they answer through your wand or through your pendulum. It gets much easier. Of course if you continue with the same process, applying this to the whole body, you would have one of the keys to levitation, where you float the bones and create a strong enough electromagnetic charge inside your body while sliding the bones so that your astral matrix exceeds gravity. When you move your mental-astral body up above your physical, that magnetic pull will lift your physical body up if that charge is stronger than gravity. So it is increasing the energies up to that point to create that type of effect.

There is a concept of the guardian angel and your inner genius. These are two separate entities. Your guardian angel is a consciousness that is connected into your family circle. In the same way that you have a physical family, you also have a spiritual family, and your spiritual family has individual entities, deities, guardians, doorkeepers, or guides as some people call them, that are there to spiritually support you. If any of these particular beings have reached a point where they have connected to their divine light, they present themselves like a guardian angel – there is this consciousness within them that is strong enough to present their inner light to you. This may act as an external consciousness which reflects information to you, or it may interact as a conscience that exists within your own awareness. Out of pure spirit divine light is the highest part of your spiritual being that people normally have access to. So it could be your own guardian angel as the essence of you, or it could be one of the doorkeepers or spiritual guides within your family circle. It could be something outside of yourself that is a guardian angel, or it could be your higher part of you which is your guardian angel. Depending on the interpretation or labelling, it can go either way.

You will notice that there is a big difference in vibration between the essence of your spirit, the angelic part of your being, the divine light, and an externalized divine light, a guardian angel. One is like it is within your own inner voice, and the other is a voice talking to you; one is more internalized and one is more externalized. You will get to know the difference between your spiritual family and your spirit.

Most people never connect to the higher part of their spirit. The closest they come to connecting to their spirit is when they experience extreme stress, which pulls their spirit into the body – when their life is threatened, the spirit comes to the fore. If you jump into a pond of cold water, your spirit gets pulled into the body and you become very self-aware, when that reptilian brain starts activating all that chemistry. So this is a very easy way to connect your spirit into an activity – but it is also a very superficial way. We need to use these methods of cold water and train to pull the spirit in and then do the mental, astral and physical training exercises to allow that spirit to come into a much more refined state and take control of three bodies: how you think, feel and act.

When you are working with ghosts, deceased beings, it is important that you have reached the point where you are cultivating light, astral light. This astral light is very helpful for lost spirits, deceased beings and ghosts. When you encounter them, you automatically generate an environment of low pressure. So you enter into prayer for the entity you are connecting with, and this makes them comfortable and makes them feel safe – then you surround them with the prayer. If you have done Akasha work, you draw an Akashic circle around them. If you are working with various forms of divine light, you draw a circle of life around them. Whatever your highest is, you draw it in a circle around, either them and yourself, or around the being that you are connecting to. Once you have drawn that circle around them and they have connected to your highest, then you make a prayer to this particular spirit and move up into light. If you were with any deities and spiritual beings, they fully understand this process and will engage with this particular spirit, hold its hand, and move it off into the light. If it is an angelic being, it will wrap its wings around the entity and dissolve it up into light. If it is a being from a religious order, it will act in accordance with the religion and connect to that particular ghost or spirit in the way it is familiar with and then move it up into that light and resolve into that light.

In this process you are demagnetizing using the Akasha; demagnetizing the static or the trauma which prevents the being from moving into its reincarnation process – the thing that made it a ghost and made it lost was some type of traumatic action. You are dissolving that energy with Akasha and releasing it, which automatically allows the spirit to continue along its incarnation process and move up the vibrational scale to where it is meant to be. This is very natural; there is nothing contrived about it. You just draw the Akasha around the ground, around the spirit, relaxing, and release. It gives you control, it has no ability to move, it has no ability to move anywhere because you have demagnetized its mental matrix. Its will to control it's own life and environment is now yours. You essentially own its ability to move by drawing Akasha around it. As it demagnetized the trauma that prevented that being from moving on you can simply make a prayer for that moving on process, and if you are connected to any particular realm system, beings of that system will be there as soon as you activate this process and help that spirit along.

You may prefer to work within the spiritual hierarchy of the individual. So if they are Christian, bring in a Christian spirit from the sun sphere – such as an angelic being – invoke it, wrap it around the person, make them feel an extreme level of love, and then move that spirit into that Christian light realm via that angelic being. Use whatever method is most comfortable for you, but really understand the metaphysical rules upon which it is working, such as why the Akashic circle is there in the first place.

Step Six: Creating Elementals from Universal Light, from Akasha or the Four Elements

Now select the skill that you want to develop – perhaps clairvoyance or anything like that – remembering that once you are in the light, you are going to invoke light with that skill that you are working on and bring it down to the elemental. Once you bring it down to the elemental, you have to bring that elemental to life. So, when we bring it to life, you want to be having an orgasm, basically – you are giving a part of your spirit to bring something to life. For example, When you look at what happens when a male ejaculates, their spirit, their mental body, puts its essence into the sperm to generate life. In our case, we are not using sperm or ovaries to generate life, we are taking the spirit and giving a jolt to put that energy into the elemental – that gives it a tangible life form. Some magicians, when building elementals, use ecstatic screams to bang the energy in, but it needs to be a very strong jolt in your field, like an Akashic volt.

As you bring that light down, let us say that I want to put consciousness into the space between my hands: I will invoke, bring the spirit in, and then reinforce that with my will and then with the consciousness in that space between my hands. So you have to use a high intensity of your spirit, of life, and have Akasha to bring it in and jolt it into physical reality. Now that energy is much more visual, you can see it a lot more clearly because it is spirit, it has consciousness in it, and if you vital breathe into the elemental, volt it, release it, stop paying attention to it so the elemental starts breaking apart and doing its – the piece is separated because you have given consciousness to the elemental, it pulls together and it has form, function, and it wants to now do its thing.

When you are invoking that spiritual essence, you want to be pulling it from the light in your spirit and then jolt it into the energy to give it life. You will want to learn how to do it quickly so that you can build your elementals for short tasks and so forth. They are very good for skills development. So when you bring the elemental to support your developmental skill – for example clairvoyance – the elemental will absorb into your body and start dissolving your belief structures about clairvoyance, remove resistance, and create a pathway for that clairvoyant energy to build. Where normally our subconscious mind has so much lack of belief, programming, and things in the way, that when we want to train clairvoyance we cannot let the frequency come pass through us, because the subconscious mind is saying that it does not believe in that – it is resisting. So the elemental gets in and dissolves this resistance. It seems really magical when you build an elemental and it does something, but all it is doing is reorganizing the qualitative patterns of the energy belief structures. The information is getting reorganized, and you know how fast this reorganizing of information is in a computer – when you press the delete button, a bunch of files are automatically gone. The elemental comes into your subconscious and deletes all resistance towards that skill and it just seems like magic. It is like, "Wow, clairvoyance is there now." But it is actually a very simple thing, you just press the delete button. They can come and reorganize information in your subconscious much better than you can, because you cannot be conscious in your subconscious. If you drop your subconscious your will is neutralized and that is what allows you to be there – that is why you cannot influence yourself. So we have this problem. We need someone else or an elemental being to come and affect your subconscious in the way that you want it to. Elemental beings are extremely good for that type of work. So you can build an elemental in a few minutes to deal with a problem that you have got right now. You could say that you are going to work with an energy but cannot get it up and develop that ability by yourself, so then you will bring the elemental to do it for you. It can work in the background and slip through the subconscious to repattern the mind.

This skill development has a lot to do with information reformatting. It reformats the information in your subconscious. For me it is one of the better functions of the elemental because it is so quick and easy, and the results are dramatic. Your form is going to be freer, your function is whatever you have chosen – we will choose clairvoyance for this particular example. The name of the elemental should be something that's in resonance with clairvoyance and with the lifespan. The process: we are going to raise ourselves up into the light, we are going to scribe, write down the shape, I draw the shape, draw it to the sphere, and then write down the function within all that. So you are scribing those qualities and the lifespan, the duration of the sit, and the name that you have chosen.

Once you have written down the light and you invoke the energy down, feel the ball and put all those conditions pre-set, then you put your spirit into it and into life at the end. Sometimes I will build the shape first, go through the vital, get all the elements, build it all up, and then once we have it built and it is tangible, they will be open to light. Bring the light down and complete it. Other times I go to the light first – it will depend on what it is for, the synchronicity and how much freedom I want to give it. If I build something to do something that is very physical outside of the white light, outside of the rules, and it is maybe something to satisfy my ego, then I will not use light, because I know it is not going to work because it is to satisfy my ego. It is something that is a bit more physical. Then I will build everything using base elements, put spirit into it, get it to do what I want it to do, and it will have the freedom to do that.

White light tends to keep everything connected to your crown chakra, regulated by your spiritual circle, your spiritual family, and it is all for the greater good, for evolution and so forth. Sometimes you might want to do things outside of that. If you want to do something that goes straight to the raw elements – say you are going to use natural spirits – you have got to charge those spirits with more energy, if you get into shamanism, nature magic and such. I do not suggest you do too much on that level, but you will work with it enough to understand it because your center of gravity will get pulled to those levels and centered there, if you do too much of one thing. If you are centering your practice within universal light, the center of gravity of the spirit, there is the center of gravity of your thinking process, it is the origin of your impetus and everything is taken care of and protected. If you start working with nature magic a lot, then you get so grounded in it, it controls you and the laws of rhythm are very extreme. In nature magic, you have things like cyclones, earthquakes, volcanoes, and all types of stuff happening that is affecting you. The rhythms in the universal light are very subtle and you are going to get that happening. When you connect to nature magic, the rhythms of nature connect to you and your astral field will go through huge upwards and downwards moves. That is why I minimize nature magic practice – it is a peripheral skill set, not a central skill set.

So, do a couple of Akasha breaths, raise open the light, open the crown, float up to the universal light, and feel in that light, feel those four qualities: shape, function, name, and lifespan. Engrave them into your light body and the universal light. Clearly scribe that intent into the light; invite that light down through you into the ball as it passes through your crown, through your mental bodies, through your astral, through your physical, into the sphere between your hands. Allow to be that size of a basketball. Use a bit of Akasha to increase the stream of light and as it is holding the purpose you've given. You can feel the shape of the sphere between the hands with your mind's eye – feel that shape, see that shape, invoke its function, feel its function, and press it between the hands, feel the shape, feel the quality, and then stretch into your willpower. Really connect it into the spirit, then use your Akasha breaths to give the jolt of life into the sphere, into the element. Hold that will intent there. Breathe with the elemental. Expand it. Give that breath of life into it. Now do the vital breath into that light sphere. Hold a very strong concentration of vital force. Your spiritual, astral and physical body is being nourished through vital breathing. Your physical body is the life force; feel the physical, astral and mental all connecting. Whatever the function of that elemental is or the skills that you chose, release the elemental off to the side. When you have a few of these elementals happening, they just tend to hover around your crown chakra and spin around the top of your head.

I have several crystal balls which I use as energy reservoirs. I have got a large one about seven inches in diameter, and then I just gather the elementals in the crystal ball, and then do Kabbalistic letters, sounds, into the balls and charge it up, and that is their energy reservoir. That is where they take your energy from. I have got like a black charcoal type of carbon crystal ball specifically for Akasha; then I got a very clear crystal ball for specific types of white light frequencies that is purely for raising the frequency, and then a universal ball for doing the universal functions. The elementals will just go into those balls and they will nourish themselves. You charge it at least once a week, with reasonably heavy charge.

You can charge the balls at the same time. Sometimes I will put the big ball in the center and the small ones on the side. I keep one in my room, so I am charging one on the room, it protects the field of consciousness while I sleep, so that my dreams go into a learning state while I sleep and I would go into any lucid type dreams that are not distracting. It depends on what functions you want. I used to connect them to amulets and put that amulet on, put an elemental skill into the amulet, connected into the body and it would support the subconscious, while the mind is focused on the skill. Those two balance each other out, you get instant success with your skill, because they have the subconscious charge supporting what you are consciously want to do. This is our biggest resistor to skills development: that we subconsciously do not believe we can do it. When we have a little bit of success we go in our head, "Ah, this is how good I am. I'm 10% there. I'm 20% there." The elemental comes in and goes, "No, you are 100% there." As soon as it tells us subconsciously and generates that emanation in the field, you consciously engage it, you can do the skill. This is why an elemental is so handy. You may want to build an elemental for every single exercise in the initiation text.

This particular elemental we have built, you want to do a sit with it, invite it into your subconscious – if it was clairvoyance, bring clairvoyant light through your pineal gland, radiate it through the field. Come to light, and let that saturate in your subconscious and get a feel for when your subconscious mind is in complete resonance with the skill – how different that skill presents itself – and then feel it, raise up the light, bring the light down in relation to the skill you want to work on, with energy behind in the subconscious that there is much more stable quietude behind you, behind the intent. So, build your subconscious and the conscious mind here, this quietude will support what you all do with the mind, it concentrates the mind. Maybe there will be a lot less static, a lot less 'monkey mind' – the energy is much more directed in the place where you will want it to be.

If that was not the case, then you have to strengthen the amount of energy within the elemental, until it can stay in control of your subconscious mind, dissolve the 'monkey mind' and accumulate and get you focused on the skill.

Kabbalistic Creation of Elementals
The next elemental we can build is something that every magician needs – it is a type of protection. Everyone has a yearning for justice; justice is a very important thing. When you are seeing negativity – seeing bad things happen around you, and bad people getting away with bad things – sometimes you want to do something about it, but in the physical realm you are not a police officer or a court judge. You are not always in power to distribute justice in the physical realm, but you are always in power to facilitate justice using the universal laws. There is a Kabbalah formula that could do that. First is the letter 'E', it is an Akashic frequency – it regulates the time continuum of an event, person, karmic field, or energy. It controls time. And then the letter 'O', it is a frequency of justice, of 'balancing the books'. We have time and we have balance, and if you apply this formula to a positive person, it will be really handy. They are just going to have incredible success and you amplify that with the intent of "May this person be happy and healthy," and you run that formula through them, and their life will smooth out and they will get what they deserve – they get good lessons, good things happening to them.

If you apply this to a very negative person – someone who is doing harm to others – they have this reservoir of negative karma and you release time from the reservoir and the justice frequency starts to manifest itself. The book starts getting balanced up, it hits them like a truck, literally – they will go on the street, bang! They'll get their karma balanced. It is just a rebalancing of energy. Sometimes it can be very subtle, sometimes – if you add a letter S onto it – they see their karma. It is more of a visual showing that they have to change what they are doing otherwise they will end up with bad repercussions. So if it is someone that you want to get to understand their own karma, if it is someone you care about and they have gone down the wrong road, we have the letter 'S' and you put the learning quality into it, they see the error in their ways. With the 'E' and the 'O' it just balances the book. They do not see it happening, it just goes up, bang, and the karma hits them in a good or bad way. Their own karma ultimately decides. You can opt for the negative karma to balance itself or you can just encapsulate them in a bubble of energy and let the universe decide. Time releases, the energy condenses in the present moment, they will experience their own karma. When that happens, it may just catch them or it may build up and they start to feel the experience and think. It might pull them into a hellhole, because that is what they are giving other people. If they are putting people in a very traumatic state through their behaviors, they will get sucked into that trauma and – depending on the way that you saturate that in – they can get stuck in a living hell for the rest of their lives.

This balancing of karmic justice is really subject to how you deliver that energy to the person, how you saturate it in them, and your underlying intent inside of it.

All that you are doing is allowing them to experience themselves. You are putting a mirror in front of them, around them. Anything that stands out, they immediately experience themselves. They are put in a bubble where there is a mirror. In this mirror, they are thinking about the experience, they are feeling the experience of causation with it, their actions experience causation. It is a one-way mirror, nothing gets out. But energy comes in. Their own karma seeps back in. So it is a very fast way for bad people to see their own doing. Your ego is going to start twisting this and adding stuff to it if you have been negatively impacted by that person. You have got to keep it as universal as possible if you are going to apply this type of work. Being neutral, when you see negativity, it can be somewhat challenging to remain neutral. You may want to add stuff to it. Be warned, if you add anything to it, then you are generating karma for yourself. You are doing things in your own field of consciousness. When you have been working with Akasha for a few years, your spirit sense will feel how karma is constantly seeking to balance itself –that energy builds and it goes past the neutral and it wants to come back to neutral. If it goes the other way and then it goes again to neutral. There is a universal magnet that is constantly balancing the book – it is always wanting to find harmony and justice and balance within all things.

So, that quality that underlies the Akasha, once you feel that quality, it becomes easy to apply this formula and connect it to a person and balance the books. Now, let us say that someone has a really good heart and they are doing a lot of good work. They are a really nice person – but their meit in this lifetime has not manifested yet. You can get some good karma and invest in their life using this "E-O" kabbalah formula. You connect to it, release time to it, and you do the justice formula. Everything will just go well for that person. Karma in the Akasha can take many life cycles to manifest. It is not something that you experience right away, Akasha is not subject to – it has a rhythm of millions of years. The energy goes and the energy comes back, it sticks to the mind substance of the source. They will come back very slowly. We can take that karma and release time and it may come back quicker.

Generally we only do this so that a person sees the errors of their ways. When you work with Akasha, that will start happening to you automatically. You will see causation, how you think, feel and act. You will know when to be more careful, how you think, how you feel, what you teach, what your actions are, and so forth. You will get a sensitivity to the outcomes just by going into Akasha every day. When you enter that stillness and hold yourself there for 30 minutes to an hour a day, your perceptions will change. All your filters will change frequency and the way that you see how you are doing things changes. Sometimes you see yourself doing stuff and your ego is the one doing it. A part of you sees the outcome and you decide that you are going to do it anyway – like when you know the coffee is bad and you are just going to drink it, you just ignore it. Another time you feel, you become in resonance with it and you will think to stop drinking coffee or whatever the situation is. It could be much more dramatic than that, of course. You have these levels of consciousness, intuitions, speaking to you – how much resonance you bring into your consciousness and intuition is up to you. Those voices are feelings, they are intuitive insights and they get stronger and stronger with Akasha. This becomes your delivery method when you want to deliver justice or rebalance and allow justice to present itself.

When you put the 'S' on the end of the formula and you build it into an elemental, you see the causation of what is going to happen before you deliver it – you can just step out of the way completely. You see a negative person hurting someone you love, you put a bubble around that person, feel your karma, cut them from the person you love, and let that person fall out of their life. It is very handy, as you do not want to see the people you love getting hurt. You have got to look at what are your options and how can you stop their behavior from happening and prevent harm to people you care about. The way that you build this elemental is what we are going to work on. Once the elemental is built, you will use the same blueprint every time. You just put the elemental over that person and when it goes and captures that person, it surrounds them, the karma starts manifesting, it will repeat the pattern. It is pre-built in the Akasha, it will release time, go into the roots of that person's karma, suck it through the Akasha, through their mental-physical body, and they will start feeling exactly what they have been giving. They will get sucked into their own reality. As long as you hold the elemental on that person, it will keep happening. Your elemental might be called balance and you direct the elemental out for personal justice. You connect the elemental through somebody who is injuring someone you love in particular.

You have to be careful as you do not want to invoke an elemental onto a person out of anger. I made a mistake about six years ago doing that. I was driving on the highway with my partner. A drunk driver knocked me off the road and I swerved with it and got pushed off and invoked ritual and put the elemental onto the person and three months later – I just forgot about it – a few months later I had a heart seizure, my whole body got paralyzed, I laid out, body shaking, I left my body, and then I watched this guy in the hospital dying of a heart attack. He drew his last breath and died and then I thought: "Why am I still connected to this guy? What's going on? It should've just balanced itself," and then he died in the hospital room. I pulled the elemental off him, as I forgot that I had put it there, and then stepped back and pulled it back to my body, I almost had a heart attack, the same way he was. My body was experiencing his death because I sent the elemental to that person while personally identifying with hate. When I came back to my own body, I pulled the elemental off and then had to go through a healing process, as this physiology was stuck to me. I had to remove all that energy, all that damage and karma because I used anger to summon the elemental onto the person around and balanced it to some of the elemental. So, when you use an elemental like this, it is easy to get wrapped up in emotions and for the elemental sticks to someone. It starts affecting your mind – it is connecting to your energy field, if there is any emotional link. Because I was really angry when I sent the elemental after that person, it stuck into him and manifested in me as well. That particular elemental was not created using this method – it's just a Akasha spirit from one of my past incarnations that stays around.

When you work with elementals, if you have any emotional connection to invoking something you have to be careful, because that emotional connection is going to reflect back into you and you can hurt yourself. That person's karma will be linked to you, so you have got to be very neutral, very much in an equanimity state, and totally disconnected from that karmic situation – you do not want their negative karma manifesting in your life. It isn't something that you do lightly, it's something that is considered as a serious situation: you have to protect them from someone or a situation and you need strategies to do that – you need methods to protect yourself and your loved ones.

With this particular letter 'E' – we are going to get through the letter 'E' first – this is to regulate time. It is not about karma, it is about your time perception. The letter 'E' allows you to investigate the astral plane, it allows you to investigate the energy underneath things, release your mental body into the universal consciousness, and get a universal perspective on things. Letter 'E' is a type of Akasha that opens up the spirit senses and allows you to see things very differently. Its function is built around invoking karma, but it is a skill you need for the next letter to invoke karma.

You want to have an elemental on hand for emergencies. Where you need some support and you invoke the spirit, you invoke the elemental, you do what you need to do very quickly. You need to draw the energy in, when you need it, with a snap of your fingers. You attach ritual to it.

You know how heavy metal people do the horns gesture where they put their hand above their crown and then make devil's horns out of their fingers, that is a demonic ritual for invoking a demon. If you do that inside of Akashic beings that are demons, then they will balance the book. There are demonic beings who will see that gesture as a karmic imbalance that needs to be balanced, when the demon shows up inside that person, the demonic beings will think that the karma is balanced, and they'll go back home. When you see that hand ritual of the devil's horn, and people do that same gesture, they are invoking their own negative karma and make their lives miserable. They do not even know it, but you now know. They may be within an environment, like a nightclub or a concert where they can easily come through and mess with their host straight away. It is almost funny when you look at someone who grabs a hammer and hits one finger, and does it to the other fingers. You will find that when you are invoking Akasha beings then one's karma is being balanced with these spirits. We are not going participate this way with such beings. They will tend to have gestures related to that shape. The finger, thumb positions in their gesture will relate to a demon and how that entity does things and what their function is. So the negative beings just work around that shape and those beings will give you the signature – if you ever get into that type of stuff. But you may need many years of Akasha work to be immune to akashic beings. You need to get into the Akasha of the sun sphere to get immune to the sun sphere before you are immune to these beings. Franz Bardon's second book *The Practice of Magical Evocation* takes you through the spheres. The book is not about talking to a spirit to get information or to have the spirit physically present itself - it is about generating immunity. You get immunity to these spheres and the beings of those spheres, you are immune to them – immunity is what you are after. When you get immune to the Akasha radiation of the sun, then the beings cannot touch you, because they are regulated by that energy. And then the rest of the spheres become easy. You blend together the Akasha work and the sun work and it will allow you to work with any energy in the solar system comfortably and safely. You do not have to worry about injuring yourself so long as you have mindfulness within your rhythms, so you do not get caught on a negative rhythm.

Elementals are very handy for that protection. Your astral ego is subject to rhythm. You are going to do very high level stuff, and then you are going to get to that high and your rhythm is taking you up and down. If your will is always on a high, there is less of a fall on the low. If you are highly polarised by travelling the saintly path within your astral nature, then it is safe. But if you are travelling the worldly path and you are doing high level light and Akasha work, that energy lets you go and you drop. You can drop into a lot of bad and crazy stuff. It only takes one bad astral trip and the rest of one's life cycle is done. The physical brain and the mental-astral matrix can burn out and you are physically risking your life. It can happen a lot of times. These very high level magical practitioners make one mistake and the rest of their lives are done. Their brains dysfunctional, their mental-astral matrices are burned. So you have got to be careful working with this type of high energy.

Elementals act as a safety net. When you work through a negative behavior, the elementals will not let it pass. The elementals will polarise that force wanting to go and let negative behaviour in your life, to create a bounce back up from the negativity. The strongest safety net to bounce back up from negativity are your precepts. Your precepts of "thou shalt not lie, thou shalt not cheat, thou shall only be in alignment with the truth," becomes the resonance of truth. Precepts remain sacred. Your fundamental precepts act as an unconscious safety net so you cannot fall below a certain level. Precepts can catch you and balance you back. If you do not have a code of living built into your psyche, you do not have a safety net and then that rudimentary swing when working with powerful energies can become detrimental.

Working with any of these forces, the biggest challenge is the effect of rhythm, as it can make you rhythmically swing if a part of you allows it. Does it make you grumpy, angry, sad, or depressed – all these negative things that come in as a counterforce towards the very high frequency? You have got to note it straight away, look at the elemental that is out of balance, dissolve it, and you may use elementals to support that. So, in the background, they are making you balanced. They will sense an energy coming into your field of consciousness before you do and they will buffer it for you. Elementals are extremely handy for practice, cause they can do some of the stuff that you will feel when it is too late. They will be fully aware of it before it happens and will buffer it for you. It is happening out of your will because you built the elemental to do those functions, so that is a part of you that is doing it –it is just an unconscious part of you and that makes the whole path easy. Anything that you feel that you cannot do and will fail on, it can be fixed. Because you can do it, you will succeed with it. You just build the elemental to buffer and change that rhythm of that belief structure – change that programming – and then you can be successful in that level.

For elementals, you want to start with the qualitative key for what you're building. When you put an elemental in your subconscious to dissolve a negative belief and reinforce a positive belief, you feel that you can affect the subconscious mind. This means that you can affect the subconscious of anyone that you are in contact with, because you can do it to yourself. That same elemental can stick to another person and remove their belief about poverty and wealth and then make them wealthy, because that is just a belief. If you dissolve that and they change frequency, you reformat the information. Changing information is exceptionally easy and you do not need a power to do that. It is actually the opposite: you need to have a connection to the Akasha and recognise how the information is written in people's subconscious minds and work with that. So it is not a power, you need quality-release skills. Even if you put a lot of quantitative power into it, it can sometimes fail at rewriting information because you try to overwhelm the system – but you do not want to overwhelm the system, you want to pull everything apart and then it will reorganise itself.

The difference between the Akasha breathing that we normally do and the letter 'E' is that the normal Akasha that we work with is a very broad spectrum of emptiness – it has got everything inside it – whereas letter 'E' is a very specific type of Akasha: it pulls things apart and allows you to see the framework of how things were built and it gets to the universal view of whatever you are looking at. Normal Akasha does not do that. So, if you take an example of normal Akasha breathing, you enter the stillness, release time, release space, work with that infinity quality. Let us say if you take a rock and the rock weighs one kilogram, you have got a negative one kilogram vacuum underneath the rock. That vacuum is a type of limited Akasha that allows the particles to vibrate into matter. When you are holding that rock, that negative one kilogram vacuum matches the form of the rock. So you have one kilogram density of form and you have one kilogram underneath it. The rock's Akashic substance will reflect the rock and allow the vibration to come in and out for it to exist and be a form. That will naturally come out of the Akasha and be there to accommodate the rock, and so forth.

That dependence between the two forms cannot exist without Akasha and Akasha cannot exist without the form. They constantly seek to reflect each other all the time. As soon as the universe reaches its neutral state through Akasha, it is generating form straight away again – then it will rise and it will pull back. So, everything is coming in and out of Akasha all the time and it is just built that way. So there is no stagnation, there is no point where things stop. Let us say you do samadhi, you concentrate on an object, and everything becomes still. You are building concentration power that is in a mental form. You automatically started to accumulate Akasha, that is why you feel the stillness when you accumulate concentration. That stillness accumulates in the background. So when you have 10 minutes of samadhi, now you have 10 minutes of Akasha which should arise as a side effect, as universal law predicates, if you accumulate that concentration. That Akasha arisen under the concentrated mind is a totally different type of Akasha to the Akasha under the rock. The Akasha under the rock is limited, while the mind substance of the universe is unlimited. So we get what was called unlimited Akasha that starts accumulating underneath the mind. That is when the mind starts developing natural skills, because the concentration gets stronger, as does the Akasha underneath, so you end up with a door that you can step through to enter into a metaphysical reality – to spiritual experiences.

When we do general Akasha breathing, we are breathing the Akasha that is similar to what is under the rock, we are breathing the Akasha that exists under the mind, so it has got this universal spectrum that fills the need of everything that exists. When you do the Kabbalistic letter 'E' it is a unique frequency of Akasha that serves a particular function: it generates types of understanding of universal law – how things pull apart, how things are created, and how they are brought back together – and there is a learning inside that type of Akasha. It is a unique spectrum of Akasha.

Akasha is not something that you can pin down easily or have labelled as easily as well. Talking about it is easy – you are just using very generalised metaphors to give the idea. When you are spending hundreds of hours working with it, it will make no sense to you whatsoever when you come back to your body. When you are inside of Akasha, it makes perfect sense. It is what it is, but as soon as you come back to the structure of your brain, your brain goes, "Huh?" There is no logical way that you can digest it. So to save yourself wasting decades of trying to figure it out – to label it, construct it and frame it – just don't bother. If you want to understand what Akasha is, go in, you will find it makes sense, and then come out, it does not make sense – and just be comfortable with that. The brain does not want to be uncomfortable, the brain is going to fight you all the way in wanting to understand it. The only thing that you will understand is the process. The process of floating down time and space, feathering off the edges of space and releasing space, engaging in that infinity quality and entering Akasha – just know the process of those three steps, as that is all that matters. Forget thinking about how you get there, what Akasha is, because it all consumes too much of your time for little-to-no results.

We start vital breathing in all of the body, check your structure, increase your vitality – you want a light and open stretched body. Whatever exercise you do, it is going to be at the expense of your physical body. You just want to stimulate more life force than normal and wake everything up. Get your spirit senses there, get your body senses there, synchronise the three bodies, enliven everything and come into a state of increased energy and sensitivity. As we breathe the astral feeling, use the three transformations so that you can drop straight into that slowness of the astral fluid – just slowing it down as it becomes thick and heavy. I want you to feel the energy of that, we are not feathering off the edges of mental space, just put it into your mind substance and relax into that empty space. And then relax the mental space, edges of the mind dissolve, and start to occupy a larger space. Visualise that violet color, breathe timelessness on the in-breath, spacelessness on the out-breath. Seam all those qualities together. Bring your body back, then a little bit forward, back and forth, in order to feel the gap between your physical body, the mind and the energy system. Gently fall into the feeling, move into that gap, move into that space. As that space gets bigger, breathe that violet energy in and breathe it out to increase the space between the bodies. While in this feeling, when it produces a sound you resonate with, spend a few minutes practicing how to make the sound of the letter 'E' – just keep tuning into the sound. Be comfortable practicing and tuning into it.

And now you do one breath where you produce the sound with the feeling, and then the second breath just calibrates the feeling. What does this do? It pulls things apart, allows you to sense, feel, see, and hear the way it is being constructed, the way they manifest, the way things come in and out of form, and how they connect to the universal laws. So I want you to take one breath, just to feel the Akasha fill the room and the spirit senses and know what you are doing. Then in the next breath, produce the sound. Take the sound and the feeling and you vibrate the sound and the feeling together. If it is too much sound, you will lose what 'E' is for and what 'E' is for is everything. Later when you have done this enough, you produce the sound and then the energy and the feeling opens the Akasha, opens the door to get to function coming out of the sound. So you have got to get these two qualities to fuse together so that they are locked. Once they are locked together, then the sound will produce the effect. You have got to get them to fuse. Pull the Akasha feelings, evaluate between your repetition, one breath feeling in, one breath out, one breath feeling in, one breath out. This will give you the time to know what you are doing and how you are fusing it together. We do not need to work in sync, so sound is always happening in the room, and it will always be one, two or three people producing the sound, while another part of the group is tuned in to feeling, so the sound never stops.

If there is a statue, an image of a deity for your practice space, always take the Akasha into the room and just sweep it and draw the strength of the deity image and allow the energy to accumulate vacuum inside that. Pull the Akasha into the image and magnetise it. This gives you a strong connection to that deity.

On Larvae and Phantoms

Every thought you have that engages your astral body, the life force of your vital field integrates with the thought, the idea of the mental body mixes into the astral, and generates a personality. This personality has a survival instinct, if you repeat the same thoughts and act upon them to generate an astral substance. These astral substances form who you are as an identity. Some of these astral substances kind of break out of your identity and individualize themselves and develop their own survival instinct. So these larvae that have formed, they are not serving or helping you – they are using you, essentially. Things like addiction to porn, alcohol or drugs – anything that disempowers you, reduces the will, the astral electromagnetic power or the vitality, this is their reducing – the larvae are feeding off that energy, taking it away from you.

To dissolve these larvae we use the same process in which it was created to 'un-create' it. We pull the mental, astral and physical parts away from each other in order to separate them. So the mental-astral matrix needs to be redissolved in the larvae, so that these layers separate and then you can simply use Akasha to neutralize and dissolve. You recognize the Akasha of the larvae and then dissolve that Akasha and the larvae get dissolved into that Akasha. So, you essentially suck the larvae into emptiness and release them from yourself. This is the most efficient way to deal with larvae within yourself, as well as within other people.

There can be a karmic consequence of sucking larvae into the Akasha of someone else. You have to be very sensitive to it. You need to look at the person who you are doing this with, have their permission, that they are wishing this to be so, they want to transcend this particular weakness and they accept the karma of you dissolving larvae into the Akasha and making them disappear, essentially.

These larvae can potentially form into phantoms. Phantoms are a little bit more subtle. They have more intelligence and consciousness, they appear and disappear. These phantoms tend to be almost like very sneaky people – they are like very sneaky ghosts, yet they are not quite on the same level of evolution that a reincarnating person who descends into becoming a ghost is. They have worked from above the larvae level and they are allowed – they are able – to appear and disappear very quickly as a consciousness; they have an astral substance, but it is not as dense and heavy and stuck to a person like larvae.

Once the larvae move into a home – a host – they suck energy out of the host for as long as possible, until the host dies or the larvae die; whereas phantoms can feed off many different people, places and situations, and their survival instinct is not restricted to one person. Phantoms can be restricted to a place, or move around and feed on whatever they can. So compared to larvae, phantoms are more subtle, a bit smarter and more free-flowing – they can move between places and between people much more easily.

Having said that, larvae do accumulate in the astral plane and within different types of group consciousness. Let us say that there is a porn actress who has been in many movies. There will be astral larvae which will form around the group consciousness when people think of that particular actress, and those larvae will move in and out of different people who attach to her. The larvae still have a centre of gravity of their consciousness and what they are and how they function, but they can move between many people, connected by one person who stimulates them. Most likely this person was completely unconscious that the larvae even exist, but they can transfer a lot of power to that person, if that actress consciously sets it up in that way.

Step Seven

The practice of elementals was extensively covered in the previous physical step, so we will not be covering that in this step. Instead, we will jump into the magical animation of pictures, statues, objects, and so forth.

The magical animation of pictures is one of the topics in *Initiation into Hermetics*. The magic animation of pictures is a waste of time if approached selfishly. For what purpose are you going to animate a picture? We do not want to look at the mundane aspects, so we are going to look at the higher frequency aspects of this teaching.

Let us say that you have an image of a deity. It may be a statue or photograph – whichever it is, that image of the deity, we want to charge that image up and give the deity expression of its teachings through that particular image, so that anyone in the room or who looks at that particular image experiences this. If this is an image on the internet, you would have to charge it through the Akasha and mental space, so that the mind gets connected to the image and the astral frequency rises. and they would start to experience as emanations, astrally as a feeling. If it is a physical object, then it will regulate the frequency of the room that the object is in, whether it is a photograph or a statue. So first we connect up to the light, we go through the three transformations exercise, feel our vital field, slow it down, release time, and go to the astral body. We slow that down to the edge of the astral body to the mental. Release space as you move through the mental, then once we hit that feeling of infinity we move into the Akasha, breathe the Akasha into the crown chakra. Then we make a prayer for light and the prayer you could use is, "May the path of light guide and protect." Once you have invoked that prayer with a deep sense of humility, either light is then going to be pulled into you or you are going to get pulled into light, depending upon your mental matrix: if your mental matrix is loose you will float up to the light; if it is tight, light will pull down into you – because it depends where that reverence and that prayer is generating effect.

Either way, if it starts pulling down through you, you will begin to invite that light down through the three bodies and then fill your three bodies. Once your three bodies are full, the mental-astral matrix will soften and equalize and your mental body will rise up – or a layer of your mental body will rise up – through the crown and enter into the ocean of light. If you are already familiar with entering into the light, then when you start the activity, your mind will float up to that light straight away. This is because you have acquired the equalization of light between those three bodies first.

Once you are in that light, you move your awareness with a deep sense of reverence towards the deity that you wish to work with. Once you have decided who and what the deity is, you would have the statute and you have drawn the deity towards you, within that light, and you go on into the union with the deity inside the light. The deity obviously knows your plan of charging a statue or a picture of the deity itself, so you go into union – once you are in union and vibrationally matched to the deity, that light will start to stream through the three bodies and you move, project your hands towards the image or the statue, and begin charging it with light.

Of course you always ensure that you have washed your hands before and so forth. I like to pick up the image and feel the weight of it, so that the light manifests physically, because I am holding the physical object – I am holding mass and weight, and my fascia is measuring it, and the light is vibrating my physical body through the life force, and is physically impregnating it. If you do not pick the object up, it is going to be more astral and you might have physical density, because your physical fascia is not stretched and stimulated. That is why I like to work with heavy objects: heavy statues, big picture frames, and so forth. You can pick it up, feel it and you charge it; you can embrace it with the left hand and charge it with the right.

So once that light has started to come down, and you start to see the light radiating around the object, from there we move into the Akasha. The light has set the fundamental function, it is there to connect to deity, to connect the teachings, and that has all been decided. From there, you load it with Akasha and the light in the Akasha starts interacting, and this is the creative cycle of light and Akasha interacting to produce form. We move down the vibrational scale of light and Akasha interacting to the Air element and start charging with the Air element; then we bring it down the vibrational scale to the Fire element, charge with the Fire, then the Water, and then the Earth. So we are working it down that vibrational scale from the crown chakra.

As that charge increases – you are still physically touching and holding the object – the glow changes. Now you will start to see the different colors of the elements glowing and radiating out of the statute of the picture. Any particular function that you want to have – let us say that you want to have a quality of universal love emanate out of this statue – you will start tuning those elements to that particular emanation. Then anyone who takes refuge or bows in front of that statue will have a deep surge of universal love flow through them. You might choose to put it in place that normal people will not see the statue or nothing will happen if they do. But if someone bows to it, the Akasha, light hits their heart center, their lower energy raises to a higher, that feeling of a deep and profound sense of universal love, and they have a spiritual experience. This is because of the reverence and the respect they showed towards the image.

So, you may be putting these things in place, so that you do not waste energy, that energy is not going out – no 'pearls' are being laid before 'swine', but energy emanates to those who respect what they are receiving and are able to receive it and then show gratitude out of the respect after they have received it. Putting these types of protective methods into place allows a larger reservoir for those who are deserving of that particular type of energy.

Once you put those protections in place, you will continue with your charging process and break down into any patterns of how you want this love to affect people. These patterns are going to expand, open their three bodies, open their heart center, and clear negative energy out of their body. What do you want to do? Is it something which opens the Akasha and allows people to make a wish, maybe for their children to have better grades at school – it will reflect that wish through that child's etheric field and generate better grades; the child's etheric blueprint changes somewhat to a higher frequency of intellect. So, any built-in magical, alchemical methods, they are going to be implanted into it at this time. It is best when you are learning to develop these skill sets to work with simple functions: a feeling of love, a feeling of happiness, making people smile – keep it simple and then, as you start to see the effects take place, you can start looking at more complex patterns, more complex alchemical releases and so forth.

So when we are working with building complex patterns, you want to look at the way the roots come from the light and through the Akasha; the way they affect the mental substance, the mental plane of the place and the person. How does it bridge into the astral and how does it bridge in the physical and create change? The feeling of how energy radiates through the planes is the essence of power – it is the essence of magic. If those bridges are not connected between the spiritual world and the physical, nothing happens. It is more about the bridge than the power. Power cannot express itself without the bridge. So how you bridge energy across is the key to success. If you want someone to look at that image and bow to it and have a profound spiritual experience, you have to have built into it the bridges between mental and physical worlds, so that energy flows through.

My method for doing this involves pressure differentials. I would have a very large amount of energy into the image and if that person wants it – depending on their level of humility and reverence within them, the depth of their prayer towards the deity they are looking at – that pressure difference opens and energy surges through the three bodies. So it generates the three transformations type effect up and down at the same time. Basically it connects and synchronizes the bodies due to their reverence so that they can have access to that reservoir of energy. If a person does not have the reverence and respect for the energy, there is no pressure difference there in order for that vacuum to open itself up. So we have to set that in place so that you are not 'casting pearls before swine'.

We do not want to give magic to people who do not deserve it – only to those who are grateful and respectful of the magic they are getting. So you put this as a subconscious pattern, that this is required before anyone gets access to a profound experience. If they are too caught up in their ego, they are not going to get anything.

The next step with this is creating the physical space around the image. You need to keep that space clean. You need to keep it so that people cannot walk too close to it. If people are walking within a metre of that particular image, their life force and energy is going to have a slight demagnetizing effect on the image. If you can, put the image inside a hollow object, where the wind does not rush onto it. If you are putting it on an altar which has a window to the right or the left and wind passes straight over the altar, your altar is going to be demagnetized and the energy is missing out a lot. So you will have to put some sort of screen there, so that wind does not directly hit the image. Having incense or candles or something around the image is convenient for people to show respect for it, because it is built into so many cultures to light a candle or light a stick of incense to make a prayer. If that is not a part of your thinking, it is not necessary. But it may be necessary for people who have that way of thinking.

Depending on what culture you are applying this to and what the situation is, consider how you connect to the physical environment and how you set up the physical environment. Having a hollow space in a wall to house a Buddha statue is ideal because that hollow will collect energy in a thermal mass of the space, and there are less air currents there, so it can radiate and cultivate energy without disturbance. That works incredibly well.

Step Eight

On the topic of the magic mirror: I prefer to use a crystal ball rather than a magic mirror, just for simplicity and ease of use and it is easy to travel with. You can buy crystal balls almost anywhere these days at New Age shops or online.

For charging a crystal ball, you place your hands over the ball in the same way that you practice to build energy between the hands, building a ball, and start creating the life force, get your whole body tuned into the feeling of life force. You are tuning into the fascia, relaxing, hanging the muscles, opening the joints and floating the bones, getting into that life force field. Now, when you are floating the bones, you float the bones on the physical-vital level and you float the bones on the astral level – the only real difference is the slowing down of time and the type of tension that you have in the fascia. The astral tension is very soft, whereas the vital tension is more taut, but the feeling of the bones floating in the fluid is very similar – there is just a different tension level around it.

Put your hands over the ball and tune your whole body into vital force and start loading the balls with vital energy. How many breaths you choose to use is up to you. If you are limited on time, do nine breaths on vital and then move to the Earth element, nine breaths, and then Water, nine breaths, and then Fire, nine breaths, and then Air, nine breaths, Akasha for nine breaths, the light for nine breaths, and the prayer for nine breaths. If you have more time, then allow more repetitions for each level. As you are breathing those energies in, you have the underlying intent of the function of a crystal ball: here is a crystal ball for clairvoyant use and you are charging that ball with the quality of clairvoyance, and you invoke that quality of clairvoyance from above the crown chakra through prayer, and you pass it through the three bodies into the element that you are charging into the ball and you charge the element in – and you follow the same process.

If you have been working with invoking the Lords of the Elements, you bring the Lords of the Element in, with that particular quality as a prayer and pass that energy through the Lords of the Elements into the ball with that particular quality, with this clairvoyance or whatever the other function is. You may be using it for mental travel, for sending healing energy to people, or for other different types of magic operations – the list is endless. It is a very handy tool. But the fundamental idea of starting with vital force and opening up the life force, and splitting off in the elements, and then working with Akasha, light and prayer remains the same.

If you are using the crystal ball for clairvoyant work, then you are going to invoke clairvoyance from above the crown. Draw that down from the universal light into the ball through each element. It needs to be filtered through each element individually, so that it harmonises that clairvoyance – they will get full quadruple amount of functioning within your clairvoyant vision.

If you are using a mirror instead of a ball, you use the same fundamental idea except that you place your hands pointing towards the mirror and charge the mirror with energy. And you can follow Bardon's advice on making a magic mirror if you are manufacturing it yourself. When you are charging the energy by pointing your hands towards the mirror, it is a very different feeling to having the ball between your hands and condensing. It is far easier to condense into a sphere between your hands than it is to project into the mirror – condense it in the mirror – due to the pressure that you feel between your hands when you hold a ball. So you get a much more powerful electromagnetic charge.

Once you have charged the crystal ball, you need to get it tuned into your consciousness. Place your hands over the ball and vital breathe with your hands, your whole body and your eyes simultaneously. As you breathe in through the eyes and out through the eyes, your energy system, your eye-consciousness and the ball will start to synchronise, so that the information can flow through the physical eyes, through the high consciousness, and mix into your intuitive field of consciousness – to your inner knowing. This needs to be done vitally, astrally, mentally, Akashically, and then in your light body. We do it inside the light body so that you can receive high level information from the Brotherhood of Light and it is clean and clear and cannot be disrupted by the lower frequencies or any other entities. This way you know that you are getting clean, clear information.

Each of these five levels needs to be tuned into the ball, with your energy bodies in the ball. This synchronicity allows for clean conduction of information. Once you have balanced the energy between the bodies and the ball, then we move on to the correct mind state that you want to use. If you are doing open-eye work – where you are gazing at the ball using peripheral vision, separating the layers of the three bodies, and then allowing the information to transfer through that separation – the energy and information will arise as an overlay on top of the ball. It is as if all those layers are pulled apart, one of those layers contains psychic information and you can view that psychic information when you use the method of transferring into the Akasha, as if your mind gets sucked into the ball and you are inside of a 3D vision of information and you are inside of the experience of what you are looking at. So this is a very different type of clairvoyance, to pulling the layers apart and viewing something – like looking at a television versus being in a 3D situation where you are inside of that particular situation you are looking at; one you have dived in and the other you are looking at it from a distance. Getting used to these two fundamental ways of using clairvoyance is important because it offers a completely different type of skill.

When you dive into the ball, into the Akasha, and you are inside of the clairvoyant information, you are interacting with it. That interaction gives you several benefits and several drawbacks. I will go through the drawbacks first. **The first drawback** is that a lot of that energy can stick to you. When you step out of the crystal ball, it is in your mental body, it will be accumulating, bubbling in your astral body, and it can affect your physiology and your karmic stream. **The second drawback** is that there is this deep subconscious memory of having been there, and when something of similar energy comes up there is a resonance that takes effect where you experience something physically. A tuning fork vibrates, or your experience inside the ball – inside of that Akashic space – vibrates. It bridges the two across and jolts a very intense memory that can stream karma from that clairvoyant vision of whatever it is into your body in the present moment, due to the law of resonance; because you had such a strong unity inside the Akasha with that particular clairvoyant thing. **Other negatives** are that the karma stream will move rhythmically in and out of resonance on an unconscious level in your body. As karma is coming up in your experience from past lives, from this life, when something comes into resonance with that particular vision etherically, you can attach to it and accelerate your own karma – and that is not a good thing. That rhythm tends to rise and fall away. So this is another setback.

One of the **positives** for this is that when you dive into the etheric situation of what you are viewing, you are able to change it – you are able to apply healing, change the karma stream of the person in the situation, interrupt a negative pattern and install a positive pattern, and take that stream of energy from where it has been, where it is and where it is going, and guide it. So you can guide positive outcomes much more efficiently than if you are observing it from a distance. This diving into the Akasha of a situation you are looking at allows you to play with that karma and the direction it is going and adjust it into positive outcomes. These are the types of things you would only do with family members you are responsible for, because the karmic responsibility of doing that is quite high. You may do it with very close friends or students, but definitely not with the general public – unless it was extremely important or the hierarchical framework required for balancing a larger situation. **Other benefits** of diving in, other than changing a karma stream, include that you achieve insight in understanding and learning about the situation on a much deeper level. There is a part of you which really knows what is happening – knows the metaphysical laws, understands the karma stream, where it has been, where it is and where it is going – and your spirit learns. When your spirit is learning, you get a type of an intuitive intellect that understands lawfulness, understands the Dharma laws. You generally do not get this effect when you are clairvoyant – you are looking at something – because the spirit is not completely immersed in it. When the spirit is immersed, understanding arises. This type of wisdom comes out of the experience. **Another positive** of immersing yourself in the Akasha of the information you are looking at is power. You get a transfer of power from the heavens and your spirit. You also get to understanding stuff *qualitatively* and are able to sit within reservoirs of power. You can bathe in it, connected to your astral field, activates skills, qualities, gifts, and powers within you that you did not previously have. That is because your etheric body is in something and you allow your etheric body to morph into what you are in. The mental-astral-physical alignment changes. You are basically adjusting your synchronicity.

Of course you are not going to be diving into someone else's karma as a skill and activating it within yourself, but what you may do is work with deity yoga, where you mentally transfer to a deity inside your crystal ball with a very strong Akashic vacuum there, and then activating, align your etheric body to the skills of that deity. So your mental-astral-physical bodies synchronize and come into resonance with their skills, with that knowledge, with that learning, with those dharma. Then your system becomes a conductor of those teachings, once it is fully absorbed into your etheric body and your mental body and radiates through the astral-physical bodies. Depending on how you are tuning the expression of those energies through which gate of the consciousness, you will want to express them as how quickly they will happen. It can come through as an Akashic volt, in one burst, or it can filter through over time for each session you sit within the Akasha of the deity that you are working with. Other benefits of this is getting to understand the layering process of creation – the way that the physical world connects to life force in the vital field, connects through the astral layers, connects through the spirit-mind consciousness, the way consciousness individualizes itself or forms group consciousness, and the way that different group consciousness connect together to form larger groups of consciousness, and so forth. When you are inside this Akashic substance and pull these layers apart, everything has an obviousness to it: "Of course it works that way, it's obvious." When you are not in the Akasha, that obviousness is not there –it is not as simple as A-B-C. When you are looking from above, when you are seeing it manifesting and things coming into form, everything appears within a state. Of course it works that way. How else could it work? Because you are at a higher vibration than the manifestation, you can see it for what it is. This type of learning is hard to get through any other method than diving into the Akashic field of a situation and observing how things manifest and transform through the Akasha.

Other benefits for this include the effects on your sense gates. When you dive into the Akasha, each of your sense gates increase their level of sensitivity, because the mental-astral matrix around the sense gates softens. So, when you are in your crystal ball, you have dived into the Akasha, you dived into this particular vision that you are looking at, your eye-consciousness expands, the mental matrix and the astral matrix affecting eye-consciousness open up, and it partially dissolves – making your clairvoyance more sensitive. Same thing happens with sound-consciousness and taste, sense and feeling. All these mental-astral matrices are connected through those gates, they open up and create more space, which means that all of your intuitive psychic faculties are amplifying during that time that you are in this etheric space. There is an amplification of your spiritual skills. This amplification is a positive or negative curve to the amplification. After a certain period of being within the Akasha, things move from synchronized sensitivity to desynchronized emptiness – so you do not want to be in the

Akasha for too long, within a particular sense gate, while you are cleaning the gate. If you are in there too long, you will lose it and go through a peak and it starts falling away. So, there is a sensitivity developed within washing Akasha through a particular sense gate and the effect it has on that gate and whether the gates are optimized.

Within each level of gain there is an ownership period in which your body has to adapt to that gain. You have to act upon that gain to take ownership of it – you make it yours. Once you have made it yours, everything is stable and you are standing on a solid platform. From there you can move on to the next level of getting more gains, building more Akasha from that gate and increasing sensitivity further. If you increase the sensitivity too much, it generates a rhythmic whiplash and you do not keep anything – it will just make your mind, emotions and body unstable. So you will get a sense of how much is enough and what is the optimum for developing each of the gates, in relation to opening an astral matrix, in relation to that gate. So you can see, feel, hear, smell, taste, and so forth, through the gates.

Fluid condensers
With fluid condensers, we start off with water. Water is your basic fluid condenser. Water is the center of gravity of life. If you have a fluid condenser that you want to use for a very specific purpose, choose the appropriate herb, boil it like tea, strain it, boil it, usually three times until you have a tincture, and then add a few drops of that to water in order to amplify it.

But let us just go to the water. You start off in the same way of preparing a magic mirror: use vital energy first, then work up the vibrational scale of the chakras. You have the Earth element, Water element, Fire element, Akasha, light, and prayer. You charge that into the fluid condenser. Once you have charged it up, you can decide on – you might do a 462 of vital, then a 462 of astral, 462 of mental, 462 of Akasha. Bardon says two Akasha, 60 mental, 400 astral. You may do 462 of vital obviously on the vital, 462 of each of the elements on the astral, 462 of Akasha, and then 462 of light. There are many combinations that work well. It will be up to you to decide which one and how you want to charge up that thought.

When it comes to using the fluid it is best to have a dropper bottle, because you only need one drop or a maximum of three drops of the fluid when you are charging up an object. Let us say that somebody says, "Can you please charge this amulet for me?" Rather than doing 462 repetitions on the amulet, you put one drop of the fluid condenser onto the amulet, then cup the amulet in your hands, load it with Akasha, and open up the power reservoir of the fluid condenser into the amulet; put a prayer over it, and invoke the related deity that will control the information field of its function. This way it can be etherically blueprinted, and then seal it in. What the fluid condenser will do, it will synchronize that information through the mental-astral-physical body of the person who wears it. So that the luck of music, the luck of study, or the luck of art – synchronicity – aligns. Luck is basically another word for synchronicity. That person will then come into perfect synchronicity with whatever that amulet is for. Fluid condensers are very handy for charging amulets because what would take many hours to normally do, you can do in seconds with one drop of the fluid condenser – invoking a related deity to it in order to change its information field and align that amulet for the person.

When you are doing healing on people, you can put one drop of the fluid condenser directly on their body – on the area that needs healing. So, if you have charged a fluid condenser for healing and you connect it to a particular deity – let us say Fudo-Myoo – by dropping a drop above the person's physical heart, it will generate a healing field around the heart and give a physical anchor for that deity to come and make changes and do 'psychic surgery' on that person's heart. So it physically links the deity connected to the fluid condenser, to function with a lot more ease, etherically, mentally, astrally, and physically.

It can be used for opening up a person's third eye. You can charge it with clairvoyance and then just put one drop on their third eye and it will absorb through the skin and into their system and have a profound effect upon their third eye. It can also be dropped into the physical eyes. You can also do for clairaudience, you can drop it into the ears. For taste, you can drop it under the tongue, and for scent you use an appropriate herb and they simply smell the fluid as it vaporizes. It can be introduced to the different sense gates for opening up different intuitive senses and creating a range of effects very quickly. So, you do all the work earlier and then you release the effect when you need to use it.

Step Nine

There are so many different ways to treat people with the electromagnetic fluid. If someone has a physical injury, where they bumped their knee and they have got a bruise, you want to do vital breathing into it. Just touch the fascia, feel a lot of force, and begin breathing and charging that local area with vital energy, and boost up their immune system lightly. Because it did not originate in the astral body, there is no need to go on to the electromagnetic fluid of the astral plane to heal the person – just go straight to the vital field, charge it up, and their body will get a burst and disappear; recovering will be accelerated. It is an easy starting point.

When we are working with astral disturbances, deep emotional patterns, diseases that originated out of the emotions – interestingly enough the emotions are not as at fault as people might think: diet, environment, toxins in the food, and so forth tend to be more responsible for diseases than emotions. When you survey people more than 100 years old, most of them are pretty grumpy and not very nice, and they are very emotional. That does not seem to disturb their lifespan at all. Your astral constitution usually causes disease – sometimes, not usually.

But in the astral plane, you can go to the root of the disease and fix it from there. So, if something has been around for a long time, you cannot fix it at the vital energy – you have to go to the astral patterns and start working with them. So, you enter the astral plane by releasing time, do the vital breath, do the full cycle breath, pausing the breath, slow everything down, take the slowness, run it through the breath, until you have moved into the astral plane. You keep cycling that slowness until you are in the astral space where you want to be.

Every astral plane has depths. There is heaviness from the bottom and light and high values on the top. And these astral planes stack on top of each other, not in a linear way, but the top edge of one layer stacks in the top edge of another. The bottom edge of one stacks in the bottom edge of another. So there is a vast overlap in the planes. They do not sit on the – the lowest of one does not sit on the highest of the next, so they are overlapping for the most part. When you are working with astral healing energy – when you go to the top of the astral plane and the top of that particular plane and work with light – it can be so far from the physical that it is not going to have much physical effect. Instead it is going to affect people's spiritual views, perception and what is sacred to the person – it is not going to affect the disease right on the bottom.

So we want to go to lower astral levels and in those lower astral levels there is a light on the top and we want to connect to that light, invoke healing from that level, and then breathe the electromagnetic fluid of that light close to the physical, bring it into resonance and affect the particular pattern of that disease, and start performing healing from that level. So we are going to tune to the level of the problem and then invoke light on that level. Most of these diseases are close to the physical level, so we are not going to high spiritual spaces in order to heal people.

If you go to high spiritual places to heal people, all you do is stimulate spirit and they turn to their religious direction more and more, and the healing does not really happen – they will just feel spiritually revived. So we have got to get onto those physical astral planes that are dense and connect to the fluids there and, moving those healing energies into the patient, rebalance them. It is all about rebalancing and bringing them into the state of equanimity. So you breath the energy, through equalizing and balancing the person.

With most diseases you are moving energy out of the body; you are rewriting information. Usually I'm charging huge amounts of energy into people, because in most people it is an excess condition, not a deficiency. With people that are deficient, you start by releasing the negative energy very softly, so that you do not drain them too much, and then you charge them with the light of the astral plane that you are working on. So you move it up to the top of that plane and you charge them up, and then you balance that level out with the rest of the levels around it. You do not have one place excessively charged with energy. The places around it work to balance all those astral planes' levels around the problem in order for equanimity to arise – thus healing arrives very quickly.

There is a certain degree of sensitivity which you need for this type of work. If you have been working with the elements and the energies inside your body, you will get a sensitivity to put in other people's bodies. If you are working with these energies with trees – working with large trees, in particular – that expanded mental, astral and vital space will open up your bodies and dramatically amplify sensitivity, so that when you go to do healing on someone, the mechanism that you need to implement is obvious. It is just part of your intuitive field of consciousness. In this case, it is just practice, practice, practice. Intuition arises and you follow that intuitive process. It will naturally unlock it and you will get the results that you are looking for.

When you are working with heavy karmic diseases you can use Akasha and light to absorb that energy into that person's own etheric and light body. You are not taking away their karma; you are giving a control point to that karma to a higher power of that being. So you draw that energy – of, say, a tumour – up into the light body and the spirit goes, "Do I need this for my learning, or don't I? Does this body need this, or does it not." From there, that spiritual consciousness can take control of it. In many cases, the spirit has simply lost control – it is not able to control the energy from the physical environment, from the astral ego, from this person's lower behaviors – and the sickness has simply risen. When the energy gets transformed up into the spirit, into the light body, into the Akasha body, then one's own spirit can manage it and say, "Okay, yeah, we're done with this, we can remove it," and dissolve the crude behaviors that caused it, and so forth. It can do the rest. So you are giving it a helping hand and there is no karmic responsibility for you. You are not taking anything away – you are just handing control from the lower mind, the lower ego, to the higher mind.

Using this technique is karmically safe and highly efficient for dealing with inside cancer and tumours, and anything that seems quite 'heavy duty'. Once you have drawn the mind substance out of the tumour, you have drawn astral substance out of the tumour, and you transform through the Akasha and to the light body of the person, the physical tumour will simply be absorbed by the body – the body will just absorb and dispose of it. The healing will be gentle and natural as the person recovers. Then they just need a good diet, clean water and air, lots of vitality in the air, and they will have a rapid recovery.

Recognize what you need to work on – is that a physical level problem, is that in the astral, is it a problem of the spirit, or just some deep karmic thing that you need to move this energy into? Once you identify that, then you select the technique: vital, astral, mental, or Akasha, light, or any healing that is appropriate for the situation you are applying to the person.

Akashic Volting
While doing this exercise, straighten the spine. If you have an amulet or

an object you want to charge up, keep it close to you if you want to do Akashic volting. Start with vital breathing and spread your awareness across the room. Get the whole body pore breathing, sensitive, go straight to the Akasha breathing, astral space-time feeling on the in-breath, spaceless feeling on the out-breath. Draw infinity in, infinity out. Sway your body front and back. Become sensitive with the gap between the three bodies. Breathe into the gap and open up the Akashic feeling. Use a dark violet color to breathe open the gap to get into the Akasha breathing.

Now breathe the Akasha into the spine, loading the spine with Akasha. Commit for about one minute, nine breaths.

Pick up the object that you want to charge, put it in your left hand, and review for a moment in your mind what effect that you want. Increase the energy conductivity through the bodies, increase energy flow through the bodies, increase sensitivity. Hold an idea of the result you seek, pull the Akasha into the body with that idea, and condense the Akasha and the idea together within your body. Get it very close to the physical. Pull the feeling, breathe the Akasha in, and condense the idea to your body.

With the last breath, you breathe the idea into the body and get to the in-breath, just pull it for a moment, stretch the spine a little bit more than usual, and then give a burst of energy from your right hand into your opposite hand – the hand that you are holding the object you are charging with.

Have a high intensity of will and relax your right hand over the left. Seal that Akashic volt into the object. Once it is sealed, place the object down. Now we can do the same for one of our elementals. If you already built an elemental for your idea, I want you to frame that elemental from above the crown down into the space between your hands. Sync yourself to it.

Once you are synchronised with it, synchronise your breathing with the elemental, Akashically breathing. From the Akasha breathing, move into the idea that you wish to charge into the elemental. On the last breath, breathe the Akasha into your body, have a clear idea of what you want to charge into the elemental, pull your breath momentarily, increase the stretching of the spine, then give it a jolt of energy of the elemental. Seal that energy in and then release the elemental off your crown.

Okay, so you take a piece of paper and write down a wish. Write it down with the idea that it is already manifested – write down in an already manifested state. If you need to break down the wish or define it in any way, write down what each word means. Maybe I'm asking for a particular skill: 'I' equals vibrational consciousness, universal mind; 'M' equals some type of masterful experience. So it is an alpha tuning fork in your astral body. Mastery is a level of skill and defines that level of skill you wish to accomplish.

Once you have gotten that statement clear, convert it into a sigil. For this example we will use the statement: "I am master of ..." Cross out any repeated letters, so that you have only one repetition of each letter. Once you have crossed out all those repeated letters, write the first letter down, and each letter has a different size and different thickness, so you make the letter into a piece of art. So, letter 'I', choose the thickness and the height, size, make it smaller. The 'A' overlap it, the 'M' overlap it, 'O' the 'F', 'S', 'T', 'E', and so on. So you use all the letters, grab your notepad, write down a statement: "I am master of ..." write down the skill and delete all the repeated letters, and make a sigil. Each letter is in different size and different thickness.

Once we have done that, look at the sigil just with the physical eyes and then start astral breathing through your eyes. Get yourself aware of the astral plane. Open the astral plane, jump to the Akasha. Release the sigil from the astral through to the Akasha. Trust in your unconscious mind – it is making an easy transition for your eye-consciousness. Akasha breathe through the eyes, looking at that sigil with peripheral vision, until that sigil goes blurry. Just allow the sigil to morph as you Akasha breathe through the eyes. That sigil starts to change shape. It takes on a new shape. Write down that new sigil. Continue to repeat this until the sigil is constant.

When the sigil is constant, place the paper in your left hand, look at the sigil again. Akasha breathe with the meaning of the sigil. Bring that statement in and tune into it – tune into what it represents as you breathe the Akasha in and out. Place your right hand above, charge your whole body with the Akasha and absorb on that frequency, absorb on that meaning. Do that through nine breaths or so.

On your last breath, breathe into your whole body with Akasha, loading your spine and breathing into the sigil. Get to the end of the in-breath, hold your breath momentarily, stretch the spine a little bit more than normal, and then put the Akasha as a jolt into the sigil.

And you can engrave that sigil into an amulet and while you are working on that exercise for a period of time, you wear that amulet, charge that before practice, and you can wear the amulet until you master the exercise. It is a very intense energy being conducted through your body. It brings you into resonance with that particular skill set.

After you have completed the mastery of your skill, one thing you can do if you like is to write it down on a piece of paper, cut the paper into a small scroll, roll it up, put the scroll in a tube and wear that tube with all the other sigils around your neck, and charge that scroll and sigils each day, for reinforcing, developing and connecting all the different skills you have been working on. If you add a drop of blood to that piece of paper, every time you charge the Akasha into it, it will make the blood coursing through your body bubble.

You can do one sigil for each exercise in the initiation text and reinforce your skills with each of the particular exercises using this method. Any other skills that you want, make a sigil accordingly. You can also make sigil engravings on stones or necklaces that you wear.

Moving on to Akasha breathing, rock your body forwards and backwards, get a sense of the degree of separation between the three bodies, feel the gaps, breathe the Akasha into those gaps, increasing the separation of the bodies.

Keep breathing the Akasha until you start to lose yourself in it. As it is with your breathing the Akasha, you forget the body and where you are, kind of like falling asleep, but it is not sleep – get to that edge, and the edge represents where you can maintain Akashic will or begin to lose that Akashic will. You want to be able to measure this Akashic will. There is a quality of infinity that underlies Akashic trance; you just want to increase that and your Akashic will, you have to invoke the Akasha – you have to release yourself into it. As you release into it, you create a feeling of a vacuum, you increase the Akasha. This vibrational scale leading to Akasha manifests as a deep sense of humility, devotion to your spiritual practice, reverence, and sacredness.

This invokes the infinity quality of the Akasha. So when you tune into that quality, the Akasha increases. You always want to work to the point where you are losing yourself in Akasha. Get to that edge, and stabilise it.

When you increase that vacuum, there is a sense of everything collapsing in on itself like a black hole. It is like your mind is collapsing upon itself, becoming smaller and smaller.

Bring your mind into a feeling of sensitivity to the Akasha, inward infinity collapsing sensation, measure its speed. How much vacuum does it have? Is it constant or it is rhythmic? Measure that with your awareness.

Once you have those measurements, increase it, create more vacuum, to empty your mind out a little bit more. The sigil that you just made, place it in the center of that vacuum, in the center of the Akasha, and collapse that Akasha into the sigil. Increasing the vacuum, moving the sigil into it, deeper and deeper.

And very gently, just sealing that with your mind, sealing that Akasha, that vacuous feeling into the sigil. Once you have mentally put your hands around it, sealed it, disconnect and return to your normal consciousness.

Step Ten

Part Three: Causation Chains is the continuation of the step Ten Physical stream of practice.

It is up to the reader's creativity to find faculties that they would like to model and emulate. You, the reader, can create a list of different faculties or layers of the five sense gates to develop your ideas. You can brainstorm, mind map and research different things you would like to progress on from different systems. Any result that a human has done in the past or the future can be modeled and replicated. Better yet, you can adapt it as you see fit, so long as it is within universal laws. For further information on modeling and emulating, you can research Neuro Linguistic Programming.

Part 3

Causation Chains

On Reverse Engineering Any Skill for Causation Chains

Let us have a look at reverse engineering different skills. Let us say that you encounter a particular skill set on YouTube, or you see a teacher perform a particular skill, and you have it intellectually figured out what is happening. The first thing we do is look at what is the outcome, what the final product is. Then we look at the physical environment of where and what is happening. Between the outcome and the physical environment, there is a causation chain. You have got movement of energy in the astral and in the mental, and movement from the Akasha. So we want to tune in to the center of gravity of that mass in the Akasha and mentally transfer into its center. From the Akasha we slowly start separating the layers. So we create space between the mental and astral matrices to reduce the clinging, to open those layers up, and as we relax into the Akasha and those layers pull apart, we will see how they are interacting.

The mental plane will have the mental patterning of how the energy is running. We ask ourselves, "What is the function? What is it doing? What is its timing? How is its space contained?" When we move into the astral it will move more into the form, the energy, the emotion, the personality, the nature of the skill and then how was that energy being fed from the astral to the physical world and the physical environment, or if the energy is coming from the astral environment to produce that result. So, there might be a bodily mechanic involved physically, there might be an astral reservoir of energy that is being released, or the energy may be stored in some type of vortex in the Akasha, and so forth.

As we pull these layers of power, we get a sensitivity to what is happening and then we can choose whether we want to replicate what is happening. Very often the energy is coming from reservoirs and those reservoirs of energy have karma – so it is connected to a particular doctrine, a particular group consciousness. That group consciousness has a lot of karma connected to it. For instance, if you walk into a Christian church and pray, you have the entire karma of Christianity expressing itself through its history and that stream moving from the past to the present, seeking to balance itself from the group conscious of Christian people. So you make a choice: do you want to engage in that karma? When they are doing hands-on healing, praying and so forth, the healing that is being given through that group consciousness has that karma stuck to it. There is a price to be paid when you receive healing from a person like that, because of the karma of what they are doing – their past, present and future functioning in a stream and these dams of reservoirs of energy that you are tapping into will always contain some form of karma. So you are better off building your own reservoirs of energy for years rather than tapping into reservoirs from others. Because once that karma flows through you, it mixes with your energy, forms a network of connections, and becomes a two-way mirror. Energy is coming in, reflecting out, and your karma mixes with their karma of the magic that you are using.

Causation Chain of Clairvoyance: Complex Breakdown of Causation Chain for Understanding the Underlying Mechanics of All Causation Chains

When we are looking at a stream of exercises that are required to develop a particular skill set, we first look at the mental stream that is required for skill, then we look at the astral stream that is required for the skill and the physical stream. Let us say the skill we are working on is clairvoyance, we look at the mental skills that are required for clairvoyance. The first one would be using eye-consciousness while observing the rising and falling of thoughts. So your eyes are open, you are taking in the information from the environment through the eye-consciousness and you are watching the accompanied thoughts arise and fall away. You stabilise the mind so that it does not touch any of the thoughts. No matter what you look at, you are not labelling, connecting any emotions or making any judgments. You are just quietly observing the rising and falling away of the information field. From there you move into one point of concentration through eye-consciousness on a meditation object. So, you do this first peripherally, where you take in the whole landscape and you observe the landscape and then you do it focally, where you take one point in the landscape – an individual object – and then focus upon the object. So you have a focal vision for the concentration, you have peripheral vision for the concentration. Both of these exercises are going to produce the type of mental vacuity or stillness around your mind. So as you are observing the rising and falling away in your first exercise, there is a vacuum of stillness forming so that no thoughts can arise, where everything becomes still.

As you progress to concentrating more upon meditation objects, you will get a stillness accumulating around such meditation objects. That one-pointed focus generates a sharper type of stillness. These two different types of stillness, we treat them as two different meditation objects, and then through the first exercise you move into that stillness and the second exercise you move into that sharper stillness and you make that your meditation object through your eye-consciousness.

The **first exercise** creates a lot more space. The **second exercise** creates a lot more inward focus and sharpness. So these two different types of stillness, you bring them into the eye-consciousness and you generate a type of equanimity. They both end up at the same place, but they take a different path to get to that equanimity within the eye-consciousness. From there you would move on to visualisation exercises. Starting with the very simple objects and progressing to more complex objects. When you start visualisation you want to use very simple shapes from the group consciousness. Squares, you know, a square with a triangle on it, which represents a house; a circle – shapes that are in the group consciousness and locked in to the basis of our psyche, the way our brain forms basic geometry, the way our brain forms basic ideas. These simple pictograms are our starting point for visualisation. Once we have mastered these very simple pictograms from the group consciousness, then we move onto more complex imagery and we add emotion to generate the complexity. If you do not have the emotion to generate complexity, the memory is not going to hold on to the visualisation, and then from there you increase the depth of the visualisation skills by working from one topic to the next.

We work from first, second, into third person. So, you are observing something, then you take a second person looking back, and a third person looking at a side angle, like the fly on the wall, the camera in the corner. You start working your visualisation exercises from these three different perspectives. It is important to master all three, for obvious reasons.

Now when you have worked through the visualising still images, then you bring things into motion – you bring activity into it. You may choose to use a repetitive loop when you start that active visualisation. So if you are engaged in an activity, you loop the activity in your mind. If you are working on your forehand in tennis, you just repeat hitting the ball with your forehead over and over and make a loop. That will give you a side benefit of making your tennis game better as well as developing the visual side of your awareness and developing a foundation for clairvoyant work.

You can do this with the eyes open or closed. And then you can look at the emptiness underneath the meditation objects. This is important because this is what releases time. So if you put an object in front of you or you visualize an object and look at it, either way it is fine but looking at a physical object is better. The stillness will accumulate around your mind and around the object in the space between you and the object. Up until the point where the object starts to flicker, when it just disappears and reappears. When it disappears and reappears, you want to take that moment of it flickering to move into the emptiness underneath the object. As you move into the emptiness underneath the object, there is this awareness that arises: *that the object is underneath, has a vacuum* and you want to bring that vacuum into your eye-consciousness. Whatever information you want to unlock, when you direct your mind to the information, you are most interested in the Akashic substance underneath the information – the vacuum underneath – because that vacuum underneath is not subject to time. It has all the layers of that object to open in that emptiness; the past, present, the future release themselves through the Akasha. So they become accessible to you as those layers pull apart. Getting this within the visual part of your training is very important to pull those layers apart. You have access to the information underneath the meditation object, or the frequency that is working under the person you are looking at, or the environment you are viewing. The separation of the layers is critical to your development.

From this mental training, we move on to the center of gravity of the object. This exists within the Akasha of the object, from the emptiness. When you meditate on an object and the flickering starts moving into the emptiness that is separating the layers, you connect to the center of the object through the Akasha, and get a sense of the center of gravity of it. This is a control point of the object and it is not the physical center of gravity we are so interested in – we are interested in the Akashic center of gravity.

From there we want to look at the astral stream in relation to clairvoyance. The astral stream has a lot to do with astral breathing through the eye-consciousness. We need to balance the elements from the astral body to generate a deeper equanimity, so we use the basic four element breathing exercises into the four regions to generate that equanimity. Then we breathe astral energy through the eyes. Breathing of astral energy through the eyes acts as a cleaning process – it releases past trauma, astral energy that is stuck to your eye-consciousness – as we are continually making judgments about things we see and attaching emotions and energy to what we see. This breaks equanimity. It contaminates the divine eye. Judgement blocks it, essentially. So we want to do this astral breathing through the eyes, to clear the eyes.

Within every astral level there is astral light. At the bottom of an astral level is dense, heavy, darker energy and at the top of each astral level is light: bright, clear light. And we want to go through each of these levels, from the lower astral levels, and breathe this clear light through which dissolves and removes contaminants and frees up the eye-consciousness. Starting at the bottom and moving all the way up. As you move up, you just simply slow things down to move into deeper levels of your astral body as you breathe that astral light through the eyes. While you are doing this, you are invoking a prayer of clairvoyance – you are inviting the quality of clairvoyance through the Akashic feeling that you developed in the mental training into your eye-consciousness. This creates a type of self-fulfilling prophecy because your astral body represents your subconscious programming. It represents your self image – how you think, feel and act. What experiences you allow into your consciousness program through your astral body. So your physical thinking, your physical feelings that you experience and your physical actions are all regulated by the astral body. We really need to program our astral body to function in the way that we want, to have the experiences that we want to experience.

This charge of astral light that we are using to wash each of these layers, we want to contain a self fulfilling prophecy within it. In this case it is clairvoyance, so we invite that clairvoyance in and out. As we wash the eyes, we wash the eyes in relation to aligning and producing that clairvoyant vision. If you are working with a particular deity, if you belong to a particular religious belief structure, you may invoke the deity of that particular system you are working with and breathe that light through in resonance with a deity and use that as a part of your own your focal point of the prayer. As you work up the vibrational scale through the astral and work towards the mental body, you will find that the energy gets softer and softer the higher you go. It does not get stronger, it gets more vast and the edges become less dense. As you move into the mental sphere, then the sense of density may disappear completely. These higher frequencies of light move much further, even though the astral plane of the physical world only extends a small distance off the planet. Remember, the light emanating from the sun has a type of gravity within that light. It is an astral substance traveling through outer space. So the astral energy moves with physical light at a very high speed. Astral energy is moving around inside our solar system. Astral energy follows light and follows gravity. If there is a meteor floating throughout space, it has a type of gravity within it and that gravity allows an astral substance to exist within it. Because everything has mind substance, energy naturally arises within that.

So, as you are breathing high levels of astral light you start connecting to astral substances that exist outside of the planet. Even though you cannot move your astral body outside of the planet, these astral energies do exist wherever there is gravity and energy moving. Basically the whole universe has astral substance and continuous flux and motion.

When we bring the training to the physical, we need to tune the peripheral receptors of the eyes. We start with vital breathing. So draw life force in through the eyes, out through the eyes, we go to a focal vision. We take a meditation object and then we just look to the left and right while we are focused and this produces half-focal receptors and half-peripheral receptors. When you look at an object focally and then become sensitive to the edges of the object, you get a perception of life force. Initially you feel that life force if you have been breathing life force through the hands and through the body, and then you begin to see that life force around the edges of things. You cannot look directly at the life force you wish to view – you have to look beside it. And by being half-focal and half-peripheral, you will be able to tune in to seeing the life force around people, objects, places, animals, plants, nature, and so forth. As soon as you have tuned in this slight displacement of the focal looking at the physical and the peripheral looking around the object, you will tune into – tune the frequency through the feeling of life force to see vital force.

From there we go a little bit wider. We start working towards the astral plane, and as we astrally breathe, the peripheral vision goes a bit wider than looking widely. And you go layer by layer and investigate what is there. Now, these layers are very subtle. You can miss them very easily. So if you move from the focal to the broad peripheral too quickly, you will miss all that data. You have to be very slow – just creep through the bandwidth of your peripheral vision while astral breathing. As soon as the eyesight goes a bit hazy, it basically means that you are touching on a frequency on a door. So go to that haziness, just stretch through it, and the metaphor of stretch through it is literal – you literally stretch from your pineal gland through your physical eyes out to meet the object you want to connect to, the frequency you want to move through, and you can open that door through this type of stretching. There is a pulling apart of the layers. Wherever you see energetic cloudiness, that is a doorway – that is something you can investigate and open up and generate more clarity by looking through it.

Once we have worked through the tuning, the peripheral receptors to astral breathing and moving those fluids in and out of the eyes, we move out to the mental plane. So, the mental plane, the peripheral vision is almost at its full extension outwards, that you are almost fully peripheral but not quite. There still requires a little bit of subtle intent to see the spiritual frequency of a person, a place, and object, and so forth. You are almost releasing the space altogether. So, breathing this mind substance in and out of the eyes and just feathering off the edges, allows you to get access to seeing the mental body. This level is quite interesting because it is the easiest type for clairvoyance to develop, for seeing spirits. When you start seeing spirits, you will see the mental silhouette of the spirit and that silhouette, you will become sensitive to its energy emanation first. So it is like a line drawing. You can just see the lines of the drawing, you cannot see the color. This silhouette represents its life force emanation coming out of its mental or astral body. So, you are really looking at the vital fields of the spiritual entity and that is what presents itself first, because it is easy to see. All spiritual beings need a type of life force in order to exist. Without that life force they would have no cohesion, they would not be able to function or use their intent to move and go about their business. So there are various levels of life force everywhere and these different types of life force each have a radiation. By doing the basics of life force breathing physically and then working through the astral-mental levels, you become sensitive to the amount of power and life force that the spiritual entity has. While the body of colors and the facial features and all the other information that comes through gives you different types of data, fundamentally life force is power. Powerful beings radiate life force in the form of the light. So if they are emitting a very powerful light, you know that they have some power. If their light is dim, you know that they do not have power. Cultivating life force ends up being one of your fundamental training exercises, because you need to have power to conduct any magical operation, to do any type of mental wandering, to do any type of magical work. You need a life force, as always an expenditure of life force and all these different types of exercises. Powerful beings have powerful life force emitting through their spirit, emitting through their astral body and their physical bodies.

This may be different levels of emanation. So, let us say a person who is an athlete will have a very strong emanation in the vital-physical body or they may or may not have a strong emanation mentally and astrally – it will depend upon how much work they have done on those levels. Whereas a lama may have a very strong emanation in his mental body and also in his astral-physical body. So depending upon where they are connecting and bridging that energy to, that is where the emanation is. It is not balanced and constant through all three bodies. Each body will emanate in accordance with the work, of what they have done on that body. So, Buddhists tend to do more work on their mental body, Taoists tend to do more work on their astral body, and then people who engage in sport do more work on their physical bodies. So we see that the life force will emanate differently in each of these three bodies, in these three different cases.

As we continue to develop the new clairvoyance, we want to start working within the Akasha. You want to start breathing the pure Akasha in through the eyes, out through the eyes, and saturating the eye-consciousness with Akasha. As it becomes saturated, the space between the mental-astral-physical eyes opens, the space between the Akashic substance and the Akashic eye, the divine eye and the mental eye opens. And as that space opens, we have access to our own latent skills. So Akasha is the most important of all the exercises, because this gives us access to all the different types of clairvoyance. The preliminary training is very limited in that it is developing a platform to stand upon. It does not actually generate the clairvoyance itself unless you have a very innate skill – if you have a past life skill, if you have a natural tendency towards something, that will activate it. But when we start the Akasha level, we can develop and form the clairvoyance in any direction we want. We can take it in the direction of prophetic vision, we can take it in the direction of medical diagnosis – to be able to see disease – and we can take it in the direction of how to teach, how to release resistance, we can bring the direction of therapy. Whatever need you have, you can tune your clairvoyance to fill that need through the Akasha work. So breathing the Akasha in and out of the eyes to pull the layers apart and go into Akashic trance in eye-consciousness gives you the freedom to develop it in whatever direction you wish.

From the Akasha work, we move on to one non-dual light. Once you have been working with the Akasha for a while, the essence of mind starts to appear, and basically it is light in its non-dual state. It is in a state of instead of fluctuating between electric and magnetic, it is just in an electric state and it is an electric state of mind substance that has not begun to vibrate. So it is just sitting there, as if it is not doing anything – but in reality it has the full plan of creation underneath it and it is seeking to express itself through that creative plan. However, the vibration is so subtle that it appears to be still. But when the mind equalizes with stillness, then you recognize that there is a subtle vibration underneath it and there is a high, vast intelligence functioning through it, seeking to express itself.

In order to bring this white light into the high consciousness, we need to create an environment that pulls it in. So you intend it, because intention will automatically generate a flux that is much stronger. We want to work with the high levels of light. You will bring it into reality if you intend it. So you need to create a vacuum through a deep form of prayer, through quietude to invite that light to arise within the eye-consciousness. You need to create a self-fulfilling prophecy before you invite that clairvoyant light to enter your eyes. So once you have created that prophecy and the prayer, then as you enter into the prayer, you go deeper and deeper into stillness, deeper and deeper into the Akasha, pulling that light into your physical eyes and to your pineal gland. You are ultimately activating the divine eye. That divine eye – because it is not subject to time and space – changes your DNA and the frequency of your spirit and makes adjustments within who you are and the way you think, feel and act. It changes the fundamental spiritual cravings that you get, and directions that you want to go. Ultimately it changes you on every level.

The more you accumulate this non-dual light inside each cell of your body, the greater reservoir of energy you have access to spiritually. When you have a spiritual need, that light comes into form. And this energy is not a physical energy, it is a spiritual energy – it is a resource of the spirit; it is spiritual nourishment of the highest form. It can come down astrally and physically and produce astral warmth and physical power when it needs to, but it ultimately is a spiritual nourishment and it activates clairvoyant senses and the clairvoyant sight when you invoke it. Once you have been working with this – working through Akasha to invoke non-dual light into the eye-consciousness – the eyes will usually become very heavy and dense, like you will have pressure inside the eyeballs. This pressure needs to be equalized. You can do this with a magnetic eye bath to wash the eyes. When doing a magnetic eye bath, you can just put your face straight into a bucket of water and do your eye exercises. This light pressure will equalise without water and depressurise the eyes, but If you do not do this, you can potentially get a lot of aching within the physical eyes, because the energy is unable to get out, so it will build and build and build. We need to demagnetise the eyes on a daily basis when doing this type of white light work very heavily.

From there we look at the stream of clairvoyance. When you invite that light down, there should be a stream that benefits more than just you. If you are a healer, you invite that light for the benefit of healing for all your future patients. If you are a teacher, you invite that light to come through your eyes for the benefit of your past, present and future students. Whatever your particular life purposes, your particular service, it is important to invite that light for their benefit. And if you are going to heal a thousand people in your lifetime, that healing will be connected straight away through your eye-consciousness. When you eventually meet the person you are going to be doing healing on, you have this instantaneous knowing what the problem is. Your clairvoyance will just simply see it, because it was already aligned to that moment a long time ago when you did these exercises.

The spirit is not subject to time in the same way that people perceive time in the physical world. Any function that your clairvoyance will have in the future, you want to align it to that moment now, so that it functions perfectly when you need it. When you invite your clairvoyance to develop and awaken now for the benefit of a person you are going to be doing healing on, or doing a reading for, or doing work with, in the future, it is perfectly aligned and that future moment is there because you aligned it right now. Dedicating that benefit in the merit of your clairvoyance skill to the people you are going to be working with in the future acts as an amplifier – it sucks this light through the three bodies, aligns it, synchronizes it, and allows that skill to function.

If any part of the mind or the astral field is clinging to the self and clinging to its own power and clinging to its own skills, you will block it. So it will not be open. We want to dedicate this skill to the people who are going to benefit from it and then the synchronicity happens, the three bodies aligned over time and space and every time it is needed, it functions perfectly for that moment.

Causation Chain of Prayer

When a person enters into prayer, they are usually directing their prayer towards a deity of some type. They are presuming that those deities are of a much higher frequency, a much higher stage of evolution, than them. There is a natural humility or humbleness that people enter into when they pray – as if they are standing in front of a God – where the mind becomes still, the ego becomes still, the body becomes still. All the static stops and everything enters into a stillness, and the stillness is initially reflected through humility.

When you are working within the Hermetic framework, the prayer is not projected outward, it is projected inwards, because the essence of you is a vibrational match to God. **The microcosm is a vibrational match to the macrocosm. So the essence of spirit has the divine spark within it.** When you pray, that prayer is directed to the microcosm within, that is a match to the macrocosm. When we were praying, we were basically praying to the essence of our own being – to the god-like nature within.

In order to generate an environment where prayer is suitable, you have got to create a temple. So if you go to church and you enter the church, you feel that temple atmosphere, you feel that sacred space, and you naturally become quiet and wish to enter into that state of prayer, that state of humility. When you are directing a prayer inward, you have got to create an inward temple, an inside sacred space. This inside sacred space is created through the four pillars: Fire, Air, Water, and Earth. Before we pray, we stabilise our will. We stabilise the Air element, we stabilise the Water element, we stabilise the Earth element, and bring them into equanimity. When they come into equanimity, then a much deeper more profound stillness can arise. So that when we reflect that prayer into the essence of the spirit, it has a much deeper and stronger connection. These four pillars of your temple must be taken into consideration.

If you are travelling the saintly path and you are very serious about your practice, then that temple must be established physically, astrally, mentally, and Akashically, so that you have a correct internal environment in which prayer can take place – that you can commune with the divine light and work within those frequencies. The **physical pillars** are going to represent your lifestyle, your speech, your connection to your community, and every physical part of your being: how you live your life. The **astral pillars** are going to represent your personality. When people think about you, what do they think about? How do you make them feel? What is your astral personality? All the emotions that you are experiencing inwardly, and emotions you are expressing outwardly, represent this astral temple. So, one needs to consider how to bring all of these aspects into balance and harmony to create a temple environment. And then the **mental body temple** is the stillness of the mind, that when you enter into prayer how much static is there? How much 'monkey mind' is there versus how much stillness exists within the mind? Most people that pray only consider the mental body – they are not considering their strong physical forms. The system you are working within will determine which one of these bodies you are going to focus upon. For instance, Buddhism will have many precepts which relate to the physical lifestyle, precepts for the astral personality, and then their releasing practices will develop their mental body. So these three different levels are all taken in consideration in different ways. Each system will address the three bodies and build this temple in a different way. This is a matter to contemplate for yourself and develop a method which fits your life's purpose and the direction you are going in with your practices. It certainly does not have a 'one model fits everyone' approach – it is very individualised. If you try to take someone else's model and you overlay it onto yourself, there is a good chance that it is going to feel out of sync and break you, and you are not going to achieve success with it. You need to individualise it according to your life's path and your life's purpose.

The next aspect of prayer is the **degrees of stillness** that you experience when you are connecting and praying to a deity or to the divinity within you. The first is obviously *humility,* that you're humbling yourself. The second is your devotion to your spiritual path. When you are truly devoted to your religious framework – to your spiritual development, no matter what system it is in – there is a type of handing over of the self. You let a part of yourself go so that the hard part of you can be in charge. So you surrender yourself. This devotion that comes from this non-self ideal – that you give up part of your own passion as part of your own attachments for the benefit of the whole – this releasing and the devotion to the path becomes the next part of that stillness. From there we have **reverence**. When you truly revere a spiritual path and you have reverence towards it, it is a two-way mirror effect. How you revere the path and the reverence which reflects within generates a stillness. If you don't revere your path, you cannot have reverence. It simply will not act in its two-way mirror function. So we need to really look at our path, revere it and then we will have reverence towards the deity, towards the divine light, towards the path we are working within. That reverence creates a vacuum which pulls you through to your spiritual goals.

From this reverence, we move into the state of sacredness. When something is truly sacred, there is a profound stillness which surrounds that sacredness. When you perceive something in this light of sacredness and you direct your mind towards it, the level of stillness is far greater than any of the levels below. The sacredness allows you to draw very deep levels of Akasha until you feel the consciousness. From the sacredness, we move into the Akashic substance itself. From the humility, devotion and reverence to the sacredness, there is some vibrational scale of stillness. Each one of these layers is accumulating a different aspect of the Akasha. The humility related to the Earth element, the devotion related to the Water element, reverence relates to the Fire element, and the sacredness relating to the Air element, working up the vibrational scale of the chakra. The Akasha basically is the sum total of those energies and the way they have been transmuting, refining and stilling themselves to work in the Akasha. The Akasha requires a release of time and space, and moving into a quality of infinity inside of the prayer. This is a natural extension out of the frequency of sacredness.

At the essence of mind is light and it is not dualistic light, it is a non-dual light. So divine light is what is on the other end of Akasha. As you move through Akasha, there is light that has not manifested yet, it is still in a zero state – it has not become singular or dual. So we have this transition through the Akasha moving through the energy slowing down – light is slowing down – until the light is reaching the zero state where it is completely manifested. So we have the light in the zero, we have the lights becoming singular and vibrating in a dual way. As you move through Akasha in deep prayer and you are connected to divine light, you will experience a slowing down of the energy within these light realms. This initial universal light is actually not non-dual. It has a flux to it, but the center of gravity of the mind and its stability within that flux is greater than the flux. So it is a force that does not carry Samsara – it will not force you to reincarnate when you leave this body, because your mind and the will of your mind is more stable than the flux of that light. If your mind was very unstable, that Samsaric force would just carry you into another reincarnation. The Samsaric forces would use that universal nature to continually reproduce the reincarnation cycle over and over again. But as the mind equalises with non-dual light, there is a tipping point at which Samsaric force becomes less than the will of the mind to equalise with this light, and the spirit becomes freed. So this is a very big platform to stand on within your spiritual progress, because this is where you actually start experiencing true freedom. Where at the end this incarnation, your mind will equalise with that light and there is not enough Samsaric force within that light to force you to reincarnate. So you can look at your spiritual growth state and choose, "I need to do more of this," and you do what is needed. Or you feel the desire to be in a part of the service and you incarnate inside the path of service.

The development of this non-dual light really is the platform you want to stand on, your first big goal with Hermetic work. Because once you are there, you will experience freedom not only within your physical, astral and mental worlds, but your spiritual, afterlife worlds as well. So your ability to generate different types of skill sets, your ability to understand, the ability to look at your spiritual development process and have insight into it. And it is regulated by this state of awareness, where you can simply see and understand more of the spiritual process.

This non-dual light state tends to reflect more through spiritual insight in understanding than physical sciences. It is obvious that many geniuses in the physical sciences have very high levels of understanding, but it is this type of light that gives understanding in scientists' spiritual evolution. This is the quality we are talking about when working with light.

Causation Chain of Samadhi

Samadhi is one-pointed concentration. With samadhi, we are very interested in looking at which gate to the mind is most important for your development. If, let us say, you are an artist, the visual part of your mind may be very important, so you are going to do most of your samadhi work with eye-consciousness. If you require feeling to be a big part of your work, then you are obviously going to use a feeling gate. If you are a qigong practitioner, you are going to work on the feeling gate, and so forth. Choose which one of the gates is going to be most beneficial for your life's purpose. Once you have that, then you decide on a meditation object through that gate which is appropriate for developing your samadhi. If you are using the visual gate, using symbols of magic are very beneficial because they give you energy to support the consciousness for the development of that concentration. If you are using the feeling gate, the obvious choice is the breath and the breath essentially is life force.

As soon as you accumulate a little breath – a little bit of breath through stretching your body – you become sensitive to life force, to electromagnetic fluids, and by making them your meditation object, you are really holding that sceptre of power in regards to health, energy work, alchemy, qigong, and so forth. So making life force your meditation object is obviously a starting point for the feeling gate. If you work with the sound gate as your meditation object, working at spiritual frequencies, mantras and various sutras, they hold power. So that power will emanate through the sound consciousness and that will make the samadhi much easier to achieve.

When you are looking at patterns of nature and places of power, you will have a lot of keys for how to develop samadhi more efficiently. For instance, if you sit next to a waterfall and practice samadhi work, you get instantaneous success – it is just easy, because of the amount of energy being produced by the waterfall and the connections to nature, as the water is hitting the rocks at the bottom of the waterfall and the negative ions are being generated. There is this bridge between the physical world, the vital world and the astral world, and that bridge opens – the waterfalls just create that opening. So the spiritual and physical worlds have these junction points that may be through vortexes, waterfalls, stupas, sacred objects, places of prayer, temples, and so forth. We have all these different places where the worlds have junction points and they become all open in one place. When we access these worlds – these places of power – we are able to train samadhi in a much stronger way because we are developing our astral body, our mental body and our physical body differently.

Now, once you have selected your meditation object and a place of power that is optimal for training, you pay attention to that meditation object, and the first thing you want to do is create stillness. You are going to bring yourself into a profound feeling of stillness. The easiest way to do that is to move into the emptiness of the object. Let us say there is an object, it is inherently empty, so you move – you merge – the center of gravity of an emptiness, and you sit in the stillness of that object. When you dive straight into that center, there is an inward vacuum at the center of all things that links to the Akasha. It is released from time and space. And moving into that center allows you to engage in samadhi very quickly. If you are just looking at an object and waiting for something to happen, it is a rather slow process to accumulate Akashic substance, which is really the pearls of samadhi. But if you move straight into the Akasha of an object, you accumulate samadhi at a very high rate. So the location is important, the meditation object, the center of gravity of the meditation object, and the Akashic trance inside the center of gravity. As soon as you hit the Akashic trance inside the center gravity of your object, you start accumulating a top-of-mind substance that comes out of the Akasha. This is one of the fastest ways to develop samadhi and to cultivate mind substance to make your mind stable and be able to concentrate for long periods of time.

Causation Chain of Inner Knowing

There is a causation chain of inner knowing, how to simply go to the heart of understanding a particular matter. And this inner knowing is developed by working with the Akasha. Akasha holds all the universal laws, all the laws of physics, all the laws of metaphysics, laws of creation, everything that exists and has yet to exist in a world, in the future, the direction in which all these laws are morphing and changing for different conditions – it is all held in the Akasha. So to understand any science or knowledge, we need to look at that science or knowledge as an existing frequency, as a form. And then we need to tune in to the Akashic substance of that form.

When we tune into the Akashic substance of a form, it starts to separate into layers. So we pull apart those layers which allow us to see how it functions, manifests, morphs, and changes, and for the cognitive mind to go, "I understand how that works." And the intuitive mind puts it all together to show you those pieces of the puzzle. Using your basic skill of mental transference, you can go into the idea that you wish to understand. Then Akashically breathing into the idea, pulling apart all the layers, you then allow the spirit to observe all those layers and have 'A-ha' moments where you understand.

The depth of the Akashic trance regulates the ability to tune in and unlock universal truths. These may be universal truths on a cosmic level or it may come down to simple mathematics. Whichever level you are working on, for divine ideas, divine inspiration and new inventions to arise, we need space. Akasha gives us space through all the layers to pull apart and for you to understand how things function on a universal or a physical level; the same rules apply elsewhere.

Causation Chain of Working with a Group

Any situation where you need to work with a large crowd of people requires you to allow your mental body to expand and occupy the space of where those people are. So if you are in a room, occupy the whole room. If you are in an outdoor space, place a bubble around the group. As soon as you have mentally occupied that space, then you will begin vital breathing into that space. The vital breathing will be in resonance to what influence you want on these people. Is it for healing? Is it for teaching? Is it for a group of people to give up smoking? What frequency do you want to bring them into?

And as soon as you have decided the frequency that you want, and you start mixing the mental space with the idea you want with life force, you begin the first transformation. You transform vital force and information together and you release time – that becomes an astral substance. This is why you magnetize a space, a group of people. The astral substance that forms directly correlates to the information, to what mental idea and effects you want to produce within that group of people.

So this mental space, mental idea, life force breathing, and life force permeates through the idea – they blend together. You slow it down, produce an astral substance and fill the astral substance into the room. Every person in that room or space becomes magnetized by the astral substance and moves it through their subconscious mind as their energy body. Their astral body is their subconscious mind. So it becomes an alpha tuning fork and they will begin to think, feel and act in resonance with that alpha tuning fork. That is just a matter of how strong you make that energy for it to become a part of those people's reality, their experience.

The highest form of ethics needs to be in place when you do any of this type of work because you can be influencing their mind stream.

Causation Chain of Invocation and Evocation

Let us consider evocation. We have invoking spirits and evoking spirits. To invoke is to bring a spirit inside you. So when you turn your mind to the frequency of a particular entity – say a deity – your mind takes on that frequency. At this point, the deity is still outside you, because you are projected towards its frequency. You have a choice: you invite that spiritual being into you and pull yourself and the deity together, so that it starts to affect your astral body, or you keep your mental body projected towards the deity, the image, the altar and then allow the resonance to form inside you, but the deity is still outside you. This difference is very important. In evoking, you are having a conversation with someone; they are in front of you and they are them, you are you – we have separation.

With invoking, you can bring the spirit into you and allow the spirit to make changes within you or you can transfer into the spirit and those changes are residue of the mental transference. These are both types of invocation.

Evocation is when you observe with the mind the spirit that you are communicating with, but it does not reach your astral body. It does not change anything within your astral form. So mental transference is your first skill with invocation. With evocation, it is more to do with how clairvoyant you are, how clairaudient you are, how strong your feeling is, and so forth – for you to interpret information coming from a spirit who is speaking in front of you.

It takes a lot more skill to evoke spirits than to invoke. Invocation is very simple: it is literally as simple as tasting a piece of cake – you just put it in your mouth and you taste it. As soon as you invite a spirit into you, you feel the spirit inside of you and it is an instantaneous reaction to the changing environment. As you mentally transfer it to the frequency of spirit, they work through your mental-astral-physical body, depending on your sensitivity to how strong that change is, but it is always a change. You will feel it instantaneously as your mental body takes on the frequency of the spirit. Your astral body starts to accommodate and become more flexible for those changes to be made. And then how you feel it radiates through your physical body.

Of course you are only going to invoke high level deities and spirits with the highest ethical fiber. You do not want to be letting spirits into you that do not have high ethics, because they can leave a residue behind and changes within you. You may be unconscious of some of their changes and they may not serve you.

Mental transference is your base skill. From there, it is about how you Akashically breathe. When you mentally transfer into a frequency, being, spirit, or place, initially there is you and there is a spirit. The two of you are initially separate. As you join with the spirit, you identify, "I am in the spirit," so your mind becomes that spirit. Then after you take it a little bit further, you want to generate more cohesion between you and the spirit, so you vital breathe into the spirit in order to make the two of you stick together, so that deity can influence your thinking, your feeling and action, to bring you into resonance for the dharma, or whatever the particular functions of the deity yoga that you are practicing. So we breathe life force, and generate similar mental-astral matrix between you and the deity.

From there, we need to yield. Whether a spirit comes into you or you are moving into a spirit, there is always going to be a difference in frequency, because it is not immediately perfect. So yielding is Akashically breathing and dissolving the difference between you and the frequency that you are tuning into. Whether you are tuning in to a person, to influence or heal them, or you are tuning to deity to invite them into you, there is an Akashic phase of yielding that equalizes this. This equalization is important because there is always going to be parts of you or parts of the frequency you are tapping into which have subconscious resistance. These pieces of subconscious resistance have survival instincts, they feel the difference and change and go, "No, what's happening? Someone is invading my space."

So if you are transferring into your pet to do healing on them, as your mind moves in, you first listen, you become sensitive as you transfer, you join, you become the pet. Then you start vital breathing to build mental-astral matrix, and by this time that animal feels something is intruding on its space and becomes uncomfortable. You yield into the Akasha of that particular animal and now you are fully joined. Then you can work through the astral layers, neutralize any negative energy, apply healing and so forth to the animal. This could be a person or a place or an object, whatever it is.

The same rules apply to invoking the deity. You have discerned a certain deity, you transfer in, you unify, you become one with the deity, you vital breathe in the mental-astral matrix, then you Akashically breathe to dissolve any differences. Then you move through the Akasha, through the mental-astral-physical planes, so that all the body is equalized with the deity. So whatever power that deity has, whatever skill it is transferring, whatever changes it is making within your three body alignment, it now has an internal environment which can do that. Once you have relaxed through the astral layers, through the mental layers, through the etheric body layer, and through the physical, you neutralize any energies which are not meant to be there, and you embed any energies which are meant to be there. And as you embed, you relax and release the energy which the influence of the deities is bestowing upon you or what you are giving to someone else. So this releasing phase or issuing phase, when you transfer the abhisheka or the abhisheka is transferred to you, or the energetic change takes place. So we start off with discernment, then we would join, then we develop life force for sticking, and then we yield inside the Akasha. Then we relax and sync through the astral layer as deep in that fusion. We neutralize any negative forces and implant more positives. Then we stimulate, we light the fire of change, whatever energy we want to manifest through those three bodies, or remove.

The first seven stages of deity yoga generate frequency – it is a frequency of change. So the next time we hit that frequency with the deity, it is automatically at the point to which that fire is burning and the energy is moving through the three bodies, and then transfer of information and chi is taking place instantly. Working with deity yoga, using this formula, you are able to look at the results you are getting and then refine those results by looking inside and hearing your inner dialogue: "Oh, okay. Mental transference, I need to work more on that. Vital breathing, generating mental matrix, I'll work more on that too." While Akasha works to yield to any differences in frequency. While we are working through the astral, mental and physical layers they are syncing, there is work to be done. Then there is neutralizing: how to really anchor something in, neutralize the negatives, create a platform for the positives, and then to light that fire, for that abhisheka energy transfer to happen. Also we see how that energy radiates through the bodies to produce whatever effect we are after. So each one of these lives can be looked at and you can train any layer, you troubleshoot with yourself, "How do I get better results? How do I make this work more effectively? How do I get it to happen quicker?" You can pull those seven stages apart and look at which one of the seven you need to work on, and then you can reflect that off the initiation text and train the exercise as needed to develop any of those seven areas.

When working with evocation, we are very often working through the planetary spheres. At first looking at evocation type of work, one would think that it is about learning. Yes, there is a transfer of knowledge and information inside of that, but what is more important than that is the immunity you get to the planetary spheres. This is because the only door to universal mind is through the sun. The center of gravity of the sun has a door to the center of gravity of all the suns, which connects to universal consciousness. That awakening opens the door to those experiences that many people are after in their spiritual work. To get to the center of gravity of the sun sphere, we need to work through the planetary spheres, work through the physical-astral worlds, work through the Moon and Mercury and Venus and so forth. You want to go through all these planetary spheres and become immune to them.

As you generate this immunity, it gradually becomes easier to enter into the sun sphere and work with the Akashic substance of the sun spheres. It gets easier to get to the center of gravity of the sun sphere and get access to the hierarchy of the sun. Once you have that access, then there is a unification of your spirit with all the other suns in the universe, and the universal mind experience starts to arise. So this universal mind experience is ultimately what we are after – the communication in evoking beings of these planetary spheres, the mental wandering within these planets that generate immunity to those energies, and this has a much higher value than any information you are going to learn from these spiritual beings.

Causation Chain of Equalizing with the Planetary Spheres

When working with the planetary spheres, before we start invoking spirits from different spheres and communicating with them, we want to equalize our spirit or mental body with the vibrations of those spheres.

If we look at the moon, for instance, and then the moon, say, becomes full, and we are starting to feel the magnetic field of a pull on the Water elements of the planet, as you connect into that moon sphere and direct your awareness – your vision – towards the moon, you feel it, feel the astral pull that it has got, you let your mental body rest within the feeling and center of gravity of that pull. And as you relax and release the space and move into this center gravity of the moon, your mental body takes on the identity of the moon, it takes some of the feeling of the moon.

If we blend the Akasha breathing into this process, we go deeper and deeper into the Akashic center of the moon. Sitting within this state for extended periods of time does several things. It makes you immune to energies of the moon and the astral effect that the moon has on the astral-physical worlds, and it also gives you a sense of mastery over the beings of the moon's sphere. So if you connect your center of gravity in the moon, fill yourself up with that light of the moon and then connect to a particular deity, they will see that bright light radiating out of you and they will recognize that you are a very highly attained magician; whereas if you just mentally connected to the moon, you would not have that density of light within you and you would be treated with a very different level of respect and a very different level of help that would come from those particular beings in relation to what you wish to learn from them and what experiences you wish to have when you connect that sphere.

The same practice applies to all the other planetary spheres. You look at the planet, it is visible, you transfer your mind to it, feel the center of gravity of that particular planet, Akashically breathe to go to the Akashic center, then sit within the Akashic center of that planet. You can breathe the vibration of the planet in and out of the Akasha straight into your physical body, making your physical body immune to the rays of energy reflecting off that planet, or you can just keep your mental body dwelling within it. It is up to you whether you pull those energies in your astral-physical form or just let your mental body be based within those frequencies. Whichever one you choose, the various levels of immunity will naturally form through the choices you make, when you bring it into your astral-physical bodies or you keep it within your mental body.

Keeping within the mental body has an interesting effect in that it makes your mental body strong. Your spiritual will peaks. When you bring it into your astral-physical form, your astral and physical body become very strong and robust, and the ability to express physical forces and astral forces increases – but that becomes a property of the physical-astral body, so your spirit is not necessarily always in charge, or the highest part of your spirit is not always in charge. When you do training where your spirit becomes extremely strong and you ignore the astral-physical form, the strength of the spirit is overwhelming over the astral-physical form, and you will find yourself being able to control the lower beings much more easily, because of the time you are spending and developing the spirit and less time developing astral-physical forms.

So, you get a benefit in both models. Whether you are training all the bodies equally, or you are training the spirit more so, you will find a big difference in your mental capacities if you are developing spirit versus astral and physical capacities in the way you express it. Developing the spirit is a much more qualitative path, while developing the astral and physical capacities is a much more quantitative path.

Causation Chain of Hermetic Evolution

When you are working with various energies, group consciousness, elements, whatever energy that has an individual identity has something protecting it – it is like it is in a cocoon. A person's physical body is slightly cocooned from the astral, there is a bridge between the two, which is cocooned from the mental. If you use mental-astral matrices between the three bodies, form a separating boundary, while also sticking the three bodies together. They act as a door between the worlds. Every group consciousness has a bubble of energy that forms that group consciousness. Every religious doctrine has a bubble around it. It is sort of you are inside the bubble or you are outside the bubble, and if you try to have one foot in and one foot out, it is like you are kind of confused. These energetic environments, these energetic bubbles or layers of group consciousness that cling together, are just a natural aspect of physics. Water, two water drops next to each other will pull towards each other and make one water drop. It will create a bubble and energy seeks to do this all the time. It is a part of survival instinct. If it did not have this surface tension for the energy to pull together, it would dissipate and become weak, but by pulling together and creating stronger tension, it develops strength.

These energy bubbles have guardians. There is an energetic principle of consciousness which lets things in and lets things out. When you are working with light and the Brotherhood of Light, you have the guardians of light, these doorkeepers that have a look at the will, at the Akashic substance, the fortitude, the qualities of your astral body, and choose: do we let this person in or do we not let this person in. Because anyone can enter into that light of that extreme will for short periods of time, they are just not able to stay for very long. We are moving in and out of Nirvana billions of times a second,, but we are not able to walk through the door and be in Nirvana, because it is such a fast fluctuation. We require a certain degree of will, a certain degree of Akasha, a certain degree of release to sit within Nirvana and not be rhythmically pulled out. These energetic substances are an energetic mind that acts as a doorkeeper for all these levels. All these different types of group consciousness need to be recognised. What are the rules these doorkeepers, these guardians of light and beings of Akasha, have as a gatekeeper for the Akasha. What rules do they abide by? What are their underlying metaphysical principles by which they operate and function? When you understand these laws, the door opens. When you do not understand these laws, you cannot step through the door.

In order to get a grasp on this we need to look at the qualities of release – how to release time to work up the vibrational scale of the astral planes, how to release space to work through the mental planes, and how to release time-space together to move between the infinity quality, to step into Akasha. This really forms the type of principle we are working with to enter into these energy bubbles. If you release time a little bit deeper than the astral space you wish to enter into, the resistance between you and the bubble disappears and you can slip in through the door. But if your mind is clinging to time, everything is running a little bit too fast, and you cannot step through – there is a type of stress that blocks you from entering. The surface tension of the energetic space balances you out. So, as we release time to work through these astral levels, we release space to work for the mental levels, and we tune into the quality of infinity to work in the Akashic levels, we get a sense of, "Okay, the door opens when I slow things down." Now what is the easiest way to slow things down, to release space and move into infinity? It is prayer. The fundamental qualities of prayer – of humility, devotion, reverence, and sacredness – will help when you are knocking at the door of a particular frequency which you want to enter; if you enter into prayer and direct that humility, that devotion, that reverence, that sacredness towards the door, the door just simply opens. You can move into that particular level.

Remember there is a vacuum principle that is operating there: as soon as you step through, you get sucked in and the door closes behind you; you are getting encapsulated inside of that particular energetic space. So when you are in that state of prayer, your prayer needs to be anchored so well, that once you are in there it is still possible to use that prayer to leave. Just because you can enter, does not mean you can get out with the same level of ease. Very often energies can get trapped in these cocoons, in these spaces. The doors are like one-way mirrors rather than two-way. Energy goes in and it cannot get out. So your level of ability to move into prayer and into Akasha has to be stable, no matter what environment or condition or stress is encountered. This gives you a sense of safety and security when you are moving through these astral levels, because it is a key – a secret opening up doors to any of these spaces and recognising the vibrational scale of prayer.

When you are entering into prayer, your negatives switch off. So, let us say that you are going into a Venus sphere and you enter into prayer, your Water element weaknesses become equalised. But when you enter into that Venus sphere and it is – they are the masters of Water and desire and passion, and it switches on, guess what? Your prayer might not be strong enough to switch it off, to exit. So you will be encapsulated while your mind and your astral form are in a physical body and can continually connect to this Venus sphere, where they feed off you and control you and your sexual desires and passions, because the prayer was strong enough to enter, but the prayer was not strong enough to leave, because your Water element became unbalanced once you entered. So your ability to pray was essentially broken. It is a good example of being able to get in, but not being able to get out. The rest of that particular incarnation you might find yourself trapped in sexual desire, inside of passions and so forth, because your ability was only strong enough one way to move through the door and not the other.

So you need to guard against these different types of effects taking place when you are working with different energies. What overrides all this is Akasha. Akasha is a substance that dissolves all the doors, so putting in a few hundred hours inside of Akashic trance – this is different to pulling energy from Akasha. When you vital breathe, you sense the Akasha around the vital force and then pull more vital force out of the Akasha into your body, then there is a sense of, "Yeah, I can take energy from the Akasha." This does not mean you are immune to the Akasha. This does not mean you have control of the Akasha. It just means that there is a part of you that recognises how to take energy from the Akasha, moving into the Akasha itself and equalising with it as your ultimate protector. When you are deep inside of Akasha, you can dissolve any energy, you can dissolve any door, you can dissolve any negative frequencies, you can dissolve a demon – whatever that force is, if your Akashic substance is strong enough, you can dissolve it. Akasha is quite a fearful frequency for many beings that have a strong form, because it threatens the immortality of their spirit. Their identity of what they are is being dissolved into Akasha when they come in contact with it. It is a very deep fear which arises for them to run away from this black hole that they are being exposed to. Akasha is your ultimate protection system because only beings that have a much deeper connection to Akasha than you are able to affect you when you are developing your Akashic skills.

One of the benefits of having a body is that you can produce thousands of times more Akasha when you have a body, than when you do not. If you do not have a physical body in your spiritual being, Akasha comes near you, it is so vast, it just pulls your spirit into it. You simply cannot develop Akasha as a spiritual being without a body. But if you have a physical body and you touch Akasha, your mental-astral matrix protects you – it keeps your spirit from getting sucked into that Akashic substance. So you can equalise with it and come back to your body. This has a huge benefit because that energy memory, that equalisation, it stays with you, it stays within your spirit. So each incarnation and between incarnations you have developed this immunity to the effects of Akasha; you have developed this Akashic trance state, where you are stable and this has huge value not only in that negative beings cannot touch you, but within all your spiritual states you can move the center of gravity in the Akasha of different frequencies and control, master, truly understand them, and extract the value for your spiritual development and spiritual development, all those through them. So the Akasha – the wuji – really is a platform that you want to become comfortable with and stand on that platform as often as possible.

Working with Akashic Beings, Beings of the Sun Sphere, and Bringing Them to Non-Dual Light

Take a look at the vibrational scale of the physical world and up the scale to the astral world, and up to the mental, and up to the Akasha. Above the Akasha are the light bodies. These light bodies are degrees of primordial light coming into form. The outermost edge is fluxing between Akasha and the mental world. It is the first touching of our innermost being, the monad. The monad activates out of the mental body. We need to work through Akasha into the lower levels of primordial light. Through those lower levels we go to brighter middle levels and the brightest upper levels of light bodies.

Through that level we connect to the Sun. The Sun sphere is regulated by the 45 hierarchy beings. Work with those 45 hierarchy beings, you draw a circle of Akasha that connects them to you. This connects you to the master of the Sun sphere. The master of the Sun sphere uses the frequency of Emnasut to emanate the divine light into the Akasha. There are two skills we need in order to move these Akashic beings from Akasha into these light levels.

The first requirement includes the fundamentals of breathing Akasha, equalizing, being sensitive to these beings, and also having a reasonable degree of immunity to them. This is so that they cannot harm us. The density of Akasha as you breathe in is equal to the density of the Akashic being that you are going to move up into light.

Then the second requirement is your connection to Emnasut – the master of the Sun sphere – to be able to reflect that energy of a Sun sphere down into the Akasha and into those beings, and raise their frequency and pop them out of Akasha into the light levels. Their rhythmic core – the rhythm caused by their merit field – determines how high they pop into those light bodies. Some will move right up to the top, others will be on the lower levels, and others would be one foot in, one foot out, and you have to transform more for them. But because they have no gravity allowing them to connect to these light levels, they are floating – they simply cannot touch them. We use our connection to gravity, the light realms and physical form to control the Akasha in order to rhythmically move them up into these light realms.

We require these two skills: skill of Akasha and the skill of connecting the light from the master of the Sun sphere through Emnasut, radiating divine light into the space or the individual entity you are working with, so that it radiates through a spirit and pulls, or creates a vacuum where they get pulled up into the light realms.

This practice leaves a residue with you. Every time that you move these beings up, a part of them stays in your karma. We need to ensure that we are doing more work with light than we are with these beings to dissolve this residue, this energy that will live with you. Every time you move a being – whether it is a low level being in the astral, a hungry ghost, an Akashic being and so forth, up in frequency, part of them gets left in your field as a byproduct of doing that. We have to ensure that we are working with light enough to clean that off – otherwise this stuff will integrate into your etheric body, into your field, and they become a part of you and your personality and form, and you start morphing into the beings you are working with. We do not want that to happen. We want to keep everything clean and clear.

As you work with moving these etheric Akashic beings up into light, we need to pay very strict attention to sitting in divine light and purifying before and after every session and do sessions of purification, cleaning all the energy bodies. This energy needs to be really cleaned in the etheric body. We need to do high levels of light in our etheric body to clean it, combust it with solar fire, and ensure that we can give our best for the beings we are working with for full safety.

The cleaning process of bringing this divine right down and cleaning your channel through the light bodies, through the crown, through the etheric bodies, through the mental-astral-physical and into the Earth – that channel through which we receive information – we receive teachings, we pass healing energies and healing for the planet through your consciousness. It all works through this channel. By simply being in a path of service where we channel this light through, that channel becomes clean and we will be much safer working with these high level Akashic beings.

When you are transforming these Akashic beings up, the level of effort that it takes to transform them is a reflection of the level of residue which remains after. If you move into the Akasha, you connect to Emnasut, you transform the being up, and they vaporize up quickly, there is little-to-no residue because it was easy. But if you are working with the beings where you really have to dig in deep to transform the energy and move it up, there is more residue which sticks and then you have to do more cleaning this light after that to ensure that karma has been dealt with.

Divine light neutralizes karma. Anything divine light touches is either going to generate karma and bring something to form, or it is going to neutralize karma and take things out of form. This is a matter of intent. When we bring divine light down, we are bringing it down in a purification path. We are creating a magnetic reversal as it comes down – it is pulling us up, it is dissolving all resistance to the vacuum which sucks us up to the divine light. This type of prayer, when we bring divine light down through the three bodies, we are praying for the counter-force of rhythm that our consciousness, our spirit gets sucked up into divine light. The creative light is in its dissolving mode in the neutralization of karma. Inside that neutralization it is like loading a slingshot into heaven, where the mind gets propelled back up after the dissolving process because there is no resistance through that channel, so your mind can shoot upwards and get released up into that primordial light.

We want to take advantage of this clearing of the channels – this elastic rhythm that shoots into light – after every clearing, just to release upwards and spend time within that light. In the same way we float up into that light, the law of rhythm is going to bring us back down again and it will bring us back down into form based on how much clearing we did and how much energy closes to pull us back into form. We want to record all these rhythms, control the rhythm to get the effect, rather than just willing yourself into light. You create a slingshot that shoots you into light and using the law of rhythm gives you a much deeper experience within your practice, rather than doing everything through pure will. Use the universal laws to your advantage.

Of course with extensive practice of using these rhythms, your mind equalizes with all the levels. It gets easier and easier to move up to a higher level, utilizing the law of rhythm. It is the easiest way to do it. Releasing it does not always work. Creating a rhythmic polarity works much more efficiently to take you up to the next level.

Let us work with the Akasha. Fill the room with Akasha and invite Emnasut to control the space. Prepare the space, pore breathe some Akasha beings up to the light realms, place your magic circles all the way around hovering. The Sun sphere beings always support this process. They sit around the circle on the outside, with prayers and energy directing into the Akasha on the inside. Then we invite these Akashic beings in, as a practice to anchor into this, we are inside of that Akashic circle with those Akasha beings. Some of these beings are highly positive, some of these are demonic, some of these are various types of dragon spirits.

As they come through, just keep this strong sense of Akasha to support the space. Once the room is full, the top of that space opens up Emnasut's divine light. It is like you are vacuuming them up. Release them all upwards, into the light realms. Their merit fields decide what level they reach. You take them as high as you can.

Close the door. Open divine light into the space that you just worked in, clear the space. Move into the physical substance of the room. Open the divine light in, bright the divine light into your body and through your three bodies, feel your etheric body through the divine light so there are no gaps. Purify and purify the physical space. Give thanks, and open your eyes, return back to the body when ready.

Part 4

Conclusion, Resources and Index

Conclusion

*(And Bonus Exercise to Build and Strengthen
your Stream of Practice)*

In conclusion of reading this book, now you have an opportunity in front of you: do you go back to the way your life was before you read this book, or do you give yourself permission to apply the wisdom in this book to massively improve your practice? Ask yourself the following questions: How would my life be different if I spent one hour a day practicing the contents of this book for the next month? How about two hours? Four? What if I practiced nonstop, from sunrise to sunset? Is it possible that the direction and capacity of my life would forever change for the better?

Since you have read this far, it is clear to the authors that you are ambitious and that you want the result of practice to be fully realized in your life. So bear with us as we take you through yet another exercise. This time, we ask that you pull out a pent and paper, or otherwise pull up the voice recording app on your phone, and record yourself responding to the following questions:

- What are twenty critical reasons that I am committed to practicing hermetics?
- What are ten ways that my life will forever be changed six months from now by practicing this system? One year from now? Five years from now? Ten years? How about twenty years from today?
- Who are all the people and sentient beings that I am benefiting through my spiritual practice, in the present and the future? (these could be family members, strangers, future students that you teach if you are a teacher, the patients you will help heal as a healer, or the lives you will improve as an inventor, so forth.

Don't read the rest of this conclusion until you've completed the previous exercise. Really. We mean it this time.

That's great if you followed the exercise and have written out all those reasons. If you didn't listen to the previous command, then we applaud that as well. We like rebels and rulebreakers – and you certainly are one since you're reading this book, aren't you? As much as we like you, we politely ask you to do the recording exercise if you haven't already.

When you answer those questions, take a moment to pause and reflect on what you have written. Really soak it in, and perhaps charge your statements with vital, astral, mental, or akashic energy if that's within your capacity at this time. Allow your willpower to lock onto these statements that you have created. Releasing time and space, allow yourself to see and experience the stream that you are creating for yourself, taking into consideration those that are benefiting by your practice. They don't need to be all humans, of course. You can take into consideration that you are benefiting other forms of intelligence and lifeforce that exist. Now fully allow yourself to immerse into this stream, into this baptism of your own stream that you have created. Allow yourself to dive deeply into this stream that belongs to you. You are the creator and facilitator of this stream – keep wisely and trust that this stream will help carry you as you swim through the physical, astral, mental streams. Perhaps you will encounter even more subtle, sublime streams as you move forward onto this journey. Akashic streams, streams of non-dual light. These subtler currents are all a part of your own stream, whether you are aware of yet or not. And that's okay. Really.

Place trust into this stream that you have created. Allow yourself to submerge into it fully, everyday. Allow yourself to be baptised by your own current, which you co-create with your highest self. When you learn to inhabit your own stream of practice, then you can progressively learn to gush this stream with untold quantity and qualities of water overtime. Because all these streams are connected to an ocean. And in this ocean has infinite possibilities. And perhaps, by learning to continually build these streams of practice, you can enter this ocean whenever you like? And perhaps by learning to build these streams of practice and by entering this ocean, you can learn to submerge out of this ocean as well? Perhaps this stream of practice was meant to bring you back into the ocean, after all? Or perhaps you were in the ocean this whole time, and now you can choose to leave it, if you like? You may be more like a flame, burning exponentially brighter, to allow a gust of spirit to blow out the candle flame that was you. And what is left of you is this stream that you created, whose momentum will continually move ever onward in service to the path of light for near infinite aeons.

"May the path of light Guide and protect."

Resources

Mark Rasmus:
www.markrasmus.org
www.youtube.com/user/SifuMarkRasmus

Jake Senn:
www.jakesenn.com/hermetics
www.youtube.com/user/jakesenn/

Franz Bardon (Czech Hermetics current and forthcoming releases):
- *Initiation into Hermetics* (IIH)
- *The Practice of Magical Evocation* (PME)
- *The Key to True Kabbalah* (KTQ)
- *Frabato the Magician* (loosely and fabricly told, but worthwhile reading, especially the unfinished fragments from *The Golden Book of Wisdom* included at the end)
- *Questions and Answers* (185 questions from students to Franz Bardon)
- *The Universal Master Key* (notes from a student attending Bardon's classes)
- *Memories of Franz Bardon* (a book by his son, Lumir Bardon)

Printable and full size Astral, Mental and Physical Study Guides:
Available at www.markrasmus.org/resources/

Index

A

air element 16, 67, 68, 71,
    85, 86, 110, 119, 121,
    127, 146, 149, 152,
    153, 155-158, 162,
    163, 165-167, 174,
    175, 188, 211, 240,
    242
Akasha 20, 32-36, 40, 41,
    42, 49, 50, 54-59,
    73-77, 81, 83-85, 87,
    88-94, 111-139, 142,
    156-167, 172-174,
    176, 184, 188, 189,
    192-197, 199,
    200-212, 214-220,
    223-227, 230, 233,
    237, 238, 239, 242,
    243, 245, 246, 249,
    251, 253-259
akashic light 32
akashic volt 194, 218, 224
amulet 51, 65, 68, 132, 183,
    197, 220, 223, 225
astral body 21, 42, 43, 50,
    53, 54, 56, 69, 70, 73,
    75, 76, 77, 80-83,
    85, 87, 88, 90-92,
    108, 109, 114, 120,
    121, 126, 131, 139,
    142, 143, 145-147,
    155, 156, 160, 165,
    166, 169, 170-173,
    178-180, 185, 187,
    191, 208, 210, 216,
    221, 225, 233-237,
    245-248, 252, 253
astral breathing 73, 145,
    146, 157, 171, 225,
    233-236
astral field 20, 32, 47, 52,
    54, 70, 155, 180, 196,
    217, 240
astral matrix 36, 47, 74, 86,
    116, 171, 172, 191,
    203, 208, 210, 218,
    219, 248, 249, 255
astral plane 20, 70, 120,
    140, 172, 173, 180,
    185, 202, 209, 221,
    222, 225, 235
astral projection 100, 105,
    135, 142, 144
astral realm 20, 124, 131

B

black and white soul
    mirror 46, 144
bone marrow 61, 63-65,
    68, 69, 183
Brotherhood of Light 32,
    50, 90, 215, 253
Buddhism 41, 49, 50, 51,
    110, 112, 117, 173,
    174, 175, 241
Buddhist 22, 41, 45, 46, 82,
    128, 145, 163, 174,
    178

C

Causation Chains 227,
    229, 230, 231
chi ball 63
clairaudience 123, 142,
    166, 167, 188, 220
clairsentience 142
clairvoyance 44, 45, 70, 72,
    100, 123, 129, 130,
    134, 137, 142, 164,
    167, 188, 193-195,
    197, 214, 215, 216,
    218, 220, 231, 233,

234, 236-239
concentration 14, 15, 48,
  55, 80, 83, 90, 93, 98,
  101, 103-105, 111,
  113-115, 118, 119,
  124, 160, 168, 174,
  175, 196, 205, 206,
  231, 244
crown 39, 42-45, 55-57,
  75, 76, 87, 90, 91,
  124, 125, 127-129,
  131, 139, 152, 166,
  171, 185, 195-197,
  202, 210, 211, 214,
  215, 224
crystal ball 110, 126, 127,
  128, 129, 131-133,
  135-137, 197,
  214-218

D

deity 41, 122, 128, 142,
  173-175, 190-192,
  208, 210, 211, 213,
  217, 218, 220, 234,
  240-242, 247-249,
  251
Dharma 46, 217
divine spark 22, 240
dual light 35, 36, 41, 42,
  50, 57-59, 75-77, 81,
  82, 90, 118, 119, 138,
  238, 239, 242, 243,
  264

E

earth element 16, 68, 84,
  85, 86, 110, 119, 122,
  123, 126, 128, 133,
  137, 146, 148, 153,
  154, 155, 157, 158,
  162, 163, 172, 175,
  188, 214, 219, 240,
  242
Elastic Force 2, 16
electric 66-68, 70, 71, 73,
  85, 129, 142, 150,
  151, 154, 169, 170,
  187, 238
electromagnetic 63, 68, 70,
  73, 87, 128, 150, 153,
  155, 176, 180, 186,
  190, 191, 208, 215,
  221, 222, 244
elemental 15, 19, 128, 144,
  146, 175, 176, 193-
  197, 198, 200-202,
  204, 209, 224
energy field 16, 72, 202
equilibrium 97, 137, 142
ethics 39, 46
evocation 159, 203, 247,
  273
evolution 27, 28, 75, 93,
  122, 138, 140, 141,
  165, 196, 209, 240,
  243

F

fascia 16, 17, 36, 38, 61-64,
  66-68, 71, 133, 137,
  149, 150-156, 159,
  160, 164, 165, 170,
  182-184, 211, 214,
  221
feeling 167
fire element 15, 16, 30,
  69, 85, 86, 119, 146,
  149, 151, 156-159,
  161-163, 174, 175,
  183, 188, 211, 219,
  242
floating the bones 61
fluid condenser 176, 219,
  220
Franz Bardon 2, 14, 18, 20,
  28, 29, 40, 52, 71, 81,
  100, 101, 103, 116,
  126, 137, 142, 161,
  163, 169, 176, 203,
  215, 219, 273

G

grounding 50, 51, 181
guardian angel 191, 192

H

healer 21, 27, 120, 129,
  239, 263
healing 16, 17, 27, 30,
  50, 92, 109, 121,
  140, 141, 160, 175,
  186, 201, 214, 216,
  220-223, 230, 231,
  239, 246, 248, 249,
  257
holographic stream 18

I

initiation 14, 18, 28, 30, 40, 41, 97, 116, 134, 143, 165, 171, 197, 226, 250
Initiation into Hermetics 14, 18, 21, 28-30, 40, 137, 169, 210, 273
intent 20, 57, 63, 64, 66, 82, 83, 88, 89, 92, 93, 94, 125, 129, 133, 144, 164, 170, 183, 188, 189, 196, 198, 199, 214, 236, 258
invocation 247

J

journal 27-33, 35, 101, 102, 116, 131, 132

L

larvae 176, 208, 209

M

macrocosm 27, 29, 122, 138
magic 31, 57, 94, 100, 113, 126, 142, 159, 176, 194, 196, 210, 212-215, 219, 231, 244, 259
magician 21, 198, 251
magnetic 20, 21, 32, 36, 63, 65, 66, 68, 70, 71, 73, 85, 86, 102, 124, 125, 129, 142, 145, 147, 148, 150, 151, 154, 157, 164, 169, 171, 190, 191, 238, 239, 251, 258
magnetic fluid 36, 65, 66, 70, 71, 86, 124, 125, 148, 154, 157, 171
marrow. *See* bone marrow
matrix 36, 38, 47, 74, 81, 86, 116, 123, 124, 125, 130, 165, 171, 172, 186, 190, 191, 193, 203, 204, 208, 210, 218, 219, 230, 248, 249, 252, 255
meditation 14, 38, 56, 61, 74, 80, 81, 97, 100-102, 104, 105, 108, 109, 112, 113, 160, 170, 171, 181, 231-233, 235, 244, 245
meditation object 14, 56, 74, 80, 102, 104, 105, 109, 112, 113, 160, 231-233, 235, 244, 245
mental body 32, 53, 54, 56, 58, 74, 76, 77, 80, 81, 83, 86-92, 98, 103, 106, 107-109, 114, 117-120, 123-126, 135-139, 149, 154, 160, 164, 169, 173, 174, 178-180, 185, 187, 191, 193, 202, 208, 210, 216, 218, 234, 236, 237, 241, 245-248, 251, 252, 256
mental matrix 36, 38, 123-125, 165, 186, 193, 210, 218, 249
mental stream 15, 100, 101
mental wandering 100, 105, 107, 123-126, 136, 137, 171, 237, 250
metaphysical 31, 45
microcosm 27, 29, 64, 66, 68, 118, 122, 123, 138, 159, 189, 240
Mona 58
moon 20, 28, 131, 135, 159, 251

N

nature 20, 32, 41, 42, 48, 57, 75, 92, 98, 102, 104, 107, 120, 159, 161, 174, 175, 185, 190, 196, 203, 230, 235, 240, 243, 244
Nirvana 31, 32, 118, 174, 175, 253
non-dual light 35, 36, 41, 42, 50, 57-59, 75, 76, 77, 81, 82, 90, 118, 119, 138, 238, 239, 242, 243, 264

P

phantom 208, 209
physical body 22, 54, 56, 61, 70–74, 76, 77, 81, 83, 87, 88, 90–92, 109, 114, 117, 119, 120, 124, 125, 139, 140, 146, 163, 166, 170–173, 175, 178, 179, 185, 187, 189, 191, 196, 201, 207, 211, 220, 237, 245, 248, 251, 252, 254, 255
Pillar of Light 52
pineal gland 54, 58, 87, 117, 129, 164, 165, 197, 236, 238
planetary spheres 251
pore breathing 55, 61, 85, 88–90, 114, 116, 147, 155, 160, 161, 171, 176, 178, 180, 181, 183, 224
prayer 32, 50, 57, 70, 72, 75, 76, 90, 91, 128, 131–133, 139, 166, 172–174, 179, 192, 193, 210, 213–215, 219, 220, 234, 238, 240–244, 254, 258
precepts 45, 51, 204
pure spirit 58, 81, 117, 118, 191

Q

quadrapolar magnet 110
qualitative key 72, 89, 90, 94, 119, 161, 174, 185, 194, 204, 252
quantitative key 72, 89, 92, 94, 185, 205, 252

R

releasing time 18, 73, 90, 156, 169, 221
resonance 21, 29, 42, 43, 46, 51, 56, 62, 63, 82, 102, 105, 110, 138, 159, 162, 163, 169, 170, 172, 175, 179, 185, 186, 187, 195, 198, 200, 204, 216, 217, 222, 226, 234, 246, 247, 248

S

sacred geometry 29, 158, 159
sacred space 20, 134, 240
samadhi 10, 103, 104, 115, 146, 244
sense gates 94, 102, 106, 107, 127, 129, 167, 168, 218, 220, 227
sight 19, 130, 239
sinking the chi 54
smell 167
soul mirror. *See* black and white soul mirror
sound 19, 45, 102, 103, 108, 124, 127, 163, 166, 182, 207, 208, 218, 244
spiritual development 22, 32, 82, 122, 242, 243, 255, 256
static 19, 50, 51, 80, 81, 87, 180, 193, 198, 240, 241
sung 64

T

tai chi 36, 54, 64, 66, 68, 71, 187
Taoist 53, 54, 65, 182
taste 167
temple 20, 240, 241
three bodies 30, 32, 47–49, 55–57, 74, 76, 81, 82, 88, 114, 115, 127, 129, 137, 139, 140, 154, 164, 165, 173, 174, 178–180, 186, 187, 192, 207, 210, 211–215, 224, 226, 237, 240, 241, 249, 252, 258, 259
Three Transformations 52, 53
training environment 42, 145
tuning fork 35, 43–49, 63, 75, 82, 216, 225, 247

U

universal law 29, 48, 93, 198, 206, 207, 227, 245, 258
universal light 193

V

vibrational scale 54, 58, 59, 79, 80, 128, 131, 133, 138, 139, 188, 193, 211, 219, 226, 234, 242, 253, 254, 256
vipassana 31, 81, 103, 104, 109, 112
vital breathing 16, 52, 66, 84, 145, 147, 148, 150, 152, 169, 170, 171, 178, 180, 183, 186, 196, 207, 221, 224, 235, 246, 248
vital energy 16, 53, 63, 85, 89, 121, 147, 148, 150, 151, 155, 159, 162, 164, 170, 186, 190, 214, 219, 221
vital essence 65
vital force 20, 65, 69, 70, 71, 89, 91, 110, 116, 121, 151, 170, 176, 183, 196, 214, 235, 246, 255
vital light 64
vortex 20, 230
vows 35, 82, 83

W

water element 15, 16, 86, 110, 119, 120, 126, 132, 146, 148, 149, 151, 157, 158, 162, 163, 167, 172, 175, 183, 188, 219, 240, 242, 254
white light 76, 83, 129, 195, 197, 238, 239
William Cook Edwards 2, 58
willpower 16, 36, 67, 84, 89, 110, 115, 120, 121, 146, 150, 170, 196, 264
wuji 54–56, 256

Printed in Great Britain
by Amazon